Tips and Traps When Mortgage Hunting

Other McGraw-Hill Books by Robert Irwin

The McGraw-Hill Real Estate Handbook (1984)

Making Mortgages Work For You (1987)

How to Find and Manage Profitable Properties (1988)

Tips and Traps When Buying a Home (1990)

Tips and Traps When Selling a Home (1990)

How to Find Hidden Real Estate Bargains, Second Edition (1991)

Tips and Traps When Mortgage Hunting

Robert Irwin

McGraw-Hill, Inc.
New York St. Louis San Francisco Auckland Bogotá
Caracas Lisbon London Madrid Mexico Milan
Montreal New Delhi Paris San Juan São Paulo
Singapore Sydney Tokyo Toronto

Library of Congress Cataloging-in-Publication Data

Irwin, Robert.
    Tips and traps when mortgage hunting / Robert Irwin.
        p.   cm.
    Includes index.
    ISBN 0-07-032248-1 (cloth) :   —ISBN 0-07-032249-X (paper)
    1. Mortgage loans. I. Title.
HG2040.15.I78   1992
332.7′22—dc20   91-25693
                                                                      CIP

        5 6 7 8 9 0   DOC/DOC   9 7 6 5 4

ISBN   0-07-032248-1   {HC}
ISBN   0-07-032249-X   {PBK}

*The sponsoring editor for this book was James H. Bessent, Jr., the editing
supervisor was Caroline Levine, and the production supervisor was
Donald F. Schmidt. This book was set in Baskerville by Carol Woolverton,
Lexington, Mass.*

Printed and bound by R. R. Donnelley & Sons Company.

This book is printed on recycled, acid-free paper containing a minimum of 50% recycled de-inked fiber.

Contents

Preface   xi

Introduction: Sorting Out the True Opportunities From the Potential Disasters   1

Too Many Options: A Problem for Consumers   2
The Time-Pressure Trap   3
About This Book   3

1. How to Get a Mortgage   4

Tip 1   4
The Seven Steps to Obtaining a Mortgage   5
Making the Decision to "Lock In"   6
Prequalifying   7
First, Know the Possible Sources of Mortgages   8
Checking Out the Sources   14

2. Learning to Speak and Understand "Mortgagese"   16

The Risk of Not Knowing   16
The Difference between a Mortgage and a Trust Deed   17
The Language of Mortgage Hunting   19

3. How to Get a Bigger Mortgage   32

A Lender's Opinion   32
The Goal—A Bigger Mortgage   33
Qualifying Ratios   35
Understanding the Ratios   35
Applying the Ratios to Yourself—Gross Monthly Income   37
First, Determine the Loan-to-Value Ratio   38
Next, Determine the Mortgage-Payment-to-Income Ratio   38
How to Find the *Maximum Mortgage Payment* You Personally
  Can Afford   39
Calculating the Maximum Mortgage Amount You Can Get Given
  the Maximum Mortgage Payment (Principal and Interest) You Can
  Afford   41
Gross Monthly Payment versus Mortgage Payment   41
Calculating Your Maximum Mortgage When You Know Only Your
  Taxes, Insurance, and Other Costs   44
Long-Term-Debt Ratio—Back End   45
Example of Debt Ratio   45
Getting the Lender to Loan You More Money   48
Front-End Flexibility   49
Back-End Flexibility   49
Jumbos—Bigger Mortgages   50
No-Qualifying   51
Lines of Credit   52
Adjusting Values   53

4. Credit Problems and Solutions   55
Brushing Up the Way You Look to a Lender

What the Lender Is Looking For   56
Bad Credit: A Lender's-Eye View   57
Some Explanations a Lender Might Accept   57
How to Fix Bad Credit   59
The Bottom Line   61

5. Adjustable-Rate Mortgages   62
Approach With Caution

Times Have Changed   62
The Advantages of ARMs   65
The "Teaser"   66
Understanding the Problems With Teasers   68
Why Keep the Teasers?   70
Easier to Qualify   72
Assumability of Fixed-Rate Mortgages versus ARMs   72
How an ARM Works   73

6. Biweekly and 15-Year Mortgages **90**
Interest Saved Is Interest Earned

Mortgage Paybacks 90
Changing the Payback 92
The 15-Year Mortgage 92
The Pros and Cons of Higher Payments 92
Why Have 30-Year Mortgages? 93
An Easier Way to Get Bigger Payments 95
Biweekly Mortgages 95
Establishing a Biweekly Mortgage 97
A 30-Year Loan in 15: Sound Finance Plus Flexibility 99
How It's Done 99

7. The Seller as a Source of Financing **102**
Be Prepared to Initiate and Motivate

What Is Seller Financing? 102
How Seller Financing Works 103
Reasons for Asking for Seller Financing 106
Lowering the Interest Rate and Reducing the Monthly
    Payments 106
Cutting Down on Costs and Red Tape 110
The Wrap 110
What to Include When You Ask for Seller Financing 113
Sellers Who Will Give Firsts 118
Assuming the Seller's Mortgage 119
How to Negotiate With the Seller 122

8. Making Balloon Payments Work **124**
Their Bad Reputation May Be Undeserved

What's Wrong With the Balloon Payment? 124
Any Mortgage Can Have a Balloon 125
Why It's Good for the Borrower 126
The Seller's Incentive 127
Paying Off the Balloon 127

9. Convertible Mortgages and Piggybacks **128**
Is Tailoring a Mortgage to Your Needs Worth the Price?

How a Convertible Mortgage Works 129
Piggybacks 131
Adjustable Convertibles 132
When Does Conversion Pay Off? 134
Is a Convertible for You? 135

10. "No-Doc" and "Low-Doc" Mortgages   137
Cutting the Time It Takes to Qualify—But at What Cost?

Self-Employed: Heavily Impacted   138
Enter the No-Document Loan   139
Low-Documentation Mortgages: All Things Being Equal, the Only
    Way to Fly   140
Advantage of Lo-Docs   140
Finding Lo-Doc Lenders   141

11. Buy-Downs   143
Getting Monthly Payments Down Can Help You Qualify

Who Pays for Buy-Downs?   144
Requirements for a Buy-Down   145
Types of Buy-Downs   146
Who Offers Buy-Downs?   146

12. Lines of Credit and Swing Loans   147
Exposure Money for Your Long-Term Needs

What Is a Line of Credit?   147
Home-Equity Credit Lines   148
Using a Credit Line as a Swing Loan   151
Problems With Swing Loans   151
Where Do You Get a Home-Equity Loan?   153
The Bottom Line on Home-Equity Lines of Credit   154

13. Refinancing   155
How to Get a Second Chance at a Good Deal

The Refinancing Decision   156
The Costs of Refinancing   156
How to Lower Your Refinancing Costs   158
How Do You Get a Lender to Pick Up the Costs?   160
Deciding What Kind of Refinancing to Do   161
How to Know How Much You'll Save on a Refinance   161
Calculating the Time Factor   163
When to Refinance   165
Making the Refinance Decision   166
Refinancing to Avoid Financial Problems   168
Refinancing to Avoid Foreclosure   169

14. Graduated-Payment Mortgages   **170**
Trading Higher Future Payments for Lower Payments Now

How the GPM Works   171
Combining the GPM With an Adjustable-Rate Mortgage   175
Advantages   175
Disadvantages   175
Who Benefits Most From a GPM?   176
Advantages of the GPM   177

15. Government Mortgages   **178**
Attractive Deals If You Can Survive the Red Tape

FHA Mortgages   178
Advantages of FHA Loans   179
Disadvantages of the FHA Loan   180
Qualifying for FHA Mortgages   180
Mortgage Premium   181
Down Payment   181
VA Mortgages   182
How the VA Program Works   182
Down Payment   182
Entitlement   183
Qualifying for a VA Loan   183
Eligibility Requirements   184
VA Appraisals   184
Automatics   184
Owner-Occupancy Requirement   185
Impound Accounts   185

16. SAM, PLAM, and Options   **186**
Mortgages for Special Circumstances

SAM (Shared Appreciation Mortgage)   186
PLAM (Price-Level-Adjusted Mortgage)   189
Option Mortgage   192

17. Reverse Annuity Mortgages   **194**
Access to Equity for the Retired Set

The FHA HECM   195
From Another Age   197

18. Mortgage Insurance Rip-Offs   **198**
Read the Fine Print and Know the Following

Conventional Loans with Private Mortgage Insurance (PMI)   199
Life Insurance   201
FHA Mortgage Insurance   202

19. Tax Considerations   **205**
How You Play the Tax Angle Can Make or Break Your Mortgage

Deductibility of Points   206
Interest Deductions   208
Taxes When You Sell or Refinance Your Property   209
Mortgage Interest versus Personal Interest   212
Other Tax Considerations   212

20. Paying Off Your Mortgage Early   **214**
The Benefits Depend on Your Circumstances

Equity Return   215
Paying Off the Mortgage   215
Tax Considerations   217
The Value of Cash   218
Consider Refinancing   219
Be Careful   219

21. Settlement Costs   **220**
Making Sure You Get a Fair Shake

RESPA   220
Good-Faith Estimate   221
Settlement Statement   222
Typical Mortgage Settlement Costs   223
Challenging Lender Fees   227
Complaints   228

Appendix 1. Amortization Table   **229**

Appendix 2. Mortgage Finder   **231**

Index   267

Preface

The book you hold represents the latest in a series going back over 10 years. The first, *The New Mortgage Game,* was written in 1981. At the time, I was really pleased with it, as *The New Mortgage Game* was one of the first books to fully describe those new-fangled "adjustable-rate" mortgages.

Adjustable-rate mortgages, however, soon became absorbed into the mainstream, as did changes in fixed-rate, government-insured, and guaranteed mortgages. Hence, five years later in 1986, I wrote *Making Mortgages Work for You* to explain the changes. At last I thought I had finally put the definitive touch on describing how to get a good mortgage.

But who could have foreseen the explosion of mortgage varieties, the changes in lending practices, and the new sources of money for borrowers that would occur in the 1990s? While the first two books sold very well, it has become apparent that a totally new book is needed to cover the new world of mortgage financing for the consumer. Hence, *Tips and Traps When Mortgage Hunting.*

One thing has not changed, however. This book is intended for *you,* the home buyer or the person who wants to refinance. It has been written to help you get the cheapest, quickest, best financing available. While lenders may indeed find this book a good resource, my hope is that the harried and confused home borrower will find it a balm and guiding light.

As with other books in the well-known *Tips and Traps* series, I've pointed out where to step to avoid the mortgage minefields and how to turn things around to your advantage. Hopefully, if you're looking for a mortgage, this book will lead you to just the right one. Good hunting!

Robert Irwin

Introduction— Sorting Out the True Opportunities from the Potential Disasters

Because you bought this book, I am going to assume that you are asking at least one of the following three questions:

1. I am buying a home—how do I get a new mortgage to make the purchase?

2. I want to refinance my present home—what's the best mortgage for me?

3. How do I get the best deal (lowest interest rate and costs) in obtaining a new mortgage?

You will find answers to these and many more questions in this book. Perhaps even more important, you will find tips that will point out ways you can save money and time in obtaining a new mortgage. And you'll be alerted to traps to avoid that could cause you to lose a deal, get you in over your head, or result in unwanted tax consequences.

1

Too Many Options: A Problem for Consumers

The real problem with mortgages today (contrary to what the press reports) is not that there aren't any out there. There are all kinds of mortgages available for people in every situation, including those who have terrible credit, even foreclosures against their name!

The real problem is that there are too many different kinds of mortgages and too many different terms available. The average person is lost at sea when trying to sort through the different kinds of mortgages. There are ARMS and PLAMS and fixed-rate and LO-DOCS and dozens and dozens more. Trying to pick between this mortgage and that gives most people a sick feeling in their stomach and results in confusion. (If you haven't obtained a mortgage for awhile, say a decade or so, you'll find it's a totally different ballgame. The days of only one kind of mortgage being available—take it or don't—are long gone.)

With all of these different kinds of mortgages, chances are that there is one that will almost ideally fit your needs. On the other hand, chances are also very high that there are probably a hundred or so that are not suited to what you want. Your real goal is to distinguish the wheat from the chaff, the right mortgage for you from the wrong one.

Unfortunately, those in the business aren't always on your side in helping you to make the right decision. When you go to a lender, such as a savings and loan or a bank, you will be told about the advantages of the mortgages they offer. But, chances are you won't be told their disadvantages. And you won't hear about other kinds of mortgages, perhaps better suited to your needs, that they don't offer but that other lenders do. To find out about all of the different kinds of mortgage out there, you might have to visit dozens and dozens of different lenders—a daunting task for even the most dedicated loan seeker.

As a result, many people seek out the services of a mortgage broker or banker (there is a distinction which we'll get to). These people deal with many lenders and, generally speaking, have a much larger bag of mortgages to offer you. But, you will find other problems here. You may be steered not toward the best mortgage for you, but the one that generates the greatest fee for the broker or banker.

In short, it's a minefield out there when you go searching for a mortgage. There are a lot of people who are eager and anxious to sell you their product and take your money. But there tends to be precious little unbiased, objective information available.

The Time-Pressure Trap

The problems of multiplicity of different mortgages and lack of accurate comparisons and decision-making guides is compounded by the fact that in most cases people who need a mortgage need one right away. If you're purchasing a house and have made an offer which was accepted, you may now only have a few weeks to secure a mortgage and close the deal. If you're refinancing, your need for money may be immediate. You don't have six months to make a thorough examination of mortgage lending to find out the best deal for you.

Most people simply don't have the time to shop around in an organized and careful manner. Even when working through a real estate broker, you may simply be given a list of lenders and told to contact them. Or you may be handed a card of the office's "resident mortgage expert" and be told that he or she will "fix you up."

Given enough time and dedication, we can all come up with the right mortgage. But, as noted, few of us have the time. (And even fewer have the dedication to do the required research.)

About This Book

Which brings us to *Tips and Traps When Mortgage Hunting*. This book contains little information that you couldn't obtain for yourself over the next six months. What it does do is save you the time and effort of looking. It puts the different mortgages in one spot for the person who is buying or refinancing a single-family owner-occupied property. It explains what a mortgage is and how to get one. It shows you what your options are if you have credit problems. It helps you deal with lenders, brokers, and bankers on an equal footing.

In short, this book is designed to help you to make the best mortgage decision for yourself.

1

How to Get
a Mortgage

Tip 1

Although it is bound to seem the case, you're not the only person doing this. Nor are you the first to ever seek a mortgage. Learn from others who have done it. Ask.

Consider These Four Scenarios

1. You've made an offer on the home of your dreams. You've been told the sellers have accepted your offer . . . the house is yours!

   Of course, you're not paying cash—almost no one does. You need to get a mortgage for 80 (or 90 or whatever) percent of the purchase price. The seller has given you 30 days to get it. Now the race begins. Where to do you start?

2. Or, you've just been hit by some medical bills that are hefty. Your savings won't cover them. You need cash, fast. Your biggest resource is your home. If you can refinance it, you can get out all the cash you need and more. Where do you go to get the loan?

3. Or, you're thinking about buying a new home. You have an existing home and a number of options. You can refinance your existing home and get the money out so that you can purchase a new one. Or

you can buy a new home and then sell your present home and get a "bridge" loan in the interim. Who do you see about all these different kinds of financing?

4. Or, you want to buy a home at an auction. But, in order to do so, you may be required to pay cash within 4 days. Of course, you don't have the cash. So what you need is to be prequalified by a lender and get a "letter of credit" or some other voucher that attests to the fact that when you need the money, the lender will fund. Who can handle that for you?

The Seven Steps to Obtaining a Mortgage

In this book we are going to talk about all sorts of different kinds of financing for single-family owner-occupied homes (properties of under four units). You'll get decision-making aids as well as a host of other self-help guides. But before we get to that, let's talk about the process of getting a mortgage and, more to the point, who you can see to get financing that works for you.

The process of obtaining a mortgage is fairly straightforward. There are seven basic steps. Sometimes these are broken down into substeps; sometimes one or more steps are skipped. But generally, when you get a mortgage, you will have to go through all seven. Here's what they are:

1. Decide on the type of mortgage you want.
2. Locate a lender.
3. Discuss "lock-ins" and "qualifying with the lender."
4. Fill out a loan application package.
5. Pay for a credit report and home appraisal (payment is not always required). This is discussed in later chapters.
6. Wait until the mortgage application is processed.
7. Sign the mortgage papers, pay the loan fees not already collected, and close the deal.

Tip

Today there are "low-document" and "no-document" loans available in many areas. These may allow you to skip through much of the application process. There will be more about these in Chap. 10.

Going through the entire process of obtaining a mortgage usually takes about 3 to 4 weeks, with 4 weeks being typical. A lot will depend on how busy the lender is.

Trap

Some lenders are terrible procrastinators. They take what seems like endless amounts of time processing your loan application. In reality they may be overwhelmed with applications.

Or, they may be out there hustling to borrow the money to lend to you. Depending on the market, they may be trying to secure the lowest possible rate to them in order to maximize their profits from you.

Further, interest rates are volatile. They are always jumping around. Therefore, it is in your best interest to do business with a lender who will lock in the rates, that is, who will guarantee you a particular interest rate for a specified amount of time.

Making the Decision to "Lock In"

Because of interest rate volatility and because of delays in securing financing, many lenders are willing to lock in a particular type of mortgage and interest rate. To lock in means that the lender will guarantee that mortgage and interest rate for a set period of time, usually no more than 30 days, but sometimes as long as 45 or 60 days.

The value of a lock-in is only as good as the credibility of a lender. Some will make verbal commitments to you. Others will write it down on paper. But, if the lender ultimately refuses to honor the lock-in, you could be up the creek without a paddle. Short of suing, there's not much other recourse.

Most lenders won't lock you in until they have qualified you and gotten a credit report on you. This can take as little as 48 hours. It may cost you a small amount to lock in, and the fee is generally refundable if you ultimately get the mortgage.

Trap

In occasional rare cases, particularly when interest rates are rising quickly, most lenders may refuse to lock in a rate. They do this to protect themselves from being hurt by giving you a low rate only to discover they have to pay a higher rate to borrow the money.

Beware of lenders who are willing to give you a lock-in in such a market. They may ultimately refuse to honor the lock-in at the interest rate originally quoted and instead demand that you pay a higher interest rate. It's not that they don't want to. It's that volatile interest rates make it virtually impossible for them to do so.

If you get a lock-in during a period of rising rates, be sure it's from a reputable lender, such as a large bank or S&L.

The way most lock-ins work is that they guarantee that for a period of time and often for a fee, the lender will not charge a *higher* interest rate. The problem is what happens if interest rates fall before you secure the mortgage?

Your options are to go ahead with the lock-in at the higher rate, or seek out another lender at a lower rate. If you are dealing with a mortgage broker, he or she may be able to switch you quickly to a lower-rate lender. If you paid a fee for the lock-in, however, it may be lost.

Lock-ins are a great device to protect you, and in most cases lenders don't charge for the privilege. They just do it as a service to secure your business. As long as you don't have to pay a fee for this privilege, it's a good idea to lock in the interest rate on your mortgage as soon as possible. Even if you have to pay a fee, it is probably worthwhile when rates are rising.

Prequalifying

Thus far, I've assumed that the mortgage application procedure begins *after* you've found a house you want to buy or have determined that you want to refinance. It doesn't have to be that way, however. In fact, particularly when you want to make a very strong offer, it's best if you go through the procedure *before* finding the house you want to buy.

Tip

Consider two offers presented for a home, yours and another buyer's. Both offers are roughly similar in price and terms. But, one offer contains a letter from a lender saying that the borrower-buyer has been prequalified and the lender will offer this person a mortgage up to the amount specified in the purchase agreement. If you were a seller, which offer would you consider the best?

Prequalifying is another tool in getting the sale you want. (It can also be helpful in negotiating price and terms.)

Prequalifying is really quite simple. You just contact a lender (described later in this chapter) and explain what you want. Most lenders will be happy to take an application, get a credit report on you, and, on the basis of your income, bills, and credit, qualify you. They will then write this down so that you can show it to a seller.

Tip

The competition for borrowers who want mortgages is so fierce that some lenders will issue prequalifying letters just on the basis of a phone call! You can call them up and describe your financial condition. They may or may not even order a basic credit report.

But they will then issue a letter which says something to the effect that based on information you've submitted (your phone call) and information they've researched (perhaps nothing at all), you are qualified to borrow up to so much money.

Trap

A letter of prequalification from a phone call may be a great tool to convince a seller to take your offer. But, don't rely on it as a guarantee of a mortgage. When you go back to the lender to get the cash, he or she will surely insist on a more detailed application.

First Know the Possible Sources of Mortgages

When you are buying a home, chances are you will quickly discover that it's up to you to locate financing. In some cases the real estate agent may direct you to another agent in the office or in another office who handles mortgages. In other cases you may be given a list of lenders and told to contact one or more.

In all cases, even when you are led to a person who handles mortgages, it is up to you to get the best mortgage for your needs. Just remember that regardless of who offers you the mortgage, there are only five basic sources of funds as described below. What you are after is the best deal for you, not necessarily the most conveniently located source.

Trap

Don't be swayed by the fact that your agent recommends one lender over another or by the fact that a lender happens to be part of the agent's office. What you are after is the least-expensive loan you can get.

Money is money. You owe it to yourself to investigate several lenders to be sure you're getting the best deal available.

Some larger real estate offices, particularly franchises, will offer "special deals" if you secure financing through them. They may advertise that you can get a mortgage, for example, for a quarter point (one-fourth of 1 percent) less through them than from other sources. Just be sure that they don't make up for this by charging you higher fees up front.

At any given time the cost of funds is roughly the same across the industry. What's usually different is how that cost is broken down—whether through up-front charges, or interest. You'll want to do some comparison of charges to be sure that you are really getting the wonderful deal that the lender may be touting.

When you apply for a mortgage on a home today, there are essentially five sources. These include

Savings banks and savings and loan associations (S&Ls)

Banks

Mortgage bankers

Mortgage brokers

Credit unions

These are called retail sources because they deal directly with the consumer, you. These sources, however, often get their money from secondary sources. Chances are that as a home-loan borrower, you will never deal with these secondary lenders. However, in order to understand the mortgage process, you should be aware of them. They include

Pools of government-qualified loans:
  Ginnie Mae
  Freddie Mac
  Fannie Mae
Insurance companies
Pools of out-of-state savings banks and S&Ls
Other large companies involved in loaning mortgage money

Depending on the size of your community, there may be literally hundreds of retail sources available to you . . . or only a few. They are all listed in your phone book and you don't have to physically go to their offices to shop for a mortgage. Most of the work can be done by phone.

Tip

Most communities have a commercial service which prints a referral sheet listing the various retail mortgage lending sources in the community as well as the rates they are currently charging and any fees they may have. These are often subscribed to by real estate agents, who usually are willing to pass them on to you. Sometimes they are free, with title insurance or escrow companies picking up the costs of compiling the information and putting out the "shopping lists." Sometimes they are offered as part of the computerized printout of a multiple-listing service. Sometimes, however, you may have to pay for them. As long as the fee is nominal, a few dollars at most, it's usually worthwhile.

Trap

These "shopping lists" are typically compiled by having a person, usually a secretary, call the various lenders and ask for the information. As a consequence, while they are generally reliable, the rates are not guaranteed. Further, some lenders have gotten quite sophisticated at putting out "teaser" rates to induce you to call or come in. When you do, you find out that there are hidden restrictions on the advertised mortgage and that the one you really want is more expensive.

Mortgage Source 1:
Savings Banks and S&Ls

By a wide measure the largest lenders on residential real estate are the savings banks or the S&Ls, even given the difficulties they have had over the past few years. They continue to lend about half of all mortgages and such lending is their primary business.

It's worthwhile noting that the term *savings bank* has generally supplanted the term *savings and loan*. What happened is that with the collapse of the Federal Savings and Loan Insurance Corporation (FSLIC) in the late 1980s, many S&Ls converted to banks and joined the Federal Deposit Insurance Corporation (FDIC). Thus, in your town yesterday's S&L may be today's savings bank. The change is more than in name only. The way the institution handles funds and makes loans may also be slightly different.

The savings banks and S&Ls typically offer a wide variety of mortgages, including both fixed-rate and variable-rate loans. (During the mid-1980s most mortgages were variable rates—where the interest rate fluctuates during the term of the loan. But more recently fixed-rate mortgages have become more popular once again.)

In the past these institutions primarily originated mortgages which they held for their own portfolio. This simply means that they did not resell the mortgages on the secondary market as described above.

Increased competition, however, has forced most savings banks and S&Ls to sell a large portion of their mortgages on the secondary market. Also, today most savings banks and S&Ls offer all types of mortgages, including "seconds," Federal Housing Administration (FHA), and Veteran's Administration (VA) loans.

Tip

Savings banks and S&Ls are "encouraged" by regulators to keep roughly 80 percent of their assets in residential mortgages. These remain their principal reason for being in business. As a consequence, although many today do sell their mortgages on the secondary market, a great many also hang onto the mortgages themselves. These are called *portfolio loans,* and such S&Ls are called *portfolio lenders.* This has certain benefits for you, the borrower.

The secondary market is standardized, and loans up to only a set maximum value can be sold on it. A portfolio lender, however, can make bigger loans or "jumbos" than can be sold on the secondary market. This is very important if you live in an area where prices are high.

In addition, the rules for qualifying a property for a mortgage that is to be sold on the secondary market are also quite strict. However, portfolio lenders can often bend these rules a bit, since they are hanging onto the mortgages themselves. If you have property with some special problems, such as unusual design, unstable soil, cracked slab, or something similar, often a portfolio lender can be the answer for you.

Mortgage Source 2: Banks

The second-biggest lender on residential real estate is the commercial banking industry. They make most of the income property loans and rank third behind S&Ls and mortgage bankers in home mortgages.

In the distant past, federally chartered banks were prohibited from making loans on real estate. Only state-chartered banks could do this, and then they could only lend a maximum of 50 percent of the property's value. Hence, most residential loans, going way into the last century, were from S&Ls.

With the institution of the Federal Deposit Insurance Corporation (FDIC) by the Banking Act of 1933, all banks could make home loans.

Thereafter banks became specialists in federally insured or guaranteed home mortgages.

Since banks are primarily looking for short-term loans, they tend not to invest their own money in real estate, instead selling most mortgages on the secondary market. They prefer commercial loans. However, when the demand for commercial loans is light, they will make some home mortgages, particularly those of a shorter variety and with adjustable rates.

Tip

If you are looking for an FHA-insured or VA-guaranteed home mortgage, a commercial bank is still probably your best source. Also, if you're looking for a construction loan, because it is of a short duration, a commercial bank will usually be in a position to offer you better terms than most other lenders.

Mortgage Source 3: Mortgage Bankers

Although well known in the lending industry, mortgage bankers are not as well known among consumers. A mortgage banker is technically an *intermediary*. This means that unlike a bank or S&L, the mortgage banker does not keep any of the mortgages it makes. It sells all of them. It does this in the following fashion. The mortgage banker may buy a forward commitment from a secondary pool of lenders such as out-of-state banks for, say, $8 million. That means that it agrees to come up with $8 million worth of mortgages at a certain yield (interest rate, points, fees, and all other return from a mortgage) over, for example, the next 6 months.

Now it goes out and secures borrowers such as yourself, lending its own money. When it has sufficient borrowers to come up with $8 million in mortgages, it sells the group of mortgages to the pool. The mortgage banker makes its money in part by getting a higher yield on the mortgages from you, the borrower, than it has to pay the pool . . . and in part by servicing (collecting payments) on the mortgage.

Mortgage Source 4: Mortgage Brokers

Some mortgage bankers, as described above, deal directly with the public, with you. Most, however, don't have the time or resources to work "retail." Instead, they wholesale the mortgages to another group called "mortgage brokers."

These are real estate people usually specially licensed to deal in mortgages. They qualify and sign up with the mortgage banker (or savings bank or other pool) to sell the mortgages at retail. They advertise themselves as "mortgage companies."

Mortgage brokers make their money by finding you, the borrower. For bringing in qualified borrowers and handling the processing work, the mortgage broker often makes between half and one-and-a-half points (percent) of the mortgage.

Note the differences between the mortgage banker and the mortgage broker. Mortgage bankers use their own funds; mortgage brokers only act as agents.

Note also the steps the mortgage money may go through before it gets to you:

Secondary lender (pool)
↓
Mortgage banker
↓
Mortgage broker
↓
Borrower

Trap

Almost any agent who has a real estate license can also get a mortgage broker's license. A mortgage broker's license entitles the agent to collect a fee for getting a mortgage for you. However, not all mortgage brokers are able to arrange loans at retail. Getting qualified with a lender is a difficult and tricky process and few agents have the skill or connections to do it.

Thus there are some agents who call themselves mortgage brokers who actually arrange mortgages at *above* retail. In other words, they do for you what you can do for yourself, and then charge you a fee for it. For example, they may arrange a mortgage for you through a savings bank and then charge you 1 point (above what the lender charges) for their services. If you had gone to the lender directly, it wouldn't have cost you the extra point.

Beware of these self-styled mortgage brokers. You don't need them. You can tell if you're getting taken if the fees charged to you are higher than they would have been if you had gone directly to the lender. A lender, who is wholesaling, will never undercut the true mortgage broker, who is retailing.

___

Use a mortgage broker when you want diversity of financing. A good mortgage broker may retail loans for half a dozen or more lenders, including many savings banks and S&Ls who don't have time or resources to do it themselves. A mortgage broker who retails for a mortgage banker may be an even better source. This person frequently can offer more competitive loans than can local mortgage brokers, banks, and S&Ls. The reason is that the broker frequently draws his or her funds from out-of-state lenders who may be able to charge less than local lenders.

Check with several mortgage brokers before getting your loan. You may find one or two whose rates are far more appealing than others.

Mortgage Source 5:
Credit Unions

Credit unions are a kind of S&L. However, unlike S&Ls, they return any profits to their members. As a consequence, they can sometimes offer more advantageous financing.

In the past, credit unions (there are more than 15,000 of them nationwide) dealt primarily in short-term consumer and auto loans. However, during the 1980s the major auto manufacturers began offering their own financing and this put a dent into the credit unions' ability to find borrowers. As a result, they have turned more and more to mortgages.

Today credit unions offer first and, in some cases, second mortgages. The big catch, of course, is that you must be a member of the credit union in order to borrow from it.

Tip
___

If you belong to a credit union, check out the terms it is offering on mortgages. When compared with other lenders, the credit union may come out looking more favorable. Remember, money is money, and if the credit union gives you a better deal, why not take it?

Checking Out the Sources

These then are the sources for mortgages. Check them out.

Savings and loan associations

Banks

Mortgage bankers

Mortgage brokers

Credit unions

Think of hunting for a mortgage as something like searching for a house all over again. You're looking for the best deal you can get.

Tip

You don't have to go physically to any lenders to check them out. As noted, there are "shopping lists" available, usually from most brokers. In addition, if you want to contact the lenders directly, you can do all your information gathering over the phone. Just go to your phone book and look up mortgage bankers, savings and loans, and banks. (Presumably you will already know if you belong to a credit union.)

Then just call a few. Ask to speak to a "mortgage loan officer."

Typically a very helpful person will get on the phone. He or she will ask you a few preliminary questions, such as how big a loan you are looking for and where your property is located. (Some lenders restrict the area in which they loan to properties near their offices.)

Then the loan officer will tell you the types of mortgages they have available, the interest rates charged, and the costs. Most, unless they are very busy, will also take some time to help educate you about the benefits of the particular mortgages they offer.

If you're going to call any lenders, be sure you call several so that you don't get a slanted picture from just one source on what's available.

2

Learning to Speak and Understand "Mortgagese"

The Risk of Not Knowing

If borrowing a mortgage is something that's new to you, the first thing you're going to discover is that lenders speak a different language. There are "points" and "origination fees" and "alienation clauses" and dozens of other terms that can make you think they're speaking some alien tongue.

While this should simply be a tiny stumbling block which can be quickly overcome with occasionally humorous results (over terms you don't understand), too often the real consequences are that borrowers don't get the best loan because they don't understand the terminology. If you don't speak "mortgagese" and you let this hinder you, you could end up paying a great deal more for your home financing than you need to. Therefore, I've chosen to explain the more common terms right up front.

Most books on mortgages put a glossary at the end of the book. However, my impression of most readers, myself included, is that we tend not to refer to the glossary unless we are absolutely desperate. Further, glossary entries tend to be short and not all that helpful. That won't do when it comes to mortgagese. So let's use a different approach.

I am going to explain the most important terms early on. I won't cover everything on mortgages by any means, just give a preview and explanation of terms and concepts that you will be encountering in pages to come. Many of you may already have encountered them. In any case, these are the essentials you will need for making intelligent mortgage-hunting decisions.

The Difference Between a Mortgage and a Trust Deed

Before actually looking at mortgage terms, let's clear up one important point. In this book I use the term *mortgage* to mean any financing that you get which is secured by real estate.

In the distant past, almost all of this type of financing was called a mortgage, hence the widespread understanding and use of the term today. However, during the latter half of this century, particularly in California, a different type of mortgage instrument came into existence called the *trust deed*. Today, chances are if you secure financing on your property, you will get a trust deed, not a mortgage. Consequently, it's important to take a few moments to understand the differences between the two types of loan instruments.

Mortgage

There are two parties to a mortgage—the borrower, or *mortgagor*, and the lender, or *mortgagee*. Skipping to an eventuality that most of us don't like to consider, the big difference between a mortgage and trust deed has to do with foreclosure.

If we don't make our payments on a mortgage, the lender can only foreclose, or take ownership of the property, by going to court. This court action can take a great deal of time, often 6 months or more. Further, even after the lender has taken back the property, we as borrowers may have an "equity of redemption" that allows us to redeem the property sometimes for years after we've lost it, by paying back the mortgage and the lender's costs. The length of time it takes to foreclose, the costs involved, and the equity of redemption make mortgages undesirable to lenders.

Trust Deed

Trust deeds came into use in the early part of this century, primarily in California, by clever and enterprising lenders. If you wanted to borrow money from them, they would say, "Yes, I'll loan you money on your property. But, to ensure that my money is guaranteed, you a sign a deed over to me. I won't record the deed unless you don't pay."

We borrowers, of course, wouldn't stand for that. If we gave the lender the deed to our property, he or she could take ownership at any time. So the lenders compromised. They said, "Okay, make the deed out to an independent third party, a stake holder. That third party will hold the deed and will sign it over to us only if you don't make your payments." That seemed fair, and borrowers went along with it. Over time the *trust deed,* as it became called, was codified into law.

There are three parties to a trust deed. There's us, the borrower or *trustor.* There's the independent third party, the stake holder, called the *trustee* (usually a title insurance company), and there's the lender, called the *beneficiary,* since it stands to benefit if the trustee turns the deed over in the event we fail to make our payments.

The advantage of the trust deed over the mortgage is that foreclosure can be accomplished without court action. The beneficiary (lender) simply informs the trustee that the borrower hasn't made his or her payments and the trustee issues the lender a deed.

Of course, strict procedures must be followed. In California, for example, the lender must allow the borrower 90 days to make the loan current. Then it must advertise the property for 21 days, during which time the borrower can redeem the loan by paying it back. Finally, it must "sell" the property to the highest bidder (usually the lender) on the courthouse steps.

Nevertheless, the process is relatively fast, there are no court costs, and we have no equity of redemption once the trustee sale is made. Once title passes from the trustee to the beneficiary (lender) we lose all interest in the property.

One other point needs to be mentioned on this subject. With trust deed foreclosure, there can be no deficiency judgment. In other words, if the property is worth less than the loan, the lender can't come back to us for the difference. In judicial foreclosure, in some instances, the lender can. It is for this reason that some lenders who hold a trust deed will opt for judicial foreclosure rather than trustee foreclosure. (See also "Purchase Money Mortgage.")

Note: Because, in this book we are mainly interested in securing the loan, *not* foreclosure, *the terms* trust deeds *and* mortgages *are used synonymously.*

The Language of Mortgage Hunting

Now, let's move forward to consider the most important terms used in *securing* mortgages on single-family residential property:

Abstract of Title

This is a written document produced by a title insurance company (in some states an attorney will do it) giving the history of who owned the property from the first owner forward. It also indicates any liens or encumbrances that may affect the title. A lender will not make a loan, nor can a sale normally conclude, until the title to real estate is clear as evidenced by the abstract.

Acceleration Clause

This "accelerates" the payments in a mortgage, meaning that the entire amount becomes immediately due and payable. Most mortgages have this clause, which kicks in if, for example, you sell the property. This is also called an *alienation clause.*

Adjustable-Rate Mortgage (ARM)

The interest rate on this mortgage fluctuates up or down according to an index and a margin agreed to in advance by borrower and lender. In some cases when there are limits to the amount of change which can be made to the interest, a change may actually be made to the principal. (See *negative amortization.*)

Adjustment Date

This is the day on which an adjustment is made in an adjustable-rate mortgage. It may occur monthly, every 6 months, once a year, or as otherwise agreed.

Alienation Clause

This is a clause in a mortgage which usually specifies that if you sell or transfer the property to another person, the mortgage becomes immediately due and payable. It is also called an *acceleration clause.*

ALTA

American Land Title Association. This is a more complete and extensive policy of title insurance that most lenders insist on. It involves a physical inspection and often guarantees the property's boundaries. A lender will often insist on an ALTA policy with itself named as beneficiary.

Amortization

Paying back the mortgage in equal installments. In other words, if the mortgage is for 30 years, you would have 360 equal installments. (The last payment is often a few dollars more or less.) This is opposed to a "balloon" payment in which one payment is significantly larger than the rest.

Annual Percentage Rate (APR)

This tells you the actual rate you will pay, including interest, loan fees, and points.

Appraisal

Lenders usually require that the property be valued by a qualified appraiser. The amount of the appraisal is the maximum value on which the loan will be based. For example, if the appraisal is $100,000 and the lender will loan 80 percent of value, the maximum mortgage would be $80,000.

ASA

American Society of Appraisers. An appraiser who displays this designation belongs to this professional organization.

Assignment of Mortgage

The lender may sell your mortgage without your permission. For example, you may obtain a mortgage from XYZ Savings and Loan. It may then sell that mortgage to Bland Bank. You will then get a letter saying the mortgage was assigned and you make your payments to a new entity. The document used between lenders for the transfer is an "assignment of mortgage." *Note:* Beware of receiving any letter saying you should send your mortgage payment elsewhere. Unscrupulous individuals have sent out such letters to borrowers in the hopes of cheating them out of payments. Verify any such letters with your old lender.

Assumption

To take over an existing mortgage. For example, a seller may have an "assumable" mortgage on a property. When you buy the property, you take over that seller's obligation under the loan. Today, most fixed-rate mortgages are not assumable. Most adjustable-rate mortgages are, but the borrower must qualify. FHA and VA mortgages may be assumable, but certain conditions may have to be met. When you assume the mortgage, you are liable if there is a foreclosure.

Automatic Guarantee

Some lenders who make VA loans are empowered to guarantee the loans without first checking with the VA. These lenders can often make the loans quicker.

Balloon Payment

One payment, usually the last, on a mortgage is larger than the others. In the case of second mortgages held by sellers, often only interest is paid until the due date—then the entire amount borrowed (the principal) is due.

Biweekly Mortgage

You make your payments every other week instead of monthly. Since there are 52 weeks in the year you end up making 26 payments or the equivalent of one month's extra payment. The additional payment significantly reduces the amount of interest charged on the mortgage and often reduces the term of the loan.

Blanket Mortgage

One mortgage that covers several properties instead of a single mortgage for each property. It is used most frequently by developers and builders.

Buy-Down Mortgage

You receive a lower-than-market interest rate either for the entire term of the mortgage or for a set period at the beginning, say two years. This is made possible by the builder or seller paying an up-front fee to the lender.

Call Provision

A clause in the mortgage allowing the lender to call in the entire unpaid balance of the loan providing certain events have occurred, such as your selling the property. An acceleration or alienation clause.

Caps

These are limits put on an adjustable-rate mortgage. The interest rate, the monthly payment, or both may be capped.

Certificate of Reasonable Value (CRV)

When getting a VA loan, the Veteran's Administration will secure an appraisal of the property and will issue this document establishing what they feel is its maximum value. In some cases, you may not pay more than this amount and still get the VA loan.

Chain of Title

This gives the history of ownership of the property. The title to property forms a chain going back to the first owners, which in the southwest, for example, may come from original Spanish land grants.

Closing

When the seller conveys title to the buyer and the buyer makes full payment, including financing, for the property. Also, the time when the deal is consummated or concluded and all required documents are signed and delivered and funds are disbursed.

Commitment

When a lender issues a written promise to you as a borrower to offer a mortgage at a set amount, interest rate, and cost. Typically, commitments have a time limit on them, for example, they are good for 30 or 60 days. Some lenders charge for making a commitment if you don't subsequently take out the mortgage (since they have tied up the money for that amount of time). When the lender's offer is in writing, it is sometimes called a *firm commitment.*

Construction Loan

A mortgage made for the purpose of constructing a building. The loan is short-term, typically under 12 months, and is usually paid in installments directly to the builder as the work is completed. Usually it is interest only.

Conventional Loan

Any loan that is not government guaranteed or insured.

Convertible Mortgage

This is an adjustable-rate mortgage (ARM) which contains a clause allowing it to be converted to a fixed-rate mortgage at some time in the future. You may have to pay an additional cost to obtain this mortgage.

Cosigner

If you don't have good enough credit to qualify for a mortgage, the lender may be willing to make the loan only if you have someone with better credit (usually a close relative) also sign. This cosigner is equally responsible with you for repayment of the loan. (Even if you don't pay it back, the cosigner can be responsible for the *entire* balance.)

Credit Report

This is a report usually made by one of the country's three large credit reporting companies, giving your credit history. It will typically state if you have any delinquent payments, any failures to pay as well as any bankruptcies and, sometimes, foreclosures. Lenders use it to determine whether or not to offer you a mortgage. The fee for the report is usually under $50 and you are charged for it.

Discount

This term has two meanings. When you borrow from a lender, it may withhold enough money from the mortgage to cover the points and fees. For example, you may be borrowing $100,000, but your points and fees come to $3000; hence the lender will only fund $97,000, discounting the $3000.

In the secondary market a discount is the amount less than face value that a buyer of a mortgage pays in order to be induced to purchase it. The discount here is calculated on the basis of risk, market rates, interest rate of the note, and other factors. See the chapter on yields.

Due-on-Encumbrance Clause

This is a little-noted and seldom-enforced clause in many recent mortgages which allows the lender to foreclose if you, the borrower, get additional financing. For example, if you secure a second mortgage, the lender of the first mortgage with the clause may have grounds for foreclosing.

The reasoning here is that the lender wants you to have a certain level of equity in the property. If you reduce your equity level by taking out additional financing, the lender may be placed in a less secure position.

Due-on-Sale Clause

This is a clause in a mortgage that says the entire remaining unpaid balance becomes due and payable on sale of the property. See *acceleration clause, alienation clause,* and *call provision.*

Escrow Company

The escrow company is the stake holder—an independent third party which handles funds; carries out the instructions of the lender, buyer, and seller in a transaction; and deals with all the documents. In most states, companies are licensed to handle escrows. In some parts of the country, particularly the northeast, the function of the escrow company may be handled by an attorney.

FHA Loan

A mortgage insured by the Federal Housing Administration. In most cases FHA advances no money, but instead insures the loan to a lender such as a bank. There is a fee to the borrower, usually paid up front, for this insurance.

Graduated-Payment Mortgage

Here the payments you make vary over the life of the loan. They start out low, then slowly rise until, usually after a few years, they reach a plateau where they remain for the remainder of the term. This mortgage is particularly useful when you want low initial payments. It is primarily used by first-time buyers. It can be and often is used in combination with a fixed-rate or adjustable-rate mortgage.

Growing-Equity Mortgage

This is a rarely used type of mortgage where the payments increase according to a set schedule. The purpose is to pay additional money into principal and thus pay off the loan earlier and save interest charges.

Index

A measurement of an established interest rate used to set the periodic rate adjustments for adjustable-rate mortgages. There are a wide variety of indexes used, including Treasury bill rates, cost of funds to lenders, and others.

Lien

A claim for money against real estate. For example, if you had work done on your property and refused to pay the worker, he or she might file a "mechanic's lien" against your property. If you didn't pay taxes, the taxing agency might file a "tax lien." These liens "cloud" the title and usually prevent you from selling the property or refinancing it until they are cleared by paying off the debt.

Loan-to-Value Ratio

The percentage of the appraised value of a property that a lender will loan. For example, if your property is appraised at $100,000 and the lender was willing to loan $80,000, then the loan-to-value ratio would be 80 percent.

MAI

American Institute of Real Estate Appraisers. An appraiser who has this designation has passed rigorous training.

Margin

An amount, calculated in points, that a lender adds to an index to determine how much interest you will pay during a period for an adjustable-rate mortgage. For example, the index may be at 7 percent. And the margin, agreed upon at the time you obtained the mortgage, may be 2.7 points. The interest rate for that period, therefore, would be 9.7 percent.

Negative Amortization

When the payment on an adjustable-rate mortgage is not sufficiently large to cover the interest charged. When this happens the excess interest is added to the principal; thus the amount borrowed actually increases. The amount the principal can increase is usually limited to 125 percent of the original mortgage value. *Anytime you have a cap on the mortgage payment,* you are looking at a mortgage which has the potential to be negatively amortized.

Origination Fee

Today this usually refers to the total costs to you when you obtain a mortgage. In the past it has meant a charge that lenders make for preparing and submitting a mortgage. It originally was used only for FHA and VA loans where the mortgage package had to be submitted to the government for approval. With an FHA loan, the maximum origination fee used to be 1 percent.

Personal Property

Any property that does not go with the land. This includes automobiles, clothing, and most furniture. Some items are disputable, such as appliances and floor and wall coverings. See the related discussion under *real property.*

PITI

This is an acronym for *p*rincipal, *i*nterest, *t*axes, and *i*nsurance. These are the major components that go into determining your monthly payment on a mortgage. (They leave out other items such as homeowner's dues, utilities, and so forth.)

Points

A point is equal to 1 percent of a mortgage amount. For example, if your mortgage was $100,000 and you were required to pay 2½ points to get it, the charge to you would be $2500. Some points which you pay when obtaining a mortgage may be tax-deductible. See your accountant.

Lenders use the term *basis points*. A basis point is one-hundredth of a point. For example, if you are charged half a point (½ percent of the mortgage), the lender will think of it as 50 basis points.

Prepayment Penalty

This is a charge made by the lender to the borrower for paying off a mortgage early. In times past (more than 25 years ago) nearly all mortgages carried prepayment penalties. However, those mortgages were also assumable by others. Today virtually no fixed-rate mortgages (other than FHA or VA) mortgages are truly assumable and, hence, almost none carry a prepayment penalty clause.

Private Mortgage Insurance

A type of insurance which protects the lender in the event you default on a mortgage. It is written by an independent third-party insurance company and typically covers only the first 20 percent of the lender's potential loss. PMI is normally required on any mortgage that exceeds 80 percent loan-to-value ratio.

Purchase Money Mortgage

When you get a mortgage as part of the purchase price of a home (usually from the seller). This is as opposed to getting a mortgage through refinancing. In some states, no deficiency judgment can be obtained against a borrower of a purchase money mortgage. (If there is a foreclosure and the property brings less than the amount borrowed, you as a borrower cannot be held liable for the shortfall.)

Real Property

Real estate. This includes the land and anything appurtenant to it, including the house. Confusion often exists when differentiating between real and personal property with regard to such items as floor and wall coverings. To determine whether an item is real property (goes with the land), certain tests have been devised. For example, if curtains or drapes have been attached in such a way that they cannot be removed without damaging the home, they may be spoken of as real property. On the other hand, if they can easily be removed without damaging the home, they may be personal property. It is a good idea to specify in any contract whether items are real or personal. This avoids confusion later on.

RESPA

An acronym for Real Estate Settlement Procedures Act. This act requires lenders to provide you with specified information as to the cost of securing financing. Basically it means that before you proceed far along the path of getting your mortgage, the lender has to provide you with an estimate of costs. Then, before you actually sign the documents binding you to the mortgage, the lender has to provide you with a breakdown of the actual costs.

Second Mortgage

An inferior mortgage usually placed on the property after a first mortgage. In the event of foreclosure, this mortgage would be paid off with funds from a foreclosure sale only after the first mortgage had been fully paid. Many lenders will not offer second mortgages, insisting instead on firsts only.

SREA

An acronym for Society of Real Estate Appraisers. This is a professional association to which qualified appraisers can belong. Whenever you hire an appraiser you are encouraged to look for the SREA designation.

Subject to

This is a phrase often used to indicate that a buyer is not assuming the mortgage liability of a seller. For example, if the seller has an assumable loan and you (the buyer) "assume" the loan, you are taking over liability for payment. On the other hand, if you purchase "subject to" the mortgage, you do not assume liability for payment.

Subordination Clause

A clause which can be inserted into a mortgage document which keeps that mortgage secondary to any other mortgages. Mortgages are valued according to the chronological order on which they are put onto a property. The first mortgage on a property is called a "first" in time. The next mortgage put on is a "second" in time. The next a "third" in time, and so forth. The order is important because in the event of foreclosure, all the money from a foreclosure sale goes to pay off the lender of the first. Only if there is any left over does it then go to pay off the holder of the second. Only if there is any left over after this does it go to pay off the lender of the third, and so forth. The earlier the number of the mortgage, the more desirable and superior the mortgage is considered.

Normally, when a first mortgage is paid off, the second advances to become the first, the third to the second, and so forth. However, since some lenders only offer first mortgages, having a second advance to the first position could prevent you from refinancing with a new first (unless the second and other inferior mortgages were fully paid off). This you might not want to do.

Hence, a subordination clause can be inserted into the second and other inferior mortgages. It specifies that the mortgage will forever remain in its current position, thus allowing you to pay off the existing first and get a new first.

This is a technique used by developers who give the sellers of land a second mortgage and then get a new first for construction. Today, most institutional lenders either will not allow a subordination clause inserted in any second or inferior mortgage they make; or if they do subordinate, they will limit the amount of the first.

Title

This is evidence that you actually have the right of ownership of real property. It is in the form of a deed (there are many different types of deeds) which specifies the kind of title you have (joint, common, or other).

Title Insurance Policy

This is an insurance policy which covers the title to your home. It may list you or the lender as a beneficiary. It is issued by a title insurance company or through an attorney underwritten by an insurance company and specifies that if for any covered reason your title is defective, the company will correct the title or pay you up to a specified amount, usually the amount of the purchase price or the mortgage.

Before issuing such a policy, for which either the buyer or the seller or both (as determined by local custom) must pay a fee, the title insurance company investigates the chain of title and notifies all parties of any defects, such as liens. These must then be paid off. Sometimes if it is not desirable to pay them off (as in the case of old bonds), a policy of title insurance with an exception may be issued.

Most states have standard title insurance policies. For example, California has a CLTA, or policy approved by the California Land Title Association. It may not be a very complete policy and may not give you total coverage. A more complete policy is the ALTA, listed above.

VA Loan

A mortgage guaranteed by the Veteran's Administration. The VA actually only guarantees a small percentage of the amount loaned, but since it guarantees the first monies loaned, lenders are willing to accept it. In a VA loan the government advances no money; rather the mortgage is made by a private lender such as a bank.

Wraparound Financing

Here a lender blends two mortgages. If the lender is a seller, then he or she doesn't receive all cash. However, instead of simply giving the buyer-borrower a simple second mortgage, the lender combines the balance due on an existing mortgage (usually an existing first) with an additional loan.

Thus the wrap includes both the second and the first mortgages. The borrower makes payments to the lender who then keeps part of the payment and in turn makes payments on the existing mortgage.

The wrap is used typically by a seller who either doesn't trust the buyer to make payments on a first or who wants to get a higher interest rate.

These then are many of the terms you are likely to run into when you attempt to secure financing. Keep in mind that we've not covered all of the terms used in real estate and financing. There are many others such as *disintermediation,* an outflow of funds from a savings and loan into short-term, higher-rate instruments, or *hypothecation,* to give property as security without giving up its use. These terms are used in mortgage lending but are really the domain of professionals. The average borrower really needn't be bothered with them.

Also, in this chapter we have covered many terms in a cursory fashion (such as *margin, index,* and *negative amortization*) which are of great importance and which warrant more detailed discussion. You will find these discussed in later chapters according to the type of mortgages to which they refer. I felt it was necessary, however, to at least mention them early on in a chapter such as this for two reasons. First, so that you, the reader, would be introduced to them and would have some familiarity with their use. And second, so that you could refer back to this section for a brief explanation when you ran across them later on.

Having thus defined our terms, let's push onward to see just how much of a mortgage you can actually get.

3
How to Get a Bigger Mortgage

Introduction

In this chapter we are going to accomplish two things. The first is that we are going to determine just how big a mortgage you can afford according to what lenders say. The second is that we are going to see how to get a bigger one!

A Lender's Opinion

The easiest way for you to determine the biggest mortgage you can afford is to ask a lender. He or she will ask you some questions about your finances, make a few calculations, and then come up with a figure.

This is quick and easy. But, there are two problems with it. The first is that you are relying entirely on the lender and don't know if he or she is right or wrong. In other words, you haven't calculated for yourself. The second problem is that doing it this way doesn't give many clues as to how qualifying for a mortgage works. As a consequence, you are lost when it comes to beating the system and applying for and obtaining a bigger mortgage than lenders say you can get.

Therefore, in this chapter we are going to go through the same steps that lenders use to qualify you for a mortgage. While at times the steps may seem strange, even arcane, hang in there. None of it is hard or impossible to understand. And the reward at the end may be a bigger mortgage than you ever thought you could otherwise get!

The Goal—A Bigger Mortgage

The bigger the mortgage you can secure, the more house you can buy or, if you're refinancing, the more money you'll end up with in your pocket. As a result, the goal of many people is to get the biggest mortgage that a lender will give them.

There are two drawbacks to this. The first has to do with payback. The bigger the mortgage, the bigger the monthly payments. For those who get in over their heads with a mortgage and payments too high, there looms the possibility of foreclosure. Therefore, the ideal for most people is not to get the biggest mortgage possible, but the biggest one you can afford.

The second problem is getting a lender to see the same way you do with regard to mortgage size. One would think that lenders would be just as interested in the true affordability of mortgages as are borrowers. However, that, surprisingly, is not often the case. Too often the mortgage lender really isn't interested in what you can truly afford. Rather, the lender is only interested in satisfying arbitrary ratios which may or may not determine what you can afford to pay back.

Getting a Mortgage Way
Back When . . .

Let's take a look at getting a mortgage historically. Back before the Great Depression in the 1930s, there were only two sources of mortgages. The first were banks which were limited to making loans of no more than 50 percent of value on houses. What was required was that the banker personally know you, meaning you had an account at the bank, and that the banker get an appraisal of the property (usually made by the banker). There was really no other qualifying.

The other source of funds for home loans was the thrifts, savings and loan associations. Here, to get a mortgage, you had to be a member. You, and thousands of others, deposited money into the thrift and it, in turn, would lend money to its members. Again, the limit was often 50 percent of the value, but in some cases it could be higher. Qualifying meant that you were a member of the thrift, were known by the officers to pay your bills, and had a property of sufficient value.

Needless to say the above "rough" system of mortgage lending might work adequately in a small society. But for our megasociety with over 60 million homeowners, it is simply too inefficient to be effective. This became quite apparent to those in Franklin D. Roosevelt's administration who were seeking to expand home financing as a way of increasing the money supply and getting the country out of the Great Depression of the early 1930s. As a result, they came up with the Federal Housing Administration.

The Lessons of the FHA

The FHA would insure loans to lenders, thus allowing them to make mortgages to buyers for up to 95 percent of a home's value. Only in order for the mortgages to work, there had to be standardized rules. These included the following, which have been adopted over time by all lenders and are in use today almost any time you get a mortgage:

Rule 1. The property must be appraised by a *qualified* appraiser to determine true market value. Then an LTV, or "loan-to-value," ratio is used to determined the loan amount. For example, if the property is worth $100,000 and the LTV is 90 percent, a maximum loan of $90,000 may be obtained.

Trap

Beware of CLTVs. Here the lender determines that the *combined* loan-to-value ratio of all loans may not be above a certain percentage. For example, you may want the seller to give you a 10 percent (of the sales price) second mortgage with you going to an institutional lender for an 80 percent first, or a total of 90 percent.

But the institutional lender may require an 80 percent CLTV. Since your combined loans equal 90 percent, the lender won't loan. You'll have to find another lender who doesn't use a CLTV or who has a higher percentage.

Rule 2. A credit report must be obtained to determine the borrower's true history of handling debt.

Rule 3. The actual income of the borrower must be established to determine how big a mortgage can be afforded as expressed in specific ratios of debt to income.

Qualifying Ratios

It is with Rule 3 that we are concerned in this chapter. Following the pattern established by the FHA in the mid-1930s, conventional lenders (those not associated with government-insured or -guaranteed mortgages) to this day follow several income ratios which they use to determine just how big a mortgage you can afford.

(*Note:* Interestingly enough, today the ratios used for FHA and VA loans are different from those used for conventional loans as outlined here. The FHA and VA guidelines are handled in Chap. 16.)

There are essentially two ratios used. These are called *front-end* and *back-end* ratios in the trade. They are the

Payment-to-income ratio—Front end

Long-term-debt (including above) ratio—Back end

Understanding the Ratios

Any time you want to get a mortgage from a lender, you're going to come up against these ratios. Consequently, it's to your advantage to know how they work . . . and how to stretch them.

Tip

While one might think that the ratios would be set in stone, the truth of the matter is that they are determined by the ultimate lender of the funds. As we saw in the first chapter, that can be a variety of lenders, including the following:

Portfolio lender (a savings bank or S&L that keeps its own paper)

A secondary government lender such as Ginnie Mae or Freddie Mac

A pool lender such as a group of out-of-state savings banks or insurance companies

These ultimate lenders establish the underwriting ratios that you must meet in order to get a loan. *Consequently, the ratios will vary from lender to lender.*

Trap

In order to have a salable mortgage in the secondary market, a retail lender (a mortgage broker, for example) must adhere to the secondary lender's (a pool of insurance companies, for example) underwriting standards. Thus, when a mortgage broker tells you that you can't qualify because you don't meet the underwriting ratios, what is meant is that you don't meet the ratios of his or her sources of funds. Another broker who has other, more liberal sources, might be able to get you a mortgage! Once again, the rule is, shop around.

Portfolio Lenders

As a side issue, portfolio lenders or those who loan their own money and do not have to answer to a secondary market also adhere to the ratios. They do so to ensure that no stockholder can later come back and accuse management of making unsafe loans. (Here we're talking about single-family residences. When it comes to commercial or income property, S&Ls in particular have a long history of unsafe lending.)

Tip

Lenders sometimes have too much money on hand. Perhaps a lender in Iowa wants to loan money out in California. To facilitate making the loans, it will relax its underwriting standards somewhat. As a result, if you find a broker who is handling this secondary lender, you may be able to get a higher loan than from a savings bank or another broker who does not handle this secondary lender.

This is yet another good reason to shop around!

Trap

Just because you do or don't fit under a certain ratio often has little to do with your real ability to repay a mortgage. For those borrowers who are very thrifty and who are applying for fixed-rate mortgages, often the ratios are too strict and unrealistically limit the amount of mortgage they can get.

On the other hand, for those borrowers who don't handle their money as well and, particularly when they are applying for adjustable-rate mortgages, the ratios often allow them to get in over their heads.

The long and the short of it is that just because a ratio tells you that you can get a certain maximum amount of money doesn't mean that you can't handle borrowing more—or that you can handle even that amount. You should make your own determination of what is the maximum you can afford and then go for that amount. (Later in this and other chapters we'll see how to get more money than the ratios say you can qualify for.)

Applying the Ratios to Yourself—Gross Monthly Income

Let's find out what the underwriting ratios say that you personally qualify for in terms of a mortgage. Once you know that, then you can begin to find ways around these ratios to get a bigger loan.

The most important element of the ratios is your *gross monthly income.* How big a loan you can get is directly derived from how much money you make, in other words, how big a monthly payment you can afford.

To find your gross monthly income, you must first determine your income both annually and monthly. To do this, you need to determine all your sources of income. These include the following.

Sources of Income

Salary (before taxes)

Profit (from a business as shown on Schedule C of your personal income tax)

Child support

Alimony

Interest, dividend, and royalty income

Any other source of income you may have

When you have all of your income sources, convert them to a monthly figure. To do this, take those which are shown annually and divide by 12. Then add them all up. This gives you your gross monthly income on which the ratios are based. *Note: Gross* means your income before tax deductions of any kind are made.

Trap

Many people today have income from other real estate. For example, you may have another home that you own and rent out. The amount of income exceeds the expenses; hence, you want to add this "profit" to the income category.

Unfortunately, when calculating rental income, you are required by most underwriting procedures to make two calculations. First, you take the income you are receiving from your rental property and multiply it by 75 percent. Then you subtract this figure from your expenses.

For example, let's say that your rental income is $1100 per month. That figure times 75 percent equals $875.

Now let's say that all your expenses, including mortgage payments, taxes, insurance, maintenance, property management, and so forth, come to $1000 a month. You now subtract the allowable income of $875 from the true expenses of $1000 and your property shows an actual loss of $125 per month—this even though in actual fact you are making a $100 a month profit! This is illustrated below.

Gross income	$1100
Multiplier	× 0.75
Allowable income	− 875
Total expenses	$1000
Net income loss	− 125

First, Determine the Loan-to-Value Ratio

The maximum mortgage payment is determined in part by the ratio of the mortgage to the value of the property. The higher the ratio (the less cash you put down), the stricter the requirements.

Generally speaking there are two separate rules, one for ratios of loan to value of over 90 percent, another for under 90 percent. Remember that the loan-to-value ratio is the percentage of the value that represents the loan. An $85,000 mortgage on a $100,000 property represents an 85 percent loan-to-value ratio.

Next, Determine the Mortgage Payment–to–Income Ratio

The first underwriting ratio we'll consider is mortgage payment to income. *Mortgage payment here means only the principal and interest on the loan. It does not take into account other expenses such as taxes, insurance, or home-owner fees.*

Mortgage payment = principal + interest

The mortgage payment–to–income ratio works like this for a *strict underwriter.* In order for you to get a mortgage, the monthly mortgage payment of principal *and* interest cannot exceed:

28 percent of your gross income for mortgages under a 90 percent loan-to-value ratio

25 percent of your gross income for mortgages of a 90 percent loan-to-value ratio

39

This establishes the basic relationship between income and mortgage (principal and interest) payment, as far as the lender is concerned. A strict lender will not give you a mortgage where the payment is more than 25 to 28 percent (depending on the LTV) of your gross income (calculated earlier). Here's an example of how to calculate the maximum mortgage payment (principal plus interest).

Gross monthly income, $	Maximum monthly payment (gross monthly income times 25–28%)
$2500	$ 625–700
3000	750–840
3500	875–980
4000	1000–1120

How to Find the *Maximum Mortgage Payment* You Personally Can Afford

To find the maximum monthly mortgage payment you can afford according to strict lenders, we apply the *above ratio.*

To Find Your Maximum Monthly Mortgage Payment

1. Find your gross income.
2. Multiply by 25 or 28 percent (depending on LTV).
3. The result is your maximum mortgage payment.

Income–to–*Maximum Mortgage Payment* Ratio Example

Gross Monthly Income $4000

80 percent LTV	90 percent LTV
$4000	$4000
× 0.28	× 0.25
$1120	$1000

Let's say your gross monthly income is $4000. The maximum monthly mortgage payment you can afford when applying for an 80 percent LTV is $1120. If you are applying for a 90 percent LTV, the amount is reduced to $1000. (See Fig. 3-1.)

Calculating Your Own *Maximum Monthly Mortgage* Payment

Your gross monthly income	$ _____
Multiplier	0.25 or 0.28
Your maximum mortgage payment	$ _____

Trap

Note that the higher the LTV ratio you go for, the lower the monthly payments you can afford. What this means is that if you opt for a 90 percent

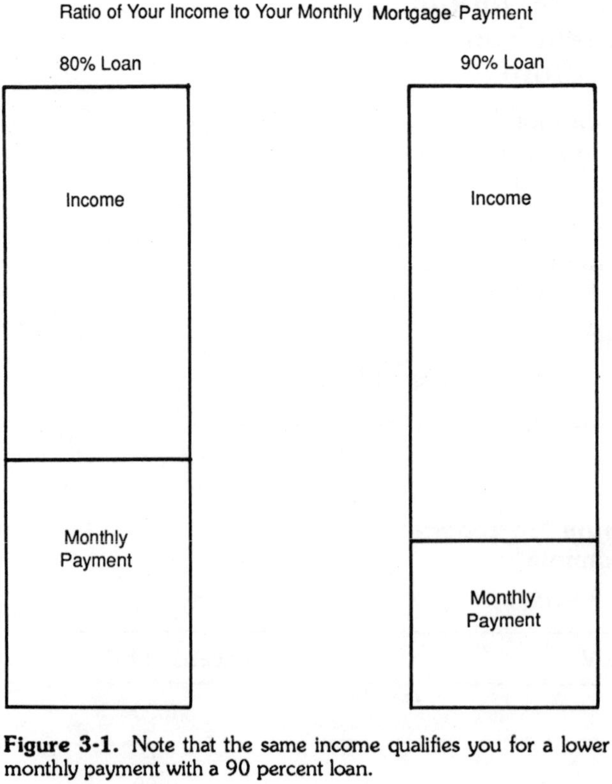

Ratio of Your Income to Your Monthly Mortgage Payment

Figure 3-1. Note that the same income qualifies you for a lower monthly payment with a 90 percent loan.

loan, the maximum loan amount will have to be lower than if you opt for an 80 percent loan.

Now you know the maximum mortgage payment (principal and interest) that you can get. The next logical question is, how big a mortgage does the payment give you?

This depends on two factors, the term of the mortgage and the interest rate.

Calculating the Maximum Mortgage Amount You Can Get Given the Maximum Mortgage Payment (Principal and Interest) You Can Afford

There are charts which give you the maximum mortgage when you know the maximum monthly payment, the term, and the interest. Check Appendix 1. It gives maximum mortgage amounts for a variety of monthly payments, interest rates, and terms. For example, if the maximum monthly mortgage payment you can afford is $1500, you can afford the following 30-year fixed-rate mortgages.

At 9% interest your maximum mortgage is $187,000

At 10% interest your maximum mortgage is   171,000

At 11% interest your maximum mortgage is   158,000

At 12% interest your maximum mortgage is   146,000

Gross Monthly Payment Versus Mortgage Payment

Thus far we have been concerned strictly with the *mortgage payment, which includes only principal and interest.* However, there's more to your gross monthly payment than just principal and interest. There are also taxes and insurance (not to mention homeowner's fees in some areas). The gross monthly payment includes your mortgage payment (principal and interest) plus these other costs such as taxes, insurance, and homeowner's dues. Figure 3-2 shows the steps in finding your gross monthly payment, which includes

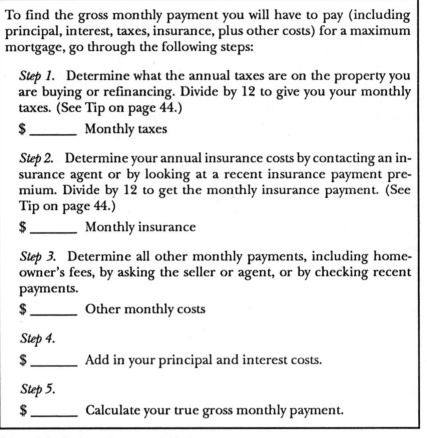

To find the gross monthly payment you will have to pay (including principal, interest, taxes, insurance, plus other costs) for a maximum mortgage, go through the following steps:

Step 1. Determine what the annual taxes are on the property you are buying or refinancing. Divide by 12 to give you your monthly taxes. (See Tip on page 44.)

$ _____ Monthly taxes

Step 2. Determine your annual insurance costs by contacting an insurance agent or by looking at a recent insurance payment premium. Divide by 12 to get the monthly insurance payment. (See Tip on page 44.)

$ _____ Monthly insurance

Step 3. Determine all other monthly payments, including homeowner's fees, by asking the seller or agent, or by checking recent payments.

$ _____ Other monthly costs

Step 4.

$ _____ Add in your principal and interest costs.

Step 5.

$ _____ Calculate your true gross monthly payment.

Figure 3-2. Finding your gross monthly payment.

Principal

Interest

Taxes

Insurance

Homeowner's fees

(For lender's purposes, it does *not* include utilities.) The earlier calculations were just for the mortgage payment (only principal and interest); many lenders use a different ratio to qualify you on the basis of your gross maximum monthly payment. Remember, I am now talking about not only principal and interest but also taxes and insurance (called PITI in the trade) plus homeowner's dues.

For your gross monthly payment (PITI + homeowner's dues) use the following new figures.

Maximum Total Monthly Payment (PITI+)

No more than 33 percent of your gross income for mortgages under 90 percent LTV

No more than 29 percent of your gross income for mortgages of 90 percent LTV

Let's now go through the same calculations as earlier, only this time for the gross maximum monthly payment.

Calculating Your Own Gross Maximum Monthly Payment (PITI+)

Your gross monthly income $ _____

Times 0.29 or 0.33

Your maximum monthly payment $ _____

To calculate the maximum mortgage you can afford given your gross monthly payment, see Appendix 2 for charts which make the calculations directly including PITI.

Typical Gross Monthly Payment

Here's the total gross monthly payment for someone buying a single-family home in a planned unit development (with a homeowner's association):

$ 23	Principal	⎫ mortgage only
764	Interest	⎬
123	Taxes	⎫ Gross
43	Insurance (fire and hazard)	⎬ monthly
25	Mortgage insurance premium	payment
93	Homeowner's association fees	⎭

$1071   *Total monthly payment*

Note that the *monthly mortgage payment,* principal and interest, is only a portion of the total payment.

Tip
_____

You can lower your monthly payments. If you have a mortgage of lower than 80 percent loan-to-value ratio, you can usually elect to pay your property taxes and insurance annually instead of monthly. You aren't saving any money, but you can schedule the payments differently in this manner. This does not change the ratios, but may help your cashflow.

Calculating Your Maximum Mortgage When You Know Only Your Taxes, Insurance, and Other Costs

If you know your taxes, insurance, and other monthly costs, you can find what you have left over for the principal and interest and work back to finding the maximum mortgage you can afford.

Step 1. Multiply your gross monthly income by either 33 percent (80 percent loan) or 29 percent (90 percent loan).

$ _____ Maximum available from income for monthly payment

Step 2. Take the figure from Step 3 in the preceding chart.

$ _____ Other monthly costs

Step 3. Subtract the other costs from your total maximum monthly payment (2 from 1).

$ _____ Maximum you have available for principal and interest (mortgage payment)

Doing the calculations in reverse, as shown above, can sometimes allow you to come out with a higher maximum mortgage payment, particularly if you happen to be in an area with lower taxes or insurance costs.

Note: Appendix 2 allows you to manipulate these figures to quickly determine

Maximum price

Total monthly payment for a given price

Income needed to qualify

Long-Term-Debt Ratio—
Back End

While the front-end ratios we've been discussing determine if you have enough gross income to qualify for a mortgage, the back-end ratio determines if you are sufficiently debt-free to make the payments. While many people have a large income, they are also so encumbered with other debts and loans that the underwriters feel they can't reasonably be expected to make the mortgage payment.

The ratio is roughly as follows: Your total mortgage payment *plus* any other obligations for which you are contracted and which will run for more than 10 months, cannot roughly equal more than 33 percent of your gross monthly income (GMI) for an LTV ratio of 90 percent or 36 percent of GMI for an LTV ratio of 80 percent.

Maximum Total Long-Term Debt

No more than 36 percent of your gross income for mortgages under 90 percent LTV

No more than 33 percent of your gross income for mortgages of 90 percent LTV

Example of Debt Ratio

Let's say that your gross monthly income is $3700. However, out of that you have a car payment of $250, a MasterCard payment of $40, and other payments totaling $130. Figure 3-3 shows steps in calculating your debt ratio.

Debt running more than 10 months

$250	Car payment
40	MasterCard
130	Other
$420	Total debt other than mortgage payment

Trap

Don't now subtract this from your gross income. Rather, it is added to the mortgage payment to figure your debt ratio. It's an important difference.

Let's say that you are contemplating purchasing a home which has a

To find *how large a monthly mortgage payment* you can afford, according to the lending underwriters, calculate the following:

Step 1. Determine your long-term debt. This includes any debt that will take more than 10 months to pay off:

$ _____ Auto payment

$ _____ Credit card

$ _____ Bank loan

$ _____ Home equity loan

$ _____ Line of credit

$ _____ Other consumer loan

$ _____ Child support

$ _____ Alimony

$ _____ Other debt

$ _____ Total long-term debt (TLTD)

Step 2. Calculate the maximum monthly payment that you can afford using the long-term-debt ratio:

Your gross monthly income $ _____ $ _____

(90%) × 0.33 (80%) × 0.36

$ _____ Maximum monthly payment $ _____ $ _____

Step 3. Subtract your total long-term debt, TLTD, from your maximum monthly payment found above.

$ _____ This is the maximum amount you can afford for your monthly payment, including principal, interest, taxes, and insurance.

Step 4. Use a mortgage chart such as supplied in Appendix 2 to look up the amount indicated here. Then read across to the maximum mortgage you can afford for the current interest rate. For example, let's say you have $789 left over *for principal, interest, taxes, and insurance.* At an interest rate of 10 percent, the maximum loan for 30 years is around $70,000.

Figure 3-3. Calculating your debt ratio.

gross monthly payment of $900, calculated as described above (PITI plus other costs). Your total debt would be the gross monthly payment ($900) plus your other long-term debt ($420).

$ 420   Other monthly debt
  900   Mortgage payment
$1320   Total debt

You must now ask yourself if this amount is less than 33 percent of your total income for a 90 percent LTV ratio or less than 36 percent for an 80 percent LTV ratio.

Total income	$3700	$3700
	× 0.33	× 0.36
	$1221	$1332

With the above income and the debt, you would qualify for the loan of your choice if the LTV ratio is 80 percent but not if it is 90 percent.

Tip

Although these ratios purport to determine what you can really afford, in reality they are nothing more than ways of assigning risk to lenders. This is evidenced by the fact that the ratios are higher if you take out an 80 percent loan than a 90 percent loan. The loan amount can be the same in both cases. For example, a 90 percent loan on a $100,000 house is $90,000. An 80 percent loan on a $112,500 home is still $90,000.

Why should you be required to have more monthly income for a $90,000 loan on a $100,000 house (25 percent ratio) than for a $90,000 loan on a $112,500 house (28 percent ratio)? The lenders argue that it is because you are putting more down on the latter than the former and, hence, are less likely to lose it to foreclosure.

That, of course, may make sense in the business world, but it makes no sense at all to a homeowner. Ten or twenty percent down doesn't make it harder or easier to make the monthly payments. From the borrower's perspective, in a truly fair system the qualifications for monthly payments should be a set amount regardless of the LTV ratio of the house. However, no one ever said lenders were fair.

Note: The maximum amount you can afford under the long-term-debt ratio may be different from the maximum you can afford according to the gross monthly income ratio. When there is a difference, you must use the lower figure.

This then is how lenders calculate your maximum mortgage amount. Admittedly it is a complicated process, but it is possible for anyone to figure out.

Having said all this, let's now see how you can stretch it to get a bigger mortgage.

Getting the Lender to Loan You More Money

We used the strictest guidelines in the calculations above, those frequently adopted in the secondary market by government pools such as Ginnie Mae. However, as noted earlier, other secondary lenders may have less strict guidelines. Furthermore, even the secondary lenders regard these ratios as guidelines rather than hard-and-fast rules. What this means is that these ratios can be bent.

If you're working with a good mortgage broker, he or she will know the underwriting guidelines of a variety of lenders and will steer you toward one who will bend your way.

Tip

Don't believe a mortgage broker or lender when it says it can't bend for you. It can.

Don't believe it when you're told all the underwriting guidelines (ratios) are the same. They aren't.

If the person you're working with tries to box you in, find another, more flexible loan person with whom to work. *Once more, shop around!*

Tip

Improve your ratios. You can quickly get better ratios by paying off short-term debt. If you owe on credit cards or have a car loan, determine if there's any way you can pay off the debt so that it doesn't show up. Paying off short-term debt can quickly improve your ratios and may mean the difference between qualifying or not qualifying for a mortgage.

Tip

If you have trouble qualifying for a big enough mortgage, look for an adjustable-rate mortgage. With an ARM, you usually get a low introductory interest rate (teaser) and you may be allowed to qualify at this lower rate.

A lower interest rate will significantly lower the monthly payments for which you need to qualify.

Front-End Flexibility

Let's take the front-end ratio, the gross monthly income. A lender may say to you, "I need to have a 25 percent ratio because you're getting a 90 percent loan-to-value mortgage." But, you may say to the lender. "I understand what you are saying. However, I have no long-term debt other than this mortgage payment. Therefore, I feel a higher ratio is justified. Please qualify me at the 28 percent ratio. Or move me up to a 30 percent ratio."

The person with whom you're working can do it, if he or she wants to. The only real question is, can the mortgage then be sold in the secondary market? Once again, *shop around* for people who work with secondary lenders with more relaxed ratios.

Tip

Look for portfolio lenders. These are typically savings banks or savings and loan associations that plan to hang onto the mortgage and not sell it in the secondary market. They can be the most flexible with their ratios. They may very well bend, *particularly if you agree to keep a large savings and checking balance in their branch.* In any event, it certainly won't hurt to ask.

Back-End Flexibility

The same holds true with the long-term-debt ratio. You can ask the lender to justify a higher ratio. For example, you can request that the lender use a 39 percent ratio or even 40 percent. (I have actually seen one lender go as high as 50 percent!) You may get your way on the basis of any of the following mitigating circumstances:

1. You have a very high income and, as a consequence, it is easier for you to spend a larger portion of it for housing expense than someone with a low income. For example, a person with a $1000 a month income who has a mortgage payment of $350, only has $650 to live for the rest of the month. However, a person with a $10,000 monthly income might pay $5000 in mortgage payments and still have $5000 to live on.

2. You have consistently lived with a higher bigger payment for years. Because of that, you feel you can handle a higher mortgage payment than the ratio allows. Be prepared to bring in receipts to prove your case.

3. You have a very large net worth. Your income may be low, but you may have a million dollars in land holdings or in stock. If times get tough, you have the ability to sell some of your assets to help make the mortgage payments. This should make you a better risk and warrant a higher ratio.

4. You have an excellent credit rating. An excellent credit rating means that you are a very good judge of what you can afford. If you say you can afford a higher ratio, a lender should be willing to listen to you, based on your past performance.

5. You have the potential to significantly increase your earning power in the future. For example, you're a professional, a doctor, lawyer, or engineer, and you're just starting out in your career. In a few years you could be making double what you're earning today. A lender should be willing to take this into account when making a judgment.

All of the above reasons can be used to justify a higher-than-normal debt ratio. However, don't expect every lender to be sympathetic to your view. Many lenders may simply scoff and say they only follow the guidelines. You want to find a lender with the courage to change the rules.

Jumbos—Bigger Mortgages

Thus far we have generally been talking about lenders who are issuing "conforming" loans. This simply means that the mortgages conform to the guidelines generally used by government pools such as Ginnie Mae or Freddie Mac. Yes, the lenders may be willing to bend the rules, if you are a particularly good borrower. But ultimately, you must still qualify under the ratios, even though they may be liberalized.

One of the biggest limitations of these conforming loans has to do with amount. They have a maximum amount. (The most recent maximum was $191,250, but it is always rising as the overall value of properties sold goes up.)

Not all lenders, however, limit themselves to the $191,250 limit. There are many private pools as well as portfolio lenders who lend much higher amounts.

Generally these are called "jumbo" loans. Usually they are conforming in all other ways (such as the ratios), except the amount is higher. Most mortgage brokers, savings banks, or other lenders offer jumbos or can direct you to a lender who does.

Tip

Some jumbos are really "piggybacks." They are two loans—a first mortgage that is conforming and a second that is not. The blended interest rate for these is usually less than for a straight jumbo. Check Chapter 9 for details.

No-Qualifying Mortgages

There is, however, a whole category of mortgages for which you as an individual don't have to qualify for at all. There is no income-to-payment ratio, no debt-to-payment ratio, often no credit check! You simply agree to pay back the money and sign a mortgage document pledging the property as security.

The key to no-qualifying mortgages is that the property is sufficiently valuable to justify the loan regardless of the buyer. To ensure this, the lender typically will only make a maximum loan-to-value of 65 to 70 percent, will often charge 3 to 5 or more points, and will have an interest rate significantly higher than for conventional fixed-rate mortgages.

Here, it is the property which qualifies, not you. For example, let's say that you own a home worth $375,000. You want as much as you can get in a refinance on it. But, you are self-employed and your tax returns don't show you making a very large income. Nevertheless, you yourself feel confident you can make the payments on this size mortgage.

You apply to a mortgage broker who has contacts with private lenders, individuals, or corporations who are interested in making high-yielding loans on real estate. An appraiser looks at the property and agrees that it is indeed worth what you say it is. The broker informs you that a 70 percent mortgage, or $262,500, is available. However, there is a catch. You will have to pay 3 percent above the going market rate for home mortgages and 3 extra points. The current rate for conforming loans is 10 percent, so your interest rate will be 13 percent. The normal points are 1½. You'll be charged 5.

Will you go along with this? You will if you want a mortgage.

Tip

Remember that in a no-qualifying mortgage, there is no qualification made as to whether or not you can handle the payments, although some states (such as California) require the lender to tell you up front that you probably cannot make the payments. Whether or not you get the loan is strictly up to you. As a consequence, some people do get in over their heads and can't keep up the payments.

Trap

No-qualifying lenders in some cases are nothing more than real estate acquirers. They *want* the borrower to default so they can take back the property through foreclosure and then resell it. Because they are operating on such a low loan-to-value ratio, in most cases they can actually make money on the resale. In fact, some lenders consider this mortgage as a way to get equity rather than as a way to lend money!

From your perspective, however, losing a property in which you hold as much as 30 to 35 percent equity makes little sense. Be sure that you can afford the payments before you get the mortgage.

Trap

Beware of lenders who, sensing you are unsure about the payments, want to impound payments out of the money loaned. I recently was talking with a lender who made a loan of $1.3 million to a widow in a house in San Francisco. I whistled to think of the payments. The lender chuckled and said her income was only $7000 a month; the payments on the mortgage alone were $10,000 a month.

I asked, How could that be? How could she pay the debt?

"Easy," he replied, "we impounded the first two years' worth of payments out of the money lent. We're holding $240,000 back to make those payments. She's tickled pink because she's getting nearly a million dollars with no payments for two years."

I asked what would happen after 2 years? He replied that she could then refinance.

This was not a sweet deal for the widow. For one thing, she lost the use of a quarter-million dollars (and the interest it would generate) for 2 years. Second, she really couldn't afford the mortgage and was, in effect, borrowing money to make payments—something you never want to do.

The only person really making a killing on this deal was the lender. It had a mortgage secured by a good property and 2 years' worth of payments in its account in the bank. How could it lose?

Lines of Credit

Finally, there is a kind of loan that goes under a variety of names, but really amounts to a line of credit. It is available from some banks.

Here, you put up your property as collateral for the mortgage. However, you also convince the bank that you have a large net worth, typically two to three times the amount of money borrowed. The bank makes you a loan without regard to income ratios.

This is a kind of cross between a personal loan and a mortgage; however, it does tie up your property. These types of loans usually involve much higher interest rates than straight mortgages.

Adjusting Values

Thus far we've been discussing how to get a bigger loan by increasing your qualifying abilities. There is, however, a different problem that may occur. It has to do with the property itself.

Let's say that you are applying for a mortgage and the lender is going to use traditional underwriting standards. Your income and credit history warrant a big loan. However, when the appraiser goes out to look at the property, he or she says that it isn't worth what you think it is. The lender, bound to a set loan-to-value ratio, offers you less than you think you should get. Let's consider an example.

Recently I sold a house in southern California. This house had been worth around $350,000 at the market's peak. However, the market had slipped recently and it sold for $320,000. The buyer applied for an 80 percent mortgage. Based on the price, the buyer was hoping to get a mortgage of $256,000.

In good times this would have been no problem. A buyer ready, willing, and able to make a purchase putting up a cash down payment normally establishes price. After all, how could anyone doubt that the house was worth $320,000, given the fact of a legitimate sale at that price?

The appraiser doubted it. When I talked with him, he said that he had been instructed by the lender to be conservative. The lender was concerned that prices might fall further in the area and didn't want to be caught with a white elephant. (The recent bad loans which have weakened S&Ls and banks were the culprit here—they made the lender wary of new loans.) Therefore the appraiser was going to give a value that would be sure not to hurt the lender. As a result, the appraiser gave the property a value of only $290,000.

This threatened to blow apart the sale. I would have to lower my price, which I would not do. Or the buyer would have to come up with $30,000 more in cash, which she did not want to do. Or I'd have to give her a second mortgage for $30,000 at virtually no interest (she couldn't afford higher payments). None of these alternatives was acceptable.

I went to speak with the lender and pointed out that we had an arm's-length sale on the house of $320,000. That should be the true value. The lender wouldn't budge. So I encouraged the buyer to apply with other lenders, agreeing to pay for additional appraisal reports.

Each lender uses an appraiser approved by that lender. We simply sought out lenders who used a different appraiser than the first one. We didn't tell them we already had an appraisal on the house, and they didn't ask. We tried three lenders. Of the three, two gave appraisals that were still lower than the sales price, but the third was right on the money. The borrower applied for and got that mortgage and I had my sale.

All of which is to say that no matter how adamant lenders are about the LTV ratio, it really all depends on the value, and the value is nothing more than an educated opinion.

Tip

If you want a higher mortgage and qualifying isn't a problem, get a new lender and a different appraisal. Just be sure that the new lender uses a different person to make the appraisal.

Consider, all lenders may insist on an 80 percent LTV ratio. If the appraisal is $100,000, the maximum loan is $80,000. But if the appraisal is $125,000, the maximum loan is $100,000. Both maintain the 80 percent LTV ratio. It's just that the first has a lower value than the second.

Values are nothing more than opinions. It's like shopping for doctors. If you don't like what one says, you can get a second opinion.

In this chapter we've examined how loans are made. We've seen what you have to do to qualify in terms of income and we've examined some of the ratios that lenders use. In the next chapter we'll move onto a bit touchier subject, your credit and how to improve it.

4

Credit Problems and Solutions

Brushing Up the Way You Look to a Lender

Introduction

Lenders want borrowers to have good credit. When you apply for a mortgage, therefore, the lender looks not only at your income, as discussed in Chapter 3, but at your history of repayment. After all, if you've got the income, but have demonstrated that you don't repay loans, the lender isn't going to be too anxious to advance you any funds.

The lender will want a "standard factual." This is a special credit report that almost all lenders use. It combines credit reports from as many as three of the nation's biggest credit-reporting agencies. It also reports judgments against you, any divorces you may have had, and it verifies your employment history. (It's really amazing the amount of information that credit-reporting agencies have today!) At some point in the loan process the lender will ask you for permission to get a credit report, and in most cases, it will also ask you to pay for that report. The cost of the report is $50 or less.

What the Lender Is Looking For

When the lender gets the credit report, a loan officer will scan it. He or she is looking to see the following:

1. You have borrowed money from a variety of sources over a period of years. At least the last 5 years should show up. A mixture of loans from credit card companies, personal loans from banks, automobile loans, and other types of borrowing should show up.

2. You show a consistent history of repaying loans borrowed when they are due.

3. You show a consistent history of paying on time.

4. You have no foreclosures or bankruptcies on your record for at least the last 7 years.

Trap
___

If you find that you're unable to pay all of your bills, at least make your mortgage payment. If there's only one bill that you can pay, be sure it's your mortgage payment.

Lenders, with proper explanation, as we'll see shortly, may forgive any late payments *except late mortgage payments.* Lenders never forgive late mortgage payments on a new mortgage application.

It only makes sense. You're coming to a lender to ask for a mortgage. The lender looks at your credit report and sees that you were late on your previous mortgage. Do you think it now wants to make a new mortgage to you? Never!

The one way to be sure of not being able to get a new mortgage is to be late on your old mortgage payments. Never be late!

Tip
___

Having no credit record is almost as bad as having a credit record with bad reports. The lender is hoping to find that you have a long history of borrowing money and paying it back when due. If you've always paid cash in the past and have no credit history to speak of, you may find that your mortgage application is denied. It's not that your credit history is bad; it's that the lender has nothing on which to base a current loan.

Bad Credit: A Lender's-Eye View

When you apply for a car loan or a credit card line of credit, often you can get by with some late payments and an occasional failure to pay, provided it was in the dim past. But when you're applying for a home mortgage, and possibly hundreds of thousands of dollars are at stake, any bad credit won't do.

Here's what could cause a lender to turn you down:

1. Late payments on a previous mortgage.

2. More than one late payment on any other loan in the past two years.

3. Any failure to repay loans in the past five years.

4. Any foreclosures at any time.

In other words, lenders are strict. They want to know that you are a sterling credit risk—that is to say, no risk at all.

However, the above list of what a lender is looking for is the ideal. In the real world, most borrowers don't have such sterling credit. Lenders understand this, and as a consequence, they are often willing to lower their standards . . . provided there are mitigating circumstances.

This means that you must provide a lender with a *written* explanation for any bad credit you have. If you have late payments, you must explain why they were late. If you defaulted on a loan, you must give all the details and include verifying information. If you had a foreclosure, you must explain how it occurred and why circumstances are different now. Here are some explanations that lenders *may* accept.

Tip

It's a good idea to provide a letter of explanation to a lender *before* it gets the credit report. Your acknowledging the problem and dealing with it puts you one leg up on it. If you wait for the credit report to show it, the lender may wonder if you're trying to conceal something.

Some Explanations a Lender Might Accept

You Were Unemployed or Sick for a Period of Time. This may be acceptable if you have a long history of excellent credit broken by a short period, say 6 months, of poor credit, followed by another long period (at least 2 years) of good credit. This explanation is particularly helpful in explaining late payments.

You Had a Divorce or Death in the Family.   Here again, you normally must show that this happened some time ago and since that time you've had excellent credit. This is particularly useful when you defaulted on loans. You had a big setback in your life, but now you're back in the saddle, as evidenced by at least 2 years' worth of good credit history.

The Bad Credit is Someone Else's Fault.   This is not a great excuse, but a plausible one. Perhaps you cosigned for someone else on a car. They ran off with the car and never made the payments. You were stuck with either making payments for 5 years on a car you didn't have and couldn't sell, or simply refusing. You refused.

This shows you had the good sense not to get in debt over your head. However, it also shows that you had the bad sense to cosign for someone else. Further, given tough circumstances, instead of plodding on and making payments, you'll bail out—something that makes good sense to you, but which lenders don't particularly like to see.

You Got in Over Your Head.   You live in California, but bought property in Oklahoma just before the oil price bust of the mid-1980s. You couldn't sell or rent it and weren't there to take care of it. Consequently, you lost it to foreclosure.

But that was 5 years ago and it was on rental real estate. Here and now you're trying to buy a home in which you plan to live. The circumstances are different. Maybe the lender will agree.

The Credit Reporting Agency Made a Mistake.   Credit reporting agencies' mistakes are legendary. They may have you mixed up with someone else. Get proof of identity on yourself and the other person. Maybe your wallet or purse was stolen a few years ago. Get verification from credit card companies. Verify any mistakes, and they shouldn't be held against you.

Tip

If you want a lender to ignore bad credit, two things you can do are to either put more money down, thus reducing your loan-to-value ratio, or get better income and debt ratios.

It's almost a sure bet that if you have marginal credit, are putting the minimum down, and are at the limit with your ratios, you will be turned down. On the other hand, if you have marginal credit, but are putting 20 percent down (instead of 10 percent) and have lower than underwriting ratios, you stand an excellent chance of getting the financing.

Tip

While lenders are on the watch for any late payments or defaults on any loans, one of the big jokes in the industry is Sears. I've seen lenders look down a credit report that has a few blemishes on it. They scrutinize each carefully until they come to the one that is a Sears late payment report, and say, "Oh, that's just Sears. Ignore it."

It seems that Sears has reported late payments on so many individuals (for whatever reasons), even those with outstanding credit, that their reports of late payments have become almost meaningless in the mortgage-lending industry.

That doesn't mean you should not pay your Sears bill. It just means that when I work with individuals whose only bad credit is Sears, I don't worry at all about their qualifying.

How to Fix Bad Credit

There are many books out there which purport to show you ways to fix your bad credit. Be aware that there's no fixing truly bad credit. What you can do, however, is correct errors and write letters to be included with your credit report which give mitigating circumstances.

For example, I recently ran into an individual who sold his home and gave the buyer a second mortgage. That buyer eventually defaulted and the seller began making payments on the existing first mortgage while attempting to foreclose on the second. He found, however, that the property had fallen in value to the point where it wasn't worth foreclosing. So he stopped making payments on the first and simply took a complete loss on the second.

However, when the first mortgage went into foreclosure, he was erroneously listed as a borrower because he had temporarily made payments on it, and the credit reporting agency put a foreclosure against his name. He discovered this when he applied for a new mortgage and was turned down by the lender.

What he had to do was to contact the lender of the first mortgage and secure an explanation from it and take that along with all the documentation from the original second mortgage and present that to the new lender. Once the new lender understood the situation, the mortgage was approved.

If the borrower had first submitted summaries of all of this to the credit reporting agency, he may never have had problems with the new lender.

Tip

The basic method of correcting bad credit is twofold. First, you have to write a letter explaining the problem and why it wasn't your fault. Second, you have to submit documentation proving what you say.

Credit reporting agencies are required by law to insert letters of explanation and to make substantiating documentation available to those who ask for reports. They are not, however, required to remove bad reports. These will tend to stay on your report usually for a minimum of 7 years.

For information on the exact procedure of dealing with a credit reporting agency, check into one of the many books on the subject. Just be sure to get a book that doesn't promise you the sky, but instead simply offers you the methods of correcting mistakes.

Trap

Beware of credit "fixers." There are big scams currently under way in the country that purport to fix bad credit. In several these advertisements ask you to call a 900 number to learn how to fix your credit. Usually you end up with a big telephone bill and no help.

Another scam is where credit "cancelers" purport to be able to remove bad credit from your credit report and to give you good credit.

Be aware that there is no legitimate way to fix bad credit. You can insert explanations, as indicated. You can also establish good credit by paying off bills on time. But, you can't remove the facts if you did, in fact, have late payments, judgments against you, foreclosures, defaults, and so forth.

This is not to say that there aren't legitimate credit counseling services available. There are hundreds of these across the country. They can help you manage your budget better and establish good credit in the future.

Tip

If you have no credit (as opposed to bad credit), obtain some well in advance of seeking a mortgage. Start out by getting a gasoline credit card. Then move up to a universal credit card such as Visa or MasterCard.

Then take out a personal loan from a bank. You can pay it back in 90 days—you only want the bank to report that they were willing to lend you money and that you paid it back. You can easily do this by borrowing an amount that you already have on deposit. This is the most secure loan possible and most banks are more than willing to make the loan.

Keep getting credit and paying it back. Within 6 months you can have the beginnings of a strong credit history, and within 2 years you can have credit enough to *get* any mortgage you would otherwise qualify for.

The Bottom Line

Credit is a judgment call on the part of the lender. As noted, extra cash down and better ratios may make up for less-than-sterling credit. If the lender has a lot of money to loan and few borrowers, it is also likely to be more lenient.

However, the bottom line is that the better your credit, the more chance you have of securing the mortgage you desire. The goal is to keep your credit good. Avoid getting bad credit at all costs.

5
Adjustable-Rate Mortgages

Approach With Caution

Introduction

In the beginning, there was the fixed-rate mortgage. This simply meant that the interest rate remained the same for the life of the loan. If your initial interest rate was 10 percent, you paid 10 percent in year 7, in year 15, in year 22, and in year 30. The rate never changed.

The fixed-rate mortgage is easy to understand. It makes sense. It's what made residential real estate so widely owned and so popular in this country.

Times Have Changed

However, back in the late 1970s something happened to the savings-and-loan industry which made the fixed-rate mortgage undesirable for lenders. Interest rates went up—sharply.

Prior to that time, interest rates had fluctuated largely within a maximum of 4 points. Between 1950 and 1975 the rates were almost never lower than 6 percent nor higher than 10 percent. This presented little problem for lenders who went with the flow.

However at the end of the 1970s, we had a dramatic, though temporary, burst of high inflation. Suddenly mortgage interest rates were 12 percent, then 15 percent, then in some rare cases for hardy individuals who were willing to risk it, 18 percent!

This put the lenders at great risk, because not only did mortgage interest rates go up, but the interest they paid to savers also went up. Because of inflation they were making a few new high-interest mortgages, but they were also paying a lot of high interest on their new savings deposits.

Unfortunately for them, the majority of their existing mortgages were at older, much lower interest rates. In some cases they were paying out 12 percent interest on a savings account and at the same time taking in an average interest rate of 9 percent on their mortgage portfolio. You can't stay in business too long at that rate. Yet, that was the position that many S&Ls found themselves in.

Many S&Ls rightly felt that when their cost of funds rose, they were put in jeopardy. They wanted their mortgage interest income to match their savings outflow. They were afraid that increased interest rates down the road would jeopardize their solvency.

Even when interest rates fell, the S&Ls didn't feel secure. They wanted a guarantee that the same problem wouldn't overtake them again. Of course, the only person who could give such a guarantee was you, the borrower.

So they shifted much of the burden of risk of interest rate volatility to borrowers. They made the borrowers liable should interest rates jump up again.

The result was the adjustable-rate mortgage, or ARM. Here the interest rate charged to the borrower fluctuates roughly in response to the cost of funds for the lender. Lenders said it was fairer. Borrowers, not knowing any better, agreed.

Tip

Almost all modern ARMs have caps or limitations on the interest rate. This puts both a ceiling and a floor on rate fluctuation (Figure 5-1). For example, the interest rate might be limited to rising not more than 5 percent nor falling not more than 5 percent from its current rate.

Tip

There's very little that's fair about the ARM. In most cases it is unfair to the borrower and a gravy train for the lender. (It's interesting to note that the S&L debacle of thousands of failed institutions did not occur until *after* the widespread adoption of ARMS.) Most ARMS do not protect the lenders much because their adjustments to interest rate spikes

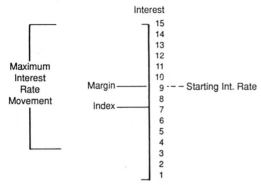

Figure 5-1. How an ARM works. The interest rate on an ARM which has a 6 percent payment cap can move up or down only 6 percent each way from the starting interest rate.

are slow and often capped. On the other hand, most borrowers are ill-prepared to make higher mortgage payments when interest rates in general move up. In the early days of ARMS, before adequate regulation, there was much ripping off of unwary borrowers by lenders offering them unrealistically low "teaser" rates to get into the ARM, and then quickly raising the interest rate and payments, driving the borrower into default. Some say that this contributed significantly to the failure of many greedy S&Ls. (These teasers are still present, as we'll see shortly.)

On the other hand, when money is tight because of high interest rates, an ARM may be the only realistic alternative available to many borrowers. And if the ARM is approached correctly, the borrower in some circumstances, which we'll discuss, can actually benefit more than the lender from its use.

Mortgage-Hunting Scenario

Perhaps an example will clarify just how an ARM actually works. Let's say you obtain a mortgage of $100,000 at 10 percent interest per year for 30 years. If this is a fixed-rate loan, your interest will remain at 10 percent for the full 30-year term. Also the monthly payment will remain at a fixed $878.

On the other hand, if this is an ARM, the interest rate may fluctuate up (for example, to 12 percent) or down (for example, to 8 percent) over the term of the loan. With an ARM, the interest rate charged is adjusted up or down at regular intervals. Similarly, your payments may fluctuate widely, for example between $600 and $1200. See Figure 5-2 for a chart of how an ARM works.

Tip

The big advantage of a fixed-rate mortgage is that you always know where you stand. If the interest rate is 12 percent and the payments are $1000 a month, they are not going to change. They will be the same at year 5 as they are at year 30. There is great peace of mind in such knowledge.

Also, as time goes by, chances are your income will grow. As your income goes up, you will be devoting less of it, proportionately, to the fixed monthly payment. As a result, you will feel—and actually will be getting—richer!

Finally, if you get a fixed-rate mortgage at a time when interest rates are low and then, subsequently, interest rates rise, you are protected. The interest rate remains at the original (now low) level. On the other hand, if this is an ARM, the interest rate could fluctuate up, to 16 percent, for example, or down, to 6 percent, over the term of the loan. In year 3 you may be paying 10 percent. In year 11 you could be paying 8 percent. In year 20 you might be paying 16 percent! With an ARM the interest rate charged is adjusted up or down at regular intervals according to the general cost of money at the time. Thus if interest rates rise, you are not protected.

The Advantages of ARMs

This is not to say, however, that ARMs have no advantages. They, too, have their place. There are two big advantages to an ARM—its low initial interest (teaser) rate and its availability.

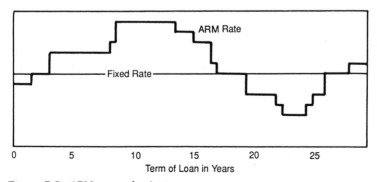

Figure 5-2. ARM rate vs. fixed rate.

Lower Rates Up Front, Short-Term

In times of volatile interest rates, such as between 1978 and 1982, lenders such as S&Ls and banks were afraid to lend money long term. They didn't want to commit themselves to a 30-year real estate loan when they had no idea where interest rates would be even 6 months into the future.

Thus, while lenders were quoting fixed rates of 17 percent (to protect themselves), they were also quoting ARMs of 12 percent. They felt comfortable with the ARM because they knew that if interest rates in general rose, the rate on the ARM would also rise. Thus, when fixed-rate loans are difficult or impossible to find, ARMS are usually plentiful.

Easier Availability

This leads to the second advantage of an ARM. As an inducement to get this type of mortgage, the lender will typically offer a discount, will initially knock off several points (a point is 1 percent of interest) from the market rate. Thus, if you find you can't qualify for the property you want with a fixed-rate mortgage, perhaps you can get the home of your dreams with a lower-initial-rate ARM.

The "Teaser"

To induce borrowers to go with their ARM, lenders usually offer a "teaser." When a borrower asks how much the ARM's interest rate is, he or she is usually told the teaser rate, which may be as much as 3 points less than the current market rate. For example, the teaser rate for an ARM may be 7 percent while the market rate for fixed mortgages is 10 percent. This is usually quite an inducement to borrowers to consider the ARM. The following is a typical ARM.

Introductory discount

Current index rate	8%
Margin	+2%
Current ARM interest rate	10%
Teaser	7%

The market interest rate for the above ARM is 10 percent. However, that may be half a point higher than the current market for fixed-rate mortgages. Few people would opt for an ARM when they can get a fixed-interest mortgage for less. Consequently, you have the teaser.

Of course, lenders don't conceal the truth. If you apply for the ARM , you will be told what the true APR (annual percentage rate) is. This is a combination of the teaser rate and the current market rate. In the above loan, it would probably be around 9.5 percent, depending on several factors. In short, you get roughly the same deal whether it's an ARM or a fixed-rate. The only real difference is the terms.

Trap

Be aware of teaser rates because they do not reflect what you will be paying in monthly payments after only a short while. If the teaser can be stretched out for years, it may be to your advantage. But if it only lasts a few months, it can result in swift payment increases.

Trap

Some borrowers think (regardless of what lenders may say) that if interest rates go down on an ARM, their payments likewise will automatically go down. This may not be the case for your ARM.

The problem here, again, is the teaser rate. If you get a teaser rate, you are paying substantially below-market interest rates. The market rate would have to go down to equal your teaser rate just for your payments to remain constant. If the market rate goes down, but not as far as your teaser, your payments have to rise. If the market rate stays the same, your payments have to rise. Table 5-1 shows why.

Note that in the table, even though the index falls, it does not fall low enough to equal the teaser until it's gone down by nearly a third. In other words, unless the index falls 3 percent, in this example, your payments are bound to rise as the teaser expires.

Of course, if the adjustment period is longer or if there is a cap, the jump may be less steep and take longer. For example, if the index remains constant and your mortgage is adjusted annually with a maximum step of 1½ percent per adjustment, then it will take 2 years for your mortgage interest rate to get from 9 percent to 12 percent.

Table 5-1. Effect of Teaser Interest Rates

Index rate, %	Margin, %	Market mortgage rate, %	Teaser, %	Difference, %
10	2	12	9	3
9	2	11	9	2
8	2	10	9	1
7	2	9	9	0

The idea to keep sight of in all this, however, is that the teaser is temporary. If the index remains constant or goes down only slightly, then your mortgage interest rate and payments must go up.

Understanding the Problems With Teasers

The problem with teasers is that they disguise the true nature of the mortgage. Borrowers are lured to the ARM by a low initial interest rate. Many never really understand that the low rate is just until the next adjustment period and that unless the index goes down dramatically, their interest rate must automatically go up each adjustment period until it reaches or exceeds the market interest rate.

Teasers and the Underqualification Problem

The worst-case scenario comes about when you are underqualified for a mortgage because of the teaser rate. Qualifying means that you must demonstrate an ability to repay in order to get a mortgage. As we've already seen, besides a good credit history and sufficient down payment, this also means that you have enough income to make the monthly payments. If you can't make the payments, ultimately, you will lose the property one way or another.

In an ARM lenders have in the past qualified borrowers not on the market rate of the mortgage (as explained above), but rather on the basis of the teaser. The result was that borrowers frequently got into trouble as soon as the mortgage rate went up. Here's how it happens.

Introductory Discount Rate

Mortgage amount	$100,000	
Teaser	9%	(True market rate: 11%)
Monthly payment (30 years)	$ 804	(True payment needed: $952)
Monthly income needed to qualify for loan	$ 2,412	(True income needed: $2856)

The monthly payment on the mortgage, just counting the teaser, is roughly $800. To qualify (assuming income must be roughly three times monthly payment and for the moment forgetting about taxes and insurance) the lender determines that the borrower should be making at least $2412. With this income the borrower, in theory, should be able to afford the initial payments.

However, as soon as the teaser vanishes, the market interest rate on the mortgage will likely rise to 11 percent. As a result, the payments rise correspondingly to $952. While a person might be able to afford $804, can that person afford $952?

Comparison of Qualifying

	Mortgage amount	Payment	Monthly income needed to qualify
At market	$100,000	$952	$2,856
Teaser	$100,000	$804	2,412
Difference			$ 444

The difference of $444 a month is what you should be making to qualify for the mortgage at market rates. If you don't make this much money, then when the rate is adjusted upward, you may not be able to afford the new, higher payment.

Trap

The above scenario is a trap for borrowers. If the lender is correct in its assumptions about what is needed in order to qualify for the mortgage, the borrower won't be able to make the payments and could lose the house.

Tip

On the other hand, you may be a better judge of your budgeting than the lender's guidelines suggest. Maybe you *can* handle the higher payments on a lower income. Being qualified for a teaser rate, therefore, may allow you greater flexibility in acquiring a mortgage. The key factor here is just to be aware up front of the dangers.

Teasers Today

In the ARM market today, most lenders are refusing to qualify borrowers at the teaser rate. However, they are not qualifying them at the current market rate either. Many use a complex formula which qualifies them somewhere in between.

Be sure you understand how your lender is qualifying you. And be sure you can truly afford the mortgage before you get it. Make your own calculations.

Why Keep the Teasers

Lenders continue to use teasers in ARMs for a simple reason. In most cases, the ARM is basically a less desirable mortgage for the borrower, and without the teaser no one would want one. The lender uses the teaser to get borrowers to take out ARMs.

It should be noted that all the problems I've been discussing should normally be contained in the loan documents. The index is specified, the margin is indicated, and the initial interest rate is stated. The only thing that is sometimes left out is a clear explanation of the consequences of the teaser. One lender I talked to, who asked to remain anonymous, said, "If the borrower wants to make false assumptions about the loan, that's his problem. All the borrower has to do is ask, and we'll clearly confirm that the monthly payment and the interest rate must rise if the index doesn't change."

In other words, *caveat emptor.* "Let the buyer (or in this case the borrower) beware." The lender will indeed confirm and explain, and the explanation may even be written down for you to read. *Take the time to ask and read.*

Tip

Here are some questions to ask about the teaser that should help you to understand it.

"If the index remains constant, what will happen to the mortgage interest rate and my payment at the next adjustment period?"

"If the index remains constant, what will be my exact mortgage payment at the next two adjustment periods?"

This should give you a pretty good idea of what to expect in terms of monthly payments.

Mortgage-Hunting Scenario

I recently was asked for some advice on a mortgage by a young couple buying their first home. It was in the San Francisco Bay area, where prices are extremely high. They could just barely afford the down payment on the house and would be struggling to make the monthly payments. The only mortgage they could qualify for was an ARM with an introductory discount (teaser) of 3 percent below market.

Their initial payments would be $2000 a month. With both of them working, they figured they could just squeak by at this. They asked if I thought they should go ahead with the loan and the mortgage.

I asked them how often the adjustment periods were and the steps. They responded, every 6 months and 2 percent.

My next question to them was, "Can you afford payments of about $2400 a month right now?"

No, they answered, they certainly couldn't. Then I asked them why they thought they could afford them in 6 months' time? In 6 months, unless the market rate fell significantly, their mortgage interest rate would rise 2 percent and their payments would go up by $400.

The best way to think of the teaser, I suggested, was as a bonus. Think of it as a Christmas present. It's great to receive, but you have to be prepared to live without it. If they couldn't handle $2400-a-month payments, which they almost surely would have within 6 months, they had no business buying the property.

Tip

Don't be like the fish who gives up its life for a juicy-looking worm with a hook hidden inside. With mortgages, the first adjustment period can pass like a flash, and then you can be up against the market interest rate. Better to face it now, before you get the loan than later when you're already on the hook.

On the other hand, teasers are not all bad. There are some benefits, if you can resell quickly.

An example of this advantage occurred with a friend of mine. He purchased a home and was given a choice of an ARM with an introductory rate of $7\frac{1}{2}$ percent or a fixed-rate mortgage at 10 percent. He selected the ARM.

The rate on the ARM would adjust upward by a maximum of 2 percent a year. Thus 2 years later he was paying a bit over 10 percent. (The ARM rate will typically end up higher than then current market interest rates to make up for the period when it was lower than those rates.)

However, the market was fairly hot in his area of the country, and after 2 years he sold at a profit. Thus, he took advantage of the low initial teaser rate and sold before the piper had to be paid.

Tip

If you are only planning to hold the property for a year or two (perhaps as an investment), then you can take advantage of the initial teaser discount. You can get the below-market-interest-rate ARM and then later, when the interest rate adjusts upward, sell the property.

Easier to Qualify

Don't entirely knock the easier qualifications of the teaser rate on ARMS. Being easier to qualify for is a real advantage of an ARM.

For example, suppose that interest rates for fixed-rate loans are 12 percent and the payment would be $1000 per month. Also suppose that the introductory rate for an ARM is 10 percent with a monthly payment of $850. It is far easier to qualify for an $850 monthly payment than for a $1000 one. The ARM might mean getting the house, whereas the fixed-rate mortgage would mean losing the deal.

Often a home buyer who can't qualify for a fixed-rate loan can qualify for a lower-introductory-interest-rate ARM. Thus the only way to make a purchase in this case may be to get the ARM.

Trap

Just because ARMs are easier to qualify for, don't think that there are no qualifications. Typically you will be asked to show your income for the previous *3 years*. It will then be averaged to give you a qualifying income.

This can be a particular problem for self-employed individuals who've just had a big year. They won't be allowed to count only that year. They have to count the previous two slimmer years as well.

Assumability of Fixed-Rate Mortgages Versus ARMS

One big disadvantage of fixed-rate loans originated in today's market is that they are, in general, not assumable. (VA and FHA loans are a limited exception.) This was not the case in the past (over 15 years ago), when many fixed-rate mortgages were assumable.

The trouble comes about when you want to sell. You may get a great 8 percent fixed-rate mortgage. A few years later, you want to sell, and the mortgage rates have risen to 12 percent. You think to yourself that you have a great selling point—a juicy 8 percent mortgage. Any buyer would love to have a house with a mortgage like that.

Only the lender is thinking differently. It absolutely does not want to continue an 8 percent mortgage when current rates are at 12 percent. So it indicates it will exercise its "due-on-sale" clause, meaning that the mortgage has to be paid off if you want to sell the home (see Chapter 2 for a more detailed explanation).

Here you are sitting with a wonderful 8 percent rate thinking you have a real selling feature only to discover that the loan is written in such a way that it all becomes due and payable at the moment of sale. Yes, you get the benefit of the 8 percent while you own the property. But the next buyer can't. (It's like the new-car warranties of some manufacturers. They apply to the first buyer, but not to subsequent owners.)

Most ARMs, on the other hand, are assumable. Assumability here means that if the buyer can qualify for the payments, as if qualifying for a new mortgage, he or she can take over the ARM. This can save the buyer some of the costs of financing a new loan.

However, most buyers aren't going to be interested in assuming an old ARM. There are several reasons. One is that most people prefer a fixed-rate mortgage if they can get it. Another is that an old ARM has lost the teaser advantage of a low initial rate, and now the payments are up there as high as (or often higher than) a fixed rate.

Trap

Some lenders point out as a supposed advantage of an ARM over a fixed-rate mortgage that when interest rates go down, the ARM goes down as well. Thus, the ARM's disadvantage of having the mortgage interest rate go up with a rising interest rate market is offset by the rate going down in a falling interest rate market. This is compared to a fixed-rate mortgage that stays the same when interest rates go down.

In theory, this argument makes sense. In practice, however, it doesn't work that way. When interest rates go down, those with fixed-rate mortgages as well as those with ARMs typically refinance to a lower fixed rate. Thus the fixed rate offers the same advantage here as the ARM. The only savings are the costs of refinancing, which you don't have to incur with the ARM. Many borrowers feel, however, that these costs are more than offset by getting a fixed-rate mortgage which will remain at the new lower rate. Remember, the ARM turns around and goes up again when the market reverses direction.

How an ARM Works

I've talked in general about ARMs versus fixed-rate mortgages. Now, let's get down to brass tacks on how ARMs actually work.

The Index

In order to determine what the interest rate for an ARM is, the mortgage has to be indexed. This means that the interest rate of the ARM is tied to some well-known economic measure called an *index*. Typical indexes include Treasury Bill rates of various lengths, the cost of mortgage funds to the lender, and the cost of funds available to the borrower from government agencies.

The way the index works is quite simple. If the index falls, the ARM's interest rate will fall. If the index rises, the ARMS interest rate will rise.

Tip

The quality of an ARM is frequently determined in part by the index to which it is tied. Lenders want their ARMS tied to indexes which record volatility in the market. But borrowers should want their ARMs tied to those indexes which tend to move slowly, if at all, in different market conditions. Finding the right index is often one of the most important features when selecting an ARM.

Stability of the index means that your payments aren't likely to fluctuate too much. A volatile index means that your payments could be all over the board. For most borrowers wide fluctuations in monthly payment are very hard to handle.

The Most Commonly Used Indexes

The agencies regulating ARMS do not specify which index a lender must use. Rather, it is up to the lender to make this selection. The regulators only specify that the index must be one over which the lender has no control, it must reflect interest rates in general, and it must be widely publicized.

The most commonly used indexes are

1. Cost of funds for the lender
2. Treasury securities indexes
   a. 6-month T-Bill
   b. 1-year treasury yields
   c. 3-year treasury yields
3. Prime rate
4. Average cost of fixed-rate mortgages
5. Libor (London Interbranch rate)

An explanation follows of what each of these different indexes covers.

Cost-of-Funds Index
Compiled by the Federal Home Loan Bank Board, this gives the average interest rate that member banks and S&Ls paid during the previous period. It is reported monthly and by district. It represents the cost to members (banks and S&Ls) of money if they have to borrow from the government.

10-Year History

- Stable, less dramatic movements up and down
- Most commonly used is the 11th District cost-of-funds index

Treasury Securities Index
Published weekly by the Federal Reserve Board, it gives the constant maturity interest rate for treasury securities. This is the interest rate that investors pay to buy these government debts.

10-Year History

  6-month T-Bill
- Most volatile of indexes
- Most closely reflects current market money conditions
- Based on the weekly auction rates

  1-Year T-Bill
- Also volatile
- Based on the weekly average of daily yields of actively traded one-year T-bills

  3- to 5-Year T-Bills
- Similarly volatile
- Based on constant maturities

Prime Rate Index
This is the lowest rate that banks charge their best customers for short-term borrowing. The rate often will vary by as much as half a point between lenders. Therefore, when used as an index, the composite prime rate as reported in the *Wall Street Journal* is usually given.

10-Year History

- Relatively stable, moves up or down in fairly large increments

Average Mortgage Rate
This is an index composed of the average interest rate for newly originated fixed- and adjustable-rate conventional mortgages of previously

occupied homes for major lenders. It is published monthly and is probably the most accurate assessment of mortgage interest changes.

10-Year History

- Very stable, particularly in the last few years
- One of the least-volatile measures

Libor Rate

Almost no one outside of the lending industry has heard of the London Interbranch (Libor) index, yet it is one of the oldest. It is also one of the most stable and the lowest. If you can find a lender who uses this rate, and if the margin is not unreasonable, it might be one of the best to use.

10-Year History

- Quite stable

Tip

When a lender offers you an index, it is required by law to show you the history of the index going back several years. Just be sure that the index history covers the volatile interest rate period of 1978 to 1982. Those years will tell you more than any others about what this index is likely to do if interest rates skyrocket.

Deciding on the Index

Obviously you can't pick an index. The lender does this. But you can shop for lenders until you find one who has the index most suited to your needs.

You want to pick a lender and an index which shows some stability over time. But be careful. An index which is volatile may, when it is down, give you a better beginning interest rate than an index which is stable but stays up.

This came home to many lenders and borrowers in 1985 and 1986. At that time one of the most stable indexes had been the cost of funds for S&Ls. However, when interest rates in general began to drop in those years, this rate stayed high. On the other hand, the Treasury rates plummeted. As a result mortgagors tied to the S&L rate retained a high interest rate while those tied to the Treasury yields saw their interest rates, and their payments, fall. Many lenders, seeing this happen, quickly switched indexes on new ARMs they were issuing. (It is not possible to switch an index on an existing mortgage.) They were thus able to offer new, lower-rate mortgages.

Of course, if interest rates rise in the future, the Treasury yields may be the first to go up and go up sharply. Hence those who have ARMs tied to Treasury yields during this latter period may live to regret it.

Tip

Considering indexes by themselves, if you plan to keep the mortgage a long time, go for the index that is most stable. If you plan to keep the mortgage a short time, consider the index that is currently the lowest.

Interest rates fluctuate up and down over time. The best time to get an ARM is when interest rates are high. That increases the odds that when they fall in the future, your payments will also go down. The worst time to get an ARM is when interest rates are low. This almost guarantees higher payments as interest rates rise in the future.

The Margin

The interest rate you pay on your mortgage is not simply the interest rate that the index reflects. Rather, the lender will add a "margin" to the index to determine your actual mortgage interest rate.

For example, the lender may specify in your ARM mortgage documents that the margin is 2.5 percent. That means that when the index is 8 percent, for example, the lender adds a margin of 2.5 percent to the 8 percent, giving you an effective mortgage interest rate of 10.5 percent.

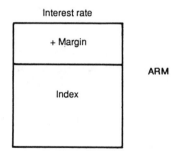

The margin is tied directly to the index used. If the index is generally low, the lender will tend to use a higher margin. If the index is generally high, the lender will tend to use a lower margin.

Trap

Don't trust lenders to look out for you. They have people working full time analyzing possible indexes to see which are the most likely to go up in the future. These people try to find indexes which are low now, so that they can put a fairly stiff margin on them and still be competitive. But they hope the index will go up in the future, trapping you with a high index *and* a high margin. As a result, you could end up paying higher-than-market interest rates in the future for the mortgage that you get today!

There is no way you can compete with the actuaries and bookkeepers that lenders employ to gain an advantage over you. If possible, however, ask to see the performance of an index going back to 1970. This should include the low interest rates of the early 1970s as well as the high-interest years of the early 1980s. See how well this index would have performed with the margin the lender wants to use. Compare it to fixed interest rates for the same period. (Something the lender should also supply.) Would you end up paying market interest rates most of the time? Or would you be ripped off by higher-than-market rates? It's worth some time investigating.

Adjustment Period

After the index, the next critical feature to look at in an ARM is the adjustment period. How frequently can the lender adjust the mortgage rate up or down?

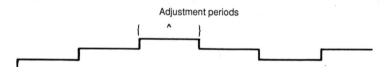

Adjustment periods

The adjustment period is non-negotiable, and each lender will specify what it wants in the loan documents. Therefore, for the borrower this is something you can pick and choose. Here are some of the more commonly used adjustment periods:

ARM Adjustment Periods

Monthly

Bimonthly

3 months

6 months

Annually

Biannually

Every 3 years

Every 5 years

Tip

Most of the time you will want the longest adjustment period possible. This gives you the greatest stability. However, most of the time lenders want the shortest adjustment period possible. This gives them the greatest protection against interest rate hikes.

Therefore, when shopping for an adjustable-rate mortgage, it is highly advisable to place the adjustment period as a big priority on the list of terms to look for.

Hybrid ARMs

There are many hybrid mortgages. Some offer an adjustable rate for a few years that can be switched to a fixed rate. Some are "called," that is, they become due in 7 years, even though they are amortized (the monthly payments are spread out) over 30 years. There are numerous variations, all with their advantages and problems, and these will be discussed at length in subsequent chapters.

Interest Rate Caps

One of the biggest problems with ARMs is the uncertainty that they produce. The borrower never really knows what his or her payments are going to be tomorrow. It's this uncertainty which causes many borrowers to forgo ARMs.

Lenders are aware of borrowers' fears of hikes in mortgage payments caused by unlimited interest rate hikes on ARMs. If the mortgage were allowed to rise without restriction, in a very volatile market you might start out paying 10 percent and end up paying 20 percent or more. Monthly payments could double! Few borrowers would take out a mortgage with such an unrestricted possibility.

To help reduce borrowers' fears, lenders frequently put *caps* on the ARM. A cap is a limit on an ARM. It limits either the amount the interest rate can rise (or fall), the amount the monthly payment can rise, or both. In this way the lender, appropriately, is assuming some of the risk for extremely volatile interest rate markets. (If there were a 6 percent cap—the interest rate on the ARM couldn't rise by more than 6 percent—and if the market rate for interest rose by 10 percent, the lender would have to assume the loss of 4 percent in interest.)

Tip

The cap puts both a ceiling and a floor on the mortgage. The interest rate can't go above a certain amount. But it can't go below a certain

amount either. If the cap is 5 percent, for example, the rate can rise
above or fall below 5 percent of the current rate. But that amounts to a
swing of 10 percent!

Mortgage-Hunting Scenario

To be sure you understand how a cap works, let's say that your ARM
has a 5 percent cap on the interest rate. That means that no matter
what happens to the index, whether it goes up or down, your mortgage can never fluctuate more than 5 percent beyond its original
rate.

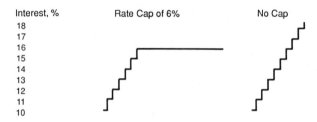

For example, you take out a mortgage with a 10 percent interest
rate and a 5 percent cap. What are the maximum and minimum interest rates this mortgage can have? For an answer, refer to Table 5-2.

In Table 5-2, the cap prevents the mortgage interest rate from rising above 15 percent. The maximum the payment could ever go
would be $1264. Without the cap, the interest rate would be unlim-
ited and theoretically could go to 20 percent or higher.

Are Interest Rate Caps Beneficial?

Nearly all borrowers would agree that interest rate caps are beneficial.
Yes, they would say, we want to be protected against runaway interest
rates.

Table 5-2. $100,000 Mortgage With an Original Rate of
10 Percent and a 5 Percent Cap

		Monthly payment for $100,000 for 30 years
Maximum interest rate	15%	$1264
Original interest rate	10%	$ 878
Minimum interest rate	5%	$ 492

However, interest rate caps are deceptive. They don't really give as much protection as they seem to. For example, the historical high on interest rates in the last 50 years was roughly 17 percent, set in the 1979–1981 period. It's unlikely that such high rates will appear again in the future.

In the example above, the 5 percent cap would put the mortgage very close to that historical high. Thus the chances of the mortgage ever getting to its maximum interest rate are fairly low. (Don't get me wrong; it could happen, but it's just not likely.) What this means is that the chances are that during the life of the mortgage, the interest rate will bounce around below or above the 5 percent cap parameters of this loan. Thus this cap may never come into play.

Many borrowers would pooh-pooh this, noting that the cap is there nonetheless in case catastrophe strikes. However, lenders are more realistic. They allow a 5 percent cap (in this case) precisely because they know it's unlikely it will ever be invoked. They give the borrower very little while taking a great deal of applause in the meantime.

Tip

From the borrower's perspective (your perspective), it's not just the fact that a mortgage has an interest rate cap that is important. Rather, it's the size of the cap that is vital.

Thus, a mortgage with a 3 percent cap is a far better mortgage than one with a 5 percent cap. And a mortgage with a 2 percent cap is better than the others. While this may seem obvious, it nevertheless is a consideration that should be taken into account as you shop around.

What this means is that you should get the lowest interest rate cap you can find.

Interest Rate Steps

I have just spoken about setting a maximum cap on the interest rate of the mortgage. But many ARMs also set a maximum limit on the amount the interest can be raised at *each adjustment period*. For example, many ARMs have a 1 or 2 percent interest rate adjustment, meaning that regardless of what the real interest rate has moved, the interest rate on the mortgage can only be adjusted in steps of 1 or 2 percent.

To see how steps work, let's say interest rates on our index have gone through the roof. Can an ARM mortgage interest rate in one adjustment period be raised to its cap? If the original rate (as per our example) was 10 percent and the cap was 5 percent, can the interest rate be hiked upward to 15 percent in one adjustment period?

If the loan did not have steps, then the answer would be "Yes!" However, nearly all ARMs have steps that limit the hikes in interest rate per each adjustment period. These limits are typically anywhere from ½ percent to 2½ percent per adjustment period. Thus, regardless of what the index the mortgage is tied to does, the interest rate cannot be hiked more than the step amount each period.

In some respects the amount of the mortgage payment steps can be more important than the cap on the interest rate!

Small Versus Large Steps

Consider two mortgages. The first has a step of 1 percent per adjustment period. The second has a step of 2 percent. Both mortgages have adjustment periods of 6 months. Notice what happens to the interest rate and payments with the two different steps.

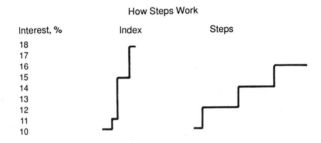

The interest rate goes from 10 percent to 14 percent over a period of time and then starts down. This is typically how interest rates behave. They don't go up and stay up or go down and stay down; they fluctuate.

A mortgage with 2 percent steps follows the rate right up and is at 14 percent within 6 months of the index. However, the mortgage with the 1 percent payment caps lags behind. Because this mortgage could only be increased by 1 percent each adjustment period, it can't rise as quickly. Hence, by the time it finally gets to 12 percent, the index is already turning down. The mortgage with the 1 percent steps never gets to 14 percent.

The point to be taken here is that the smaller the steps, the greater the lag time when there is a sudden jump in interest rates. (Of course, a sudden decline would not be felt as quickly, either.) If it is assumed that interest rates will tend to move both up and down, the smaller the steps, therefore, the more stable the mortgage. Small steps, in fact, can have a far greater impact on the stability of the mortgage than can an interest rate cap.

Typically, you would prefer a mortgage with small steps over one with larger payment caps.

Trap

Many ARM lenders are naturally concerned about the lag in mortgages with small steps. They see that they could lose out on interest during spikes in interest rates. Naturally enough they want the mortgage interest rate to keep pace with the index and they saw that mortgages with small steps would lag behind, causing them to lose interest.

As a consequence, some ARMS are written with "catch-up" clauses. These clauses provide that even though the step doesn't rise fast enough to keep pace with the index, any interest lost to the lender in this fashion would be carried over to the next adjustment period.

With a catch-up clause in a mortgage, the beneficial effects of smaller steps are nullified over a long period of time. In the previous example, the mortgage with 1 percent steps would continue to increase toward the maximum even after the index had turned down. It would continue on up until all the interest due to increases in the rate had been given to the lender. If you had this mortgage, you would lose in the long run all the benefits you gained in the short run from small steps.

In addition, this catch-up effect has proved to be extremely confusing to borrowers who find their interest rates and mortgage payments rising just when the index has turned and is beginning to fall. Borrower lawsuits and public complaints quickly convinced many lenders that catch-up means trouble.

Consequently, in recent years lenders have tended to reduce the number of catch-up clauses in mortgages. Today, instead of ARMs having catch-ups, many simply opt for bigger steps. Two percent steps are common.

Tip

Shop for a lender that offers both small steps and no catch-up clauses. They are hard to find, but sometimes they do exist.

On the other hand, if at all possible, avoid mortgages with catch-up clauses.

Note: Although in the long run, catch-up clauses tend to nullify the beneficial effect of smaller steps, they don't do so in the short run. If you plan to sell the property fairly quickly, small steps, even with a catch-up clause, can prove beneficial.

Mortgage Payment Caps

I have spoken about setting a maximum cap on the interest rate of the mortgage. But some ARMs also set a maximum limit on the amount the monthly payment can be raised each adjustment period regardless of what happens to the interest rate.

A monthly payment cap states that the payment cannot rise beyond a certain percentage of the previous period's payment. The most common payment cap is 7.5 percent. The payment in the new adjustment period cannot increase the payment in the preceding period by more than 7.5 percent.

To see how payment caps work, let's say interest rates on the index have gone through the roof. You have a maximum step of 2 percent per adjustment period. So, the lender raises the interest rate a full 2 percent.

However, you also have a cap on the mortgage payment. It can't be raised more than, for example, 7.5 percent each period. Here's what happens:

Effect of Capping the Mortgage Payment ($100,000 mortgage for 30 years with 7.5 percent payment cap)

Step = 2%

Cap = 7.5% (of mortgage payment)

Required increase in mortgage payment = $151

Maximum increase in mortgage payment = $66

Without the payment cap, the mortgage payment would rise $151. With it, the maximum rise is $66.

When interest rates rise dramatically, the monthly payment cap keeps the payment relatively stable. In the above example the payment cap kept the payment from rising by an additional $85.

Trap

Beware of "negative amortization." Borrowers who are scrimping to make the monthly payment and who are terrified of payment increases often jump at the chance to get a monthly payment cap. They feel that in so doing they are taking a major step in protecting themselves. I don't

Mortgage Payment Caps

agree with this at all. Understand when negative amortization can take place and be wary of it.

Negative Amortization

Negative amortization today occurs in a substantial number of ARMs. It is something which is often hidden from view, unless you know what to look for in the documents. Although the negative amortization terms are fully explained in those mortgages in which it occurs, many people simply don't understand the implications. Many still fail to see the dangers.

Negative amortization means that instead of the mortgage going down, it goes up! Each month instead of paying off some of the loan, you add to it. You end up owing more than was originally borrowed and/or having a longer borrowing period. Even worse, you end up paying interest on interest.

The Cause of Negative Amortization

Negative amortization typically comes about because your payments are capped and the cap is lower than the interest rate rises.

Wanting such caps, as we've seen, is only natural. You want to be able to control your monthly payment. The big concern is that the monthly payment not rise too swiftly. Typically you have limited ability to increase your income. You are afraid that sudden large monthly payment increases could cause you to lose your property. You are seeking protection.

Tip

If you get a mortgage that has a *payment cap,* you can be almost certain that it has negative amortization. In fact, the best way to determine if a mortgage has negative amortization is to look for a payment cap. If you find it, you should immediately know what's in store for you.

Trap

It's important to remember that a monthly payment cap alone does not limit interest rate increases. What a monthly payment cap does is to restrict that portion of the interest rate increase that you immediately pay. The portion that you do not pay, however, does not go away. Rather, it is added to the mortgage.

In the illustration below, the amount owed depends on changes in the interest rate. If the interest rate exceeds the payment cap, the unpaid interest is added to the principal, increasing the amount owed. The original amount borrowed in this example is $80,000.

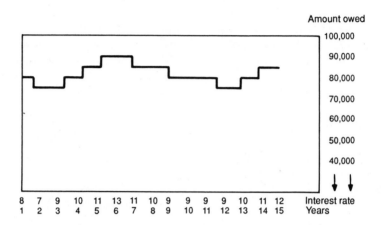

Here is an example of the effect of capping a mortgage payment on a 30-year, $50,000 ARM. The initial interest rate is 12 percent. The example was supplied by the Federal Home Loan Bank Board.

Year	Rate, %	Monthly payment, $		Remaining balance, $	
		5% cap	7.5% cap	5% cap	7.5% cap
1	12	514	514	49,818	49,818
2	13.5	540	552	50,079	49,915
3	15	567	594	50,837	50,295
4	16.5	595	638	52,180	50,977
5	18	625	686	54,236	51,992
6	18	656	738	56,284	52,534

Note: Federal lender regulations prohibit negative amortization from increasing beyond 125 percent of the original mortgage balance. For example, if your original balance was $100,000, negative amortization can increase the mortgage to a maximum of $125,000.

In the above example the remaining balance on the mortgage will increase over a 6-year period by $6466 with a 5 percent monthly cap, or by $2716 with a 7.5 percent monthly cap. The reason the increase is so dramatic is that the borrower is paying interest on interest.

(*Note:* The above example uses only a $50,000 mortgage. Double the effects for a $100,000 mortgage. Triple them for a $150,000 mortgage.)

Will Appreciation Offset Negative Amortization?

Often an argument used by lenders to justify the bad effects of negative amortization is that housing price increases will more than offset it. Yes, you might be adding to the mortgage amount, but your house will be worth more anyhow, so why worry?

This argument is obviously fallacious in light of recent housing slumps across the country. Housing prices certainly do not always go up.

Additionally, from the borrower's perspective, price increases in property have traditionally been a way of increasing equity. In fact, one of the principal reasons for buying real estate has always been to take advantage of the profit potential in price increases.

With negative amortization, however, the mortgage increase eats into that equity, into the potential profit. With negative amortization the lender, in effect, shares some of the increase.

Tip

In very few cases do you need negative amortization. If your desire is to control the monthly payment on your mortgage, you can do this even better by shopping around for an ARM that has small adjustment steps.

A mortgage in which the steps for each adjustment period are not more than 1 percent will actually provide smaller monthly payment increases per adjustment period than a similar mortgage that uses higher steps and a monthly payment cap of 7.5 percent.

Think about it. With just a little bit of shopping around you could avoid the negative amortization trap.

Other Problems With Mortgage Payment Caps

Mortgage payment caps are often a trade-off for other, more important benefits. A lender who offers a monthly payment cap as an inducement to a borrower then often feels justified in asking for more restrictive terms in other areas. For example, such a lender may want bigger steps or more interest. The borrower may give up these vital benefits for the apparent benefit of a monthly payment cap.

Finally, the ultimate monthly payment may be higher with a cap than without. Consider Table 5-3 prepared by the Federal Home Loan Bank

Table 5-3. Cap Rate Comparison Chart
($50,000 30-Year Mortgage)

Year	Interest rate, %	Monthly payment, $			
		7% cap	7.5% cap	10% cap	No cap
1	12	514	514	514	514
2	13.5	540	552	565	572
3	15	567	594	622	630
4	16.5	595	638	684	689
5	18	625	686	753	748
6	18	656	738	753	748
10	18	797	800	753	748
15	18	1018	800	753	748
20	18	1112	800	753	748
25	18	1112	800	753	748
29	18	1112	800	753	748

Board. In this case various interest rate caps are given, and the monthly payment is shown over a period of 29 years. The chart assumes that interest rates start at 12 percent, then rise to 18 percent at year 5 and remain there. It also assumes that there is no interest rate cap on the mortgage.

Notice that the lower the monthly payment cap, the lower the monthly payments initially. But over the long run, the lower the monthly payment cap, the higher the monthly payments as the lender plays catch-up trying to recoup interest not received because of the payment cap. In the example, a 7.5 percent cap (the most commonly used today) will result after year 10 in a payment of $800. Without the cap, the payment would only have been $748.

Tip

Monthly payment caps can mean lower monthly payments at first, but higher monthly payments later on.

Monthly Payment Cap With an Interest Rate Cap

The above example was exaggerated to make a point. (No one expects interest rates to move to 18 percent and stay there.) An important consideration was also overlooked—a mortgage might have *both* a monthly payment cap *and* an interest rate cap.

Some lenders use this combination, and borrowers sometimes think that it is a significantly better loan. With the interest rate capped, the loan is indeed better for the borrower. But it is questionable how significant the benefit is when there is also a monthly payment cap.

To see why, look back at the previous example. Let's say that in addition to the monthly payment being capped, the interest rate was capped at a 6 percent maximum change with steps of 1½ percent per year. The chart would work out exactly the same! The interest rate cap would have no effect since the interest rate only rose to the maximum (from 12 percent in our example to 18 percent) and the increases were never beyond the 1½ percent steps.

Only if the interest rate cap were lower, in our example less than 6 percent, would it act to mitigate the negative effects of a monthly payment cap. For example, a 5 percent interest rate cap would limit the interest rate from rising above 17 percent in the above example. This would reduce the total negative interest under the monthly payment cap.

Tip

When a mortgage has both an interest rate cap and a monthly payment cap, you automatically should know that the interest rate cap is set higher than the monthly payment cap and that negative amortization could take place. The reason is simple: If this weren't the case, if the interest rate cap were set sufficiently low that no negative amortization could take place, then no monthly payment cap would be necessary.

My suggestion is to avoid monthly payment caps. Look instead for lower interest rate caps, longer adjustment periods, and lower steps.

Conclusion

ARMs have their place. But generally speaking, they are ugly loans. Lenders like them because they reduce lenders' concerns over volatility. Agents like them because they help make sales that otherwise might fall through. Borrowers like them because they mean initially low payments and the ability to get financing that otherwise might not be available.

But don't think of them as a panacea. They are not. They can solve a particular mortgage problem that you might have. But, they won't solve all of your problems. And likely as not, after a few years, they will end up causing more problems than the solutions they originally seemed to offer.

6
Biweekly and
15-Year Mortgages

Interest Saved
Is Interest Earned

Introduction

One of the most popular mortgages to be "discovered" in the last few years is the "biweekly." Here the borrower makes a payment every other week instead of the traditional once-monthly payment. The result is that over the life of the loan an amazing amount of interest is saved and the mortgage can actually be paid off years early.

For many people, how the biweekly mortgage works is a mystery. How can making a payment every 2 weeks instead of every month make such a big difference?

In this chapter we'll look at how the biweekly works, what its benefits really are, and we'll also look at some of the more dramatic pitfalls that have emerged regarding it.

Mortgage Paybacks

Most first mortgages on real estate are fully "amortized." That means that the payments are arranged so they are all equal (except sometimes for a slight difference in the last one), and the mortgage gets fully paid off. In other words, there is no balloon payment.

What many people don't realize, however, is that while the payment remains essentially the same over the term of the mortgage, the separation between what goes to principal and what goes to interest changes markedly.

During the early years of a mortgage, virtually all of the monthly payment goes toward interest. It is only in the very last years that the majority of the payment begins adding up to principal. Figure 6-1 is a graphic portrayal of a typical 30-year mortgage.

If the mortgage is for $100,000 at 12 percent interest, the monthly payment is $1028. However, of that amount only $28 initially goes to principal. Roughly $1000 goes to interest.

As you can imagine, reducing the $100,000 by $28 isn't going to make much of a difference . . . at first. However, over time it adds up. Each month the mortgage is recalculated, and each month the amount that goes to principal increases while the amount going to interest declines. By year 10, for example, nearly $100 of each payment is going to principal with only $900 going to interest.

This steady increase in the amount going to principal continues over the life of the loan but actually begins to accelerate by year 20. Then nearly $300 is going to principal with only about $700 going to interest.

What's happening is that as the amount of money going to principal increases, the amount owed decreases and, consequently, the interest charged goes down. As is seen in Figure 6-1, this process accelerates dramatically at the end of the loan period. By year 25 of a 30-year loan, you're actually paying more than half of the payment to principal and only half toward interest. By the final payments, virtually all is principal.

What this means is that the vast majority of the interest paid on the mortgage over its life is paid during its first years. And that interest

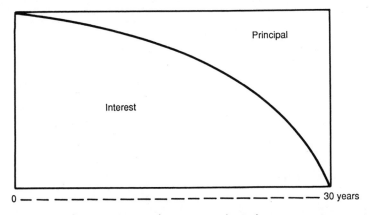

Figure 6-1. In the early years of a mortgage, almost the entire payment goes to interest. Only in the later years does principal begin to be significantly paid back.

charge is hefty. For example, after 30 years on a $100,000 mortgage at 12 percent, the total amount of interest charged during the time was $270,016. The interest charged was nearly three times the total amount borrowed!

Changing the Payback

What some people have discovered is that the term of the mortgage can be significantly shortened and the total interest significantly reduced, if more money is paid up front toward principal.

Tip

Simply making one additional payment in the first year *that goes entirely toward principal* can reduce the time it takes to pay back the loan by over a year and reduce the interest paid over the term of the mortgage by over $10,000!

The 15-Year Mortgage

One way to pay more money up front is by taking a shorter payback period, 15 years instead of 30. This increases the monthly payment, but decreases the interest charged as well as results in a quicker payoff of the mortgage. The following is a comparison of 30- and 15-year mortgages of $100,000 at 12 percent, fully amortized.

	30-year	15-year
Total interest	$270,016	$116,032
Interest saved		$153,984

Note that by making a higher payment, not only does a 15-year mortgage get paid off in half the time, but it also saves nearly $154,000 in interest. Figure 6-2 is a graphic portrayal of how this works.

The Pros and Cons of Higher Payments

Of course, the problem with a 15-year mortgage is that it has higher payments. In our example of a $100,000 mortgage at 12 percent interest, that's an increase in monthly payment from $1029 to $1200.

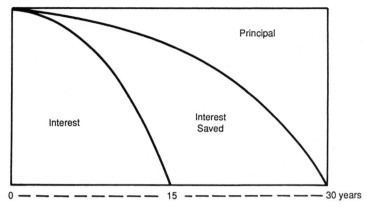

Figure 6-2. Interest saved on a 15-year term.

Tip

On any mortgage, when you cut the mortgage term in half, the monthly payment only goes up about 15 percent. In other words, by opting for a short 15-year mortgage and paying roughly 15 percent more in monthly payments, the borrower pays the loan off in half the time and saves roughly half the interest charged when compared with a 30-year term!

The reason an increase of only 15 percent per month can cut the mortgage term in half and the interest in more than half is because virtually all of that 15 percent increase goes to principal. In the first month of a 15-year mortgage, nearly $200 goes to principal as opposed to less than $30 on the 30-year loan. If you can envisage it, a 15-year mortgage is sort of like taking a 30-year mortgage and starting to make payments at year 15. You get the benefits of the last 15 years when more and more of the payment goes toward principal and less and less toward interest.

Why Have 30-Year Mortgages?

The reason 30-year mortgages are popular has to do with monthly payments (Figure 6-3). Thirty years is the optimum time for getting a minimum payment. You can see this clearly when you look at various payments at different terms for a $100,000 mortgage at 12 percent interest.

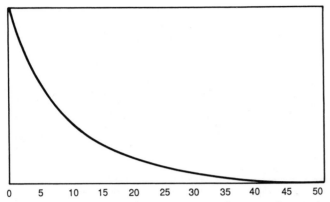

Figure 6-3. Relationship of payment to term. Increasing the term lowers the payment for any mortgage. The maximum reduction, however, is achieved by year 30. After that any further reduction in payment by increasing the term is minimal.

10 years	15 years	20 years	25 years	30 years	35 years
$1435	$1200	$1101	$1053	$1029	$1016

Note, for example, that when you go from a 10-year loan to a 15-year loan, the payment drops by $235. As you move from 10 to 15 to 20 years, you significantly reduce the monthly payment. However, as you approach a 30-year term, the amount of reduction in payment for each year added gets smaller. Once you reach 30 years, you are at the optimum point on the curve. Any further extensions of term reduce the monthly payment only insignificantly. For example, going from a 30-year term to a 35-year term, an addition of 5 more years on the mortgage, only reduces the monthly payment by about $13 a month. The law of diminishing returns begins to take a hand the further out you go. Mathematics and common sense have determined that the optimum term for the lowest payment is 30 years.

Tip

Lenders like the shorter 15-year mortgages. If you can afford the slightly higher payments, a lender will often give you a lower interest rate, fewer points, and fewer fees if you go 15 years. It's something worth considering.

An Easier Way to Get
Bigger Payments

Those in the mortgage field have long known that it makes good financial sense to secure a 15-year mortgage instead of a 30-year one. However, the increased monthly payments have always been a stumbling block. Whether buying a home or refinancing, higher monthly payments are usually the last thing a borrower wants. In fact, most borrowers, just to qualify, must have the lowest monthly payments possible.

For just this reason, a couple of years ago a new kind of mortgage came into existence, the "biweekly." This mortgage keeps your payments the same. However, it also pays more into the mortgage, thus shortening the term and allowing for greatly reduced total interest and a quicker payback.

Biweekly Mortgages

In the biweekly mortgage plan, you make a payment every 2 weeks instead of once a month. For example, let's say your payment would be $1000 a month on a straight monthly basis. Instead of paying that amount, you pay $500 every 2 weeks. That shortens the term and reduces the interest.

Crazy, you say?!

You may be scratching your head wondering what difference it makes whether you pay $1000 a month or $500 every 2 weeks.

The difference is the fact that there are only 12 months in a year, but there are 52 weeks; 52 weeks work out to 13 months.

Tip

Our calendar is based on 364-plus days per year. The breakdown into weeks is precise, 52. But the breakdown into months is imprecise, with some months longer than others. The shortest month is 28 days, exactly 4 weeks. But the longest months have 31 days, an extra three, which when added up throughout the year make for an additional 4 weeks. It would make more sense to have 13 months rather than 12. But custom is hard to break. Consequently we have 12. along with 12 monthly mortgage payments.

When you make biweekly payments, you are actually making two additional payments each year. This amounts to the equivalent of one additional monthly payment, which for practical purposes, all goes toward principal. Thus the biweekly mortgage allows many people to painlessly and effortlessly increase their principal payments, dramatically reducing the time to pay off and cutting the total interest paid.

For example, if you borrow $75,000 at 10 percent interest, making the equivalent of one extra payment each year will mean you can pay off your 30-year mortgage in just 21 years and save a whopping total of $75,000 in interest charges over that term. Figure 6-4 illustrates this graphically.

No, a biweekly doesn't pay off as fast as a 15-year mortgage. But it pays off nearly 10 years faster than a 30-year mortgage, and you can save tens of thousands of dollars in interest.

Trap

A biweekly mortgage is not for everyone. It works best when you are salaried and getting paid on a weekly or biweekly basis. You can easily budget your money to take care of the payment that way and probably won't feel the extra expense very much.

On the other hand, if you're paid monthly or work for yourself, the biweekly setup can be a no-no. Making payments once each month will seem natural. On the other hand, a biweekly schedule will have you making payments more often, probably at times when you don't have money coming in. A biweekly schedule can be a nightmare for someone who is self-employed or who is paid monthly.

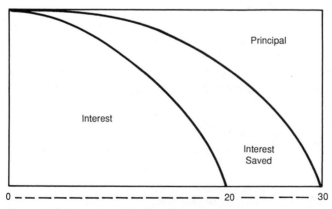

Figure 6-4. Interest saved in biweekly mortgage.

Establishing a Biweekly Mortgage

Biweeklies are offered by several mortgage lenders. They are set up right from the start with payment coupons that require you to make a payment every 2 weeks. The mortgage company takes care of the bookkeeping, and as long as you keep making those payments, you are shortening the term of your loan as well as the total interest you will have to pay. Check with a mortgage banker for this type of loan.

Trap

A biweekly can be used to reduce the size of your payments instead of shorten your term and cut interest. Say the payments on a 30-year mortgage are $1000 a month and $500 biweekly. On a yearly basis paid monthly, you will have paid in a total of $12,000. However, biweekly that comes to $13,000. The extra thousand dollars can be used to reduce your biweekly payments by $42. Some lenders have encouraged borrowers to try this.

This defeats the entire purpose of the mortgage. You might just as well pay monthly as to pay a reduced amount biweekly. You will not save anything on interest and will not have your mortgage term reduced. The only advantage I can see is for those borrowers who prefer biweekly payments for simplicity of bookkeeping and budgeting.

Biweekly mortgages are touted throughout the loan industry today, not because they are really that wonderful, but because they are new and because the public has latched onto the concept. What the public wants, it typically gets.

However, before you decide that a biweekly mortgage is for you, check into the modified 15-year mortgage described at the end of this chapter. It's another option.

Trap

Beware of firms, particularly those which telemarket, which offer to set up a biweekly mortgage for you. They will say that they will "take over" the payments of your mortgage and that you can then pay them biweekly and reap the benefits. Typically, they will charge a whopping fee, sometimes as much as a $1000 or more. Plus, they may require a biweekly charge for the service.

This is a scam pure and simple. It does for you what you can do for yourself. Only it charges for it and puts you at risk. Here's how.

First, a true biweekly mortgage is arranged between you and the lender at the time you secure financing. The lender agrees to accept payments every 2 weeks, and you agree to make payments on that schedule.

In the scam, you make biweekly payments to an independent company. It then makes your regular monthly mortgage payment, withholding extra money until the end of the year when it makes an additional (13th) payment.

During that time this firm has control over your money. That means it earns interest on money that you've paid in, but that it has not yet paid to your mortgage company. Further, if the firm has financial difficulties and goes broke, you could lose all the money you paid in which it did not forward to your lender of record. Finally, for this it expects a service charge.

Tip

You can set up the equivalent of a biweekly mortgage plan all on your own. It's not hard to do and only takes a few moments of time. There is one big catch, however. You must first check to be sure that your lender allows increased frequency and "prepayment" without a penalty. Most modern mortgages do, but it won't hurt to check. Here, then, are three ways to create your own biweekly mortgage:

1. Make an extra payment once each year. Each month, simply pay into a separate account an amount equal to one-twelfth of your monthly mortgage payment. Then send that money at the end of the year with your twelfth payment. Be sure you *instruct your lender to apply it to principal.* Otherwise, it may simply be considered an early monthly payment.

2. Divide the amount you pay each month by 12. Then add that amount to your monthly mortgage payment. For example, if your monthly payment is $720, you would send in $780. ($720 ÷ 12 = $60; $720 + $60 = $780.) In this way you'll be paying one-twelfth more each month, the rough equivalent of a biweekly schedule. Be sure your lender doesn't object to this.

3. Send in payments every 2 weeks to your mortgage company. This plan, which duplicates the biweekly mortgage, requires your lender's consent. After all, your regular mortgage calls for monthly payments, and you're asking to send in half that amount every 2 weeks. Call your lender and see if they will accept this plan. Some will. Others may charge you a small fee to set up a separate bookkeeping system to handle it. Some may simply not go along.

4. Ask the lender to set up a biweekly plan and volunteer to have the money automatically withdrawn from a savings or checking account. The lender might very well do this, simply because it would be able to avoid losing the "float." (The float is the interest on the money during the grace period, typically 2 weeks after it's due but before the late payment applies.)

Note: All of the above plans will save you money. However, number 3 will save you the most since the amount you are adding to principal goes in sooner (than waiting until the end of the year) and, consequently, acts to increase principle and thereby reduce interest sooner.

Keep in mind that you can accomplish all of the above on your own. You do not need anyone to help you do it. You certainly shouldn't pay anyone to set this up for you. To get a true biweekly mortgage, however, you must set up it up with the lender.

A 30-Year Loan in 15: Sound Finance Plus Flexibility

A variation of the biweekly mortgage that's been available for a long time is the 30-year mortgage paid back in 15. I can remember very sharp borrowers doing this as long as 30 years ago, often over the objections of the lender. Even back then, when most mortgages had prepayment penalties, they did allow up to the equivalent of 6 months interest to be paid in advance and people took advantage of that clause. Today, with most mortgages not having prepayment penalties of any kind, it's even easier to do.

Here's how this plan works.

You get a 30-year mortgage (with a no prepayment feature). But you pay it off using a 15-year payment schedule. If you borrowed $100,000 at 12 percent for 30 years, your payments should be $1029 a month. However, instead of paying $1029 per month, you pay $1200 a month—$171 extra.

30-year monthly payment	$1029
Extra principal	+ 171 (prepaid monthly)
Total monthly payment	$1200

How It's Done

When the monthly payment stub comes from the lender, it usually contains two extra lines. One is for additional payments paid in advance.

The second is for extra principal. On the latter you list the extra amount you are paying, thus notifying the lender that you want it to go to principal. You can find the extra amount to pay by simply checking with an amortization schedule for your loan amount and interest rate. The schedule will give payments both for 30 and 15 years. Use the latter amount.

In the case of the $100,000 mortgage at 12 percent, by paying an extra $171 per month to principal, you will, in effect, pay off your 30-year loan 15 years early. You will have converted your 30-year loan into a 15-year term, plus saved yourself more than half the interest that would otherwise be spent.

Double-Bonus Tip!

Many people want 15-year loans because of the shorter term and the savings of interest. For this reason, they opt for these mortgages when they buy or refinance. They tell the lender: Make my term 15 years.

My suggestion is that you hold back and instead opt for a 30-year term and then schedule a 15-year payback period all on your own. This could save you a lot of grief later on.

The reason is that doing it this way, the loan is written for 30 years with payments still set at a lower amount, $1029 a month in our example of a $100,000 mortgage at 12 percent. You make the higher payments, $1200 in this case, at *your* option.

However, if at any time the higher payments become a burden—let's say you lose your job or get sick—you can drop back down to the lower 30-year term payments. There's no penalty for this; it's at your option. You can't do this if you are fixed into a 15-year mortgage.

Tip

Paying off a 30-year loan as if it were 15 years by increasing the amount to principal will work for any mortgage that has no prepayment penalty. To find the exact amount you need to pay additionally, check the amortization schedule found in Appendix 2. Or, if you don't mind approximations, simply pay an additional 15 percent of each monthly payment.

Biweekly and 15-year mortgages are becoming increasingly popular, and for good reason. Borrowers are simply tired of paying huge amounts of money for interest over the life of a mortgage when, either by restructuring the frequency of the payment or by adding a small additional amount to each payment, they avoid that. Think of it this way

... paying every other week or paying an extra hundred dollars a month probably isn't going to kill you. But paying tens, sometimes hundreds of thousands of dollars extra in interest over 30 years can put a real dent in your estate.

Tip

You don't have to own the property for 15 years or longer to get the benefits of biweekly or 15-year mortgages. Everything that you pay immediately goes to principal and increases your equity as soon as you make the payment. The sooner you pay or the more you pay, the lower the mortgage and the more of the house that you really own.

7
The Seller
as a Source
of Financing

Be Prepared
to Initiate and Motivate

Question. What is your source of the cheapest, no-qualifying, quickest-to-get mortgage money when you buy a home?

Answer. The seller.

Getting the seller to finance your purchase of his or her home is one of the best ways to get financing. If the seller is willing to give you a mortgage, either a first or more likely a second, you can get in quickly and without a lot of hassle.

In this chapter we're going to examine what you should ask for in seller financing. We'll also take a close look at how realistic your chances are of getting seller financing, depending on market conditions.

What Is Seller Financing?

It goes by many names. However, about a dozen years ago someone came up with the monicker "creative financing." At the time, this was an appealing term to sellers. It meant that they could more quickly secure a sale by helping the buyer get a mortgage.

Tip

Seller financing is almost always short-term. Few sellers will go longer than 3 years. Almost none will go longer than five.

However, in practice the connotation quickly changed until it became widely perceived as "seller rip-off." The reason was that some unscrupulous buyers and brokers connived to use this tool to cheat sellers out of their equities. So many sellers lost money on "creative" or "rip-off" financing that for the last 5 years it has been difficult for an honest buyer to get *any* seller to go along with it.

Today, however, most of the rip-offs are gone and many sellers are once again willing to help buyers purchase their homes. This is particularly true since the onset of the cold real estate market over much of the country with falling prices and few qualified buyers.

How Seller Financing Works

As those familiar with real estate financing know, when a seller "carries back paper," he or she is creating a mortgage with the buyer as the borrower. The buyer, in essence, is loaned a portion of the seller's equity in the home.

Tip

The terms *hard-money second* and *soft-money second* have come into vogue. A soft-money second is one which the seller offers to the buyer. A hard-money second is where the buyer-borrower goes to a lender (not the seller) and obtains funds. The hard-money second is usually harder to get and has a higher interest rate as well as points and other costs.

Let's take an example of a seller's second.

Mortgage-Hunting Scenario

Helen wanted to purchase a home for $200,000. However, she only had $20,000 to put down (plus money for closing costs.) That meant that she would have to get a 90 percent mortgage. The problem with this was that any bank or savings and loan required Helen to pay for private mortgage insurance (PMI) on any loan with less than 20 percent down. PMI would cost roughly ½ percent of the mortgage bal-

```
┌─────────────────────┐
│ 10% Down            │
│ ($20,000)           │
├─────────────────────┤
│ 90% Mortgage        │
│ ($180,000)          │
│                     │
│                     │
│                     │
└─────────────────────┘
```

ance, payable monthly. In the case of a $180,000 mortgage, that
came to $900 annually, or an additional $75 a month.

Helen was stretching to get into the property, and an additional
$75 a month was more than she could afford, according to the
lender. When PMI was added in, she wouldn't qualify for the mortgage and no deal would be made.

Needless to say, Helen was upset . . . and so was the seller. So
Helen came to the seller with this proposition.

"Mr. Seller. I need to put 20 percent down in order to avoid paying PMI and thus disqualify myself from the mortgage. But I only
have 10 percent. Will you lend me the additional 10 percent on a second mortgage? I'll pay you the same interest rate I would pay the
holder of the first mortgage."

The lender wanted to make a sale. In addition, the lender wasn't
buying another house, so he didn't need all the money from the sale
in cash. An agreement was struck. Here's how the new deal looked:

Helen still ended up financing the same amount of money,
$180,000. However, in the second case, 10 percent of it came from
the seller. This meant the lender of the first mortgage was only making an 80 percent loan and no PMI was required, thus saving Helen
½ percent in interest, or $75 a month. She now easily qualified.

```
┌─────────────────────┐
│ 10%Cash             │
│ ($20,000)           │
├─────────────────────┤
│ 10% Second          │
│ ($20,000)           │
├─────────────────────┤
│ 80% Mortgage        │
│ ($160,000)          │
│                     │
│                     │
└─────────────────────┘
```

Trap

Many lenders today are applying a combined loan-to-value ratio (CLTV) to their first mortgages. What this means is that all loans on the property cannot exceed a certain percentage. If a lender of a first had an 80 percent CLTV, the type of financing shown above would not work because it would require the buyer to put 20 percent cash down.

If you need to work with a second mortgage, be sure the lender of the first does not use CLTV.

Tip

Most lenders of firsts have some specific rules regarding seconds. Yes, they will allow you to use a second mortgage for a portion of the down payment. But generally speaking, they will require that the second mortgage *must be for a term of at least 5 years, although a few will allow as short a term as 3 years.*

Their reasoning is that if the second is for any shorter, when it comes due, your house will not have appreciated sufficiently to allow you to refinance. You may need to pay off the second and not be able to secure cash to do it. As a consequence, the seller-lender might foreclose, which could threaten the stability of the first.

Trap

Some sellers will not want to give you a second for 3 to 5 years as described above. They may insist on an 18-month or 2-year second. When you point out that this will preclude you from getting a first, they may recommend a "trick" or a "silent" second.

A trick second is where the sales agreement shows a 3- to 5-year second. But you and the seller agree that you will have a shorter term, and when all the documents are recorded, you record a shorter second than the agreement calls for. Since the lender of the first rarely sees all the documents recorded, you end up with the desired first and shorter second, in spite of the lender's rules.

A silent second is where you record the 3- to 5-year second, as agreed. Then, a month or so after the transaction, you and the seller record a new second for a shorter term or sign a separate agreement to pay off the second earlier. Again, you have subverted the rules of the lender of the first.

Beware of either the trick or the silent second. True, you may get away with it because the lender of the first simply won't know what's happened. However, some first lenders are now requiring that they get to see *all* the documents recorded, thus putting a crimp into the trick second. Further, if you ever get into trouble and go into foreclosure, particularly during the early years of ownership, everything will come to light and the holder of the first, besides foreclosing on the property, may charge fraud. Facing fraud means that you could be liable both civilly and criminally and that you could be forced to defend yourself against the federal government! (Most lenders of firsts are protected against fraud by federal law.)

While getting a seller to take back a longer second may be difficult, it could be a whole lot easier than the trouble you could get into from a trick or silent second.

Trap

Many mortgages are available only if you occupy the property. Some borrowers lie about their intent to occupy a property in order to get a better mortgage.

Never lie about your intent to occupy the property. It's a federal offense. The government prosecutes it vigorously, and the penalties are severe.

Reasons for Asking for Seller Financing

In our example above, Helen asked for seller financing in order to help her qualify for her first mortgage. There are, however, other reasons why you may want to use seller financing:

To help you qualify (as in Helen's situation)

To get a lower overall interest rate and reduced monthly payments

To allow you to put less cash into the property

Lowering the Interest Rate and Reducing the Monthly Payments

Another use of seller financing is to help you reduce your monthly payments. This can be an extremely helpful means of financing a home, particularly in a soft market. Here's how it works.

Mortgage-Hunting Scenario

David wanted to buy a home for $150,000. However, he had to sell his own home. The idea was that he would take $50,000 of equity from his present home and then place it into the new home. All he had to do was to wait for his home to sell.

The problem was that he wanted to move right away. Interest rates were currently low and the market was soft. He could get a great deal on a new home.

On the other hand, there was every indication that in a few months the market might get tighter (more buyers, fewer sellers). That would be a good time for him to sell his current home.

Ideally, what he needed to do was to buy the new house now and sell the old house later. He needed to reverse the usual order of things.

The problem was that he couldn't buy the new house until he sold his own (so he thought) because he needed to get his equity out in order to come up with a down payment. A friendly broker gave him a couple of options.

A Swing Loan

The first option was to get a swing loan. David would refinance (hard-money second) his old house to get enough money out to make the down payment on the new house. He wanted to put 20 percent down, so he would need to get $30,000 out.

Trap

Swings loans are costly and tricky. They are not for the unsophisticated borrower. Go for a line of credit before you try for a swing loan.

He could certainly do this. However, he would be making payments on the $30,000 as well as on the mortgage on the new house. That meant a lot of payments.

Swing Loan
($30,000 @ 13%)
$309 Payment

First Mortgage
($120,000 @ 10%)
$1,054 Payment

If David simply sold his old house, got his equity out in cash, and used it as a down payment, his total mortgage payments would be

$1054 on a first mortgage. However, if he got a swing loan, he would be making payments on that as well, in this case an additional $309 per month.

The payments on the swing loan jeopardized his qualifying for the new first mortgage. In addition, he wasn't sure he could handle such a high amount of payments.

Tip

If you're interested in a swing loan, ask for one with "no payments." Some lenders will calculate one year's worth of payments into the mortgage amount. That way you will have no payments for the first year, during which time you can, one hopes, sell the property and pay back the swing loan.

Trap

Don't fall into the trap of thinking that because there are no payments on a swing loan (see above), there's no interest. You pay roughly the same interest whether it's paid monthly or annually.

The swing loan can be a good mortgage for those who can handle it's extra interest charge. However, there might be a better way.

No-Interest, No-Payment Second

Since the market was weak, David decided to try something different. He decided to ask the seller to finance the purchase, at least until he could sell his old home.

The deal that David presented to the seller was this:

1. The purchase price would remain the same—$150,000.
2. However, David would only put 5 percent, or $7500, down. (That's all the money he had without the equity in his present home.)
3. The seller would give David a second mortgage for 15 percent of the sales price, or $22,500. That, and David's cash down, equaled 20 percent. David would then get a regular 80 percent first mortgage.

The catch was that the seller's second was to be written with the following conditions:

1. No interest
2. No monthly payments

```
┌─────────────────────────────┐
│        $7,500 Down          │
├─────────────────────────────┤
│      No Int/Payment         │
│     Second ($22,500)        │
│       No Payment            │
├─────────────────────────────┤
│                             │
│      First Mortgage         │
│    ($120,000 @ 10%)         │
│     $1,054 Payment          │
│                             │
│                             │
│                             │
│                             │
└─────────────────────────────┘
```

Tip

No seller will accept a no-interest, no-monthly-payment second mortgage in a strong market. There's no reason to. Good buyers will be coming in with cash.

However, this plan may fly in a weak market when there simply aren't any buyers around. Consider it whenever you buy and the residential housing market is cold.

Notice that what's really happening here is that David is getting the seller to finance the swing loan. A regular hard-money lender would certainly charge interest. But a desperate seller might not.

Trap

Everything in this world has both plusses and minuses. The no-interest, no-payment second is a real plus for you, the buyer and seeker of mortgage funds. However, it's obviously a real minus for the seller, who would most certainly want to get all cash.

In order to use it, therefore, you must look for two things. First, you need a seller who doesn't need all the cash out of a property in order to move on to another. Remember that most sellers are selling only to buy again somewhere else.

Second, a seller is going to consider the no-interest, no-monthly-payment second a negative when looking at the overall deal. Therefore, you will want to sweeten up the offer in some other way. That usually means price.

The trade-off is in terms of price. Expect to pay a higher price with a no-interest, no-monthly payment second than if you offer straight cash.

It's very rare that you'll be able to get both this kind of a second and a good price, too.

Tip

Sometimes a seller will balk at giving a buyer so large a second with only 5 percent down. One way to get the seller to accept might be to put the second not on the new home, but on the seller's (David's) old home. This assures that the second is protected by more equity. It also guarantees the seller that the second will be paid off as soon as David's old home sells.

Another alternative is a "blanket" second that covers both the house in question and another house that the buyer might own. Blanket seconds give the seller additional security because they cover two properties.

I have seen no-interest, no-monthly-payment seconds written fairly frequently in a cold market. Often it may be the only way the seller is going to be able to sell the property and for that reason may be acceptable.

Cutting Down on Costs and Red Tape

There is one additional advantage of having the seller carry back the mortgage and that comes from the fact that the seller will not normally charge any fees for the service. It would be a rare seller indeed who charged points, for example, for a carry-back second—or who charged processing or document fees, something that institutional lenders charge all the time. When you have the seller finance the sale, among other things, it also means that the financing is a lot cheaper for you.

The Wrap

Thus far, we've been assuming that the seller would be thrilled to give you a second mortgage when you offer to buy his or her property. However, some sellers are quite wary. They are concerned about your ability and desire to repay the mortgage. For example, what if the seller gives you a big second mortgage and then you don't make the payments on the first?

This puts the seller in a difficult position. The seller must learn about the default and foreclose on you, all the while fending off the institutional lender of the first.

Many sellers who would otherwise be willing to help buyers with financing won't do it because of their fear of the buyer not living up to the obligations on the first mortgage, forcing them into a difficult foreclosure. The wraparound or "all-inclusive second mortgage" is a solution to this problem.

Tip

The wrap blends two mortgages. Since one of the mortgages is usually of a lower interest rate than the overall wrap rate, it provides the lender with a much higher yield. Because of this, the lender can sometimes offer the borrower a lower interest rate. Thus, a wrap can benefit both borrower and lender.

The wrap has been used for years in commercial financing of real estate. It gained popularity in residential property in the mid-1970s as a way of getting around "due-on-sale" clauses (preventing assumptions), thus allowing buyers to assume sellers' existing low-interest-rate mortgages.

It fell out of vogue in real estate when the due-on-sale clause in existing mortgages was widely upheld in precedent-setting court cases. And once again it is coming back into vogue as the real estate market goes slow and sellers look for new and creative ways of helping buyers purchase their homes.

How a Wrap Works

In its simplest form, the seller gives you a single mortgage which includes a new second as well as an old, assumable first. However, instead of making two mortgage payments, you make one . . . to the seller. The seller then makes the payment on the existing first and keeps the difference, which is the payment on the second.

Notice the difference here between a wrap and a traditional second. In the traditional second, you are the borrower of record on both the first and the second and make two payments, one on each mortgage. In the wrap you are the borrower of record on only one mortgage, the wraparound. The seller then forwards your payments to the lender of the first.

Typical Wrap

In this example, you put 10 percent down, wrap an existing first of 70 percent of the sales price with the seller advancing 20 percent of the equity. It looks like this:

10% Down
W 20% Seller **R** Financed **A** **P** **A** 70% Existing **R** Assumable **O** First **U** **N** **D**

Trap

You can get in trouble trying to wrap around an existing *non*assumable first mortgage. The reason is simple. As soon as the sale is recorded, it gives the lender of the first mortgage constructive notice that the property has changed hands.

If the lender discovers what you've done, it can then exert the *due-on-sale* clause found in almost all nonassumable mortgages and call in the loan. (Remember, nonassumable means that as soon as the property is sold, the mortgage must be paid off. Putting the wrap on the property, in effect, results in the first becoming immediately due and payable.)

In actual practice, according to lenders with whom I've talked, most discover the wrap less than 50 percent of the time. And those that do discover it frequently overlook the problem if their loan is current and paid on time. Their philosophy is that they'd rather keep a good paying borrower than get into the hassle of a foreclosure.

In order for a wrap to work easily, the first mortgage must either be new or, if it's existing, must be assumable. (FHA and VA loans are often assumable and may be wrapped in this fashion.)

In the case of a new mortgage, often both the seller and the buyer are named in the mortgage. In the event the borrower doesn't make payments this allows the seller the right to make payments on the first and keep it current while foreclosing on the wrap.

In the case of an assumable mortgage, such as an FHA-insured or VA-guaranteed loan, often no notice of the wrap need be given to the lender. The new wrap loan is simply placed on the property and the seller continues making payments on the existing first.

Trap

Sometimes a seller will want to wrap around a nonassumable first mortgage. You may be told that to avoid accelerating the mortgage because of the due-on-sale clause, the title won't actually be transferred to you. Rather, it will be held in escrow or will be in some other form, until you can pay off the equivalent of the second-mortgage portion of the wrap. Then the seller will transfer and you can get a new first mortgage.

Remember, the problem here is caused by the fact that the existing mortgage cannot be assumed. The wrap in this case is a ploy to get around the nonassumption problem.

Beware of this kind of a deal, as it may end up costing you a lot of money as well as the house. In real estate, your interest in the property is evidenced by title, which means a recorded deed in your name. If you don't have title, you don't effectively own the property. Without your knowledge, the seller, conceivably, could refinance it or even sell it to someone else! Without title, you aren't properly protected.

In a nonrecorded wrap, the best you are likely to have is a contract with the seller. However, no matter how ironclad the contract may appear to be, your only recourse in the event the seller fails to live up to the terms, may be to take the seller to court—a long, arduous, and costly process with unpredictable results.

What to Include When You Ask for Seller Financing

It's important to understand that everything in real estate is negotiable. That includes the second mortgage (or wrap) that you seek from the seller.

What this means for you is that you can plan the terms and conditions of the loan so that they give you, the borrower, the greatest advantage. This is not to say that the seller will accept your terms. However, unless you have terms, how will you know?

Interest Rate

Of course, one of the most important items to consider is the interest rate. As with most things, this is a trade-off. The higher the interest rate, the more likely the seller is to accept this kind of financing. The lower the interest rate, the less likely. In other words, the more interest you are willing to pay the seller on this note, the more desirable it is.

Tip

___

The trade-off is usually between purchase price and interest rate. If you are offering a good purchase price (close to market or what the seller is asking), you are more likely to get a low interest rate. On the other hand, if you are low-balling the seller and demanding a low price, you are better off offering a higher and more appealing interest rate on the second.

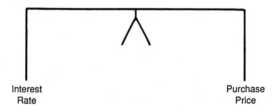

Interest   Purchase
Rate   Price

Tip

___

Be aware of usury laws. Some states have laws which limit the amount of interest that a seller can charge on a second mortgage. Any amount over that rate is considered usurious and unlawful. (These same laws may not apply to first mortgages offered by institutions.) The seller may insist on an interest rate that is above the usury rate for your state.

You can then inform the seller of the problem and in this way get a lower interest rate on your mortgage than you might otherwise secure.

Note: Other states, such as California, specifically exempt seller financing from usury laws. Here, as a seller, you can charge any amount of interest you want.

Term

Another negotiable item is the term. A second or wrap can be for any length of time. It can be for 3 months or 3 years or 30 years. It's all up to what you and the seller agree upon.

In most cases the longer the term, the better for you, the borrower. Most sellers want seconds for a relatively short time, 18 months to 5 years. Usually during that time you pay interest only, which means at the end, you still owe the full amount that you borrowed. (Balloon payments are discussed in Chapter 8.)

As a result, you must usually refinance or sell the home before the term of the seller's financing runs out. Naturally, the longer the second, the better it is for you.

On the other hand, sellers usually, but not always, want their money out quickly. Thus, the shorter the term, the more appealing the second is likely to be. Again, if you ask for a longer second, be prepared to give someplace else, such as offering a higher interest rate or perhaps a higher price. On the other hand, if you're willing to settle for a short-term second, say a year, you may be able to negotiate for a lower interest rate (or no interest) and a lower purchase price.

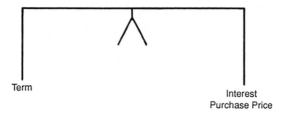

Term

Interest
Purchase Price

Tip

Most sellers want their money as soon as possible so that they can put it into another home. But sometimes a seller has different ideas. Sellers who are retiring or who have other assets often want a long-term mortgage at a good rate so that they can collect interest, which is usually better than they can get at the bank.

Find out your seller's motivation. If, indeed, the seller is looking for interest income, a long-term second may be to both parties' advantage.

Trap

Beware of short-term seconds. You can never know what the market will be like 3 years, or 2 years, or even 6 months in the future. You may say to yourself, "Sure, it'll be a cinch to refinance when the short-term second comes due." But by then, interest rates may take a jump up and you won't be able to refinance. Or you could be laid off and not have the income to qualify for a new mortgage. Or the market may head into a tailspin and you may not be able to sell.

Always allow yourself as much of an escape route as possible. In terms of seconds, this means getting enough time to ride out most adversities. *I consider any second for less than 5 years to be risky.*

Tip

Many institutional lenders today are giving long-term (15- to 30-year) seconds at competitive interest rates. If there is a problem with seller financing, see if a lending institution can help out.

Conditions

Finally, there are the conditions of the second. Keep in mind that whatever conditions are imposed in the second are strictly a matter of negotiation between you and the seller. Unlike a first mortgage from an institutional lender, where federal law may require certain conditions, with a second almost everything is negotiable.

In most cases buyer and seller will simply fill out a "standard" second mortgage agreement that a title insurance, escrow company, or broker will provide. However, you can easily deviate from the printed text. Be sure you have a good real estate attorney working with you.

Late Payment Penalty

One matter you will want to consider is that of late payment. In almost all first mortgages, there is a provision that if your payment is more than 2 weeks late, you will be fined a penalty usually equal to 5 percent of the mortgage payment ($50 on a $1000 payment).

This clause does not have to be inserted into the second. Unless the seller insists upon it, it would be to your advantage, in fact, to have it left out.

Tip

Some states have a limit on the amount of a late payment penalty. In California, for example, the limit is 6 percent. Also, the penalty may or may not be applicable to a balloon payment in your state. Check with a local attorney.

Tip

The penalty for late payment can be a negotiating point. If the seller intends to sell the second to an investor, it is vital to have the penalty. Most investors either will not buy or will pay less for a second without a penalty clause. Therefore, if the seller insists on a penalty clause in the second, you may agree, for a better term or interest rate.

Subordination Clause

This a clause that you may very well want to have in the second, but which the seller, if he or she is bright at all, will usually frown upon (depending on the circumstances—see the discussion in Chapter 2). It is difficult to get sellers to agree to subordinate, but if you can, it can be a real plus for you.

A subordination clause means that the second remains in place if you refinance the first.

While this may seem obvious, it is not. To understand why, it is necessary to remember how mortgages are placed on real estate. They flow chronologically in the order in which they were recorded. What makes a first a first is not so much anything which is stated in the paperwork, but the fact that it was recorded first, before any other mortgages. A second was recorded second. A third was recorded third, and so on. A first is not even necessarily the largest loan, although usually it will be.

Let's say you have a first and a second and you want to refinance the first. In order to do this, you have to pay off the existing first and get a new mortgage. However, as soon as you pay off the existing first, the existing second moves up and becomes "first" in chronological order. Therefore, you could not refinance the old first mortgage with a new first mortgage.

The solution is the subordination clause. When put into a second, it requires that mortgage to hold its place. The second remains a second regardless of what happens to the first. If you pay off the first, you can then refinance and get a brand new first and *the second holds its position.*

The importance to you of this is the fact that you can usually get a first mortgage for a lower interest rate, longer term, and higher amount than a second. Also, by keeping the second in its position, you can refinance, get more money out, and not have to pay off the second!

This latter, of course, is why sellers don't like it. A subordination clause weakens a second.

Tip

A seller might be induced into taking a subordination clause if you limit it. For example, you could insert a clause saying that you will get a first of no more than a certain amount. Limiting the amount of the first protects the seller's second.

Refinance Clause

This is a tricky little clause that some shrewd borrowers have been inserting into second mortgages of late. If it gets past the seller, it could be worth its weight in gold.

The refinance clause simply states that when the second comes due, the seller agrees to refinance it. In other words, your second may be for 3 years. At the end of the 3 years, at *your* (the borrower's) option, it can automatically be refinanced for an additional 3 years.

Why would the seller accept such a condition?

Usually the clause states that the refinance will be at or slightly above the then-current mortgage market rate for first mortgages. In other words, if at the end of 3 years (in this case) the market rate for conventional first mortgages is 10 percent, the second will be refinanced at, say, 12 percent.

If the seller doesn't need the cash, this is an excellent way to lock in money for an additional period of time.

If you get a refinance clause inserted into your second, be sure that the future interest rate is as low as possible and that it is tied to a standard index which can be provided by any lender. Such indexes include the current T-Bill rates, the average yield of mortgages for the previous 30 days, the lender's cost of funds from the government, or some similar economic measure. Also, try to get a margin as low as possible.

Tip

If you're daring, you may agree to a very high interest rate on the refinance, say 5 percent above going mortgage market rates!

The seller may think that he or she is getting a real bonus here, which you can use as a negotiating tool elsewhere in the deal. In reality, of course, the seller is getting nothing since the refinance is at your option. You can choose not to exercise it and instead to refinance elsewhere or sell the property.

Size of Second Relative to Down Payment

While it's true that everything is negotiable, some things are harder to negotiate. For example, it may be to your advantage to offer a 5 percent down payment and a 15 percent second. However, if the seller wants to dispose of that second, he or she will find it almost impossible to do if you put only 5 percent down. In order for a second to be marketable to an investor, the buyer must typically put at least 10 percent down.

Sellers Who Will Give Firsts

Thus far we've been discussing sellers who are willing to give part of the equity to you in the form of a second mortgage. But there's another, though much smaller, class of sellers who are willing to make first mortgages.

These sellers are typically older people who have been in the property for 20 to 30 years and have either paid off or almost paid off their existing mortgage(s). These people may not have any use for a large amount of cash, as they would receive in an all-cash sale. But instead they may be interested in a kind of annuity. They want so much each month on which to live. A first mortgage is an ideal answer for them . . . and for you as well.

The reason for this is that if the sellers carry the first, you may get the mortgage for slightly below market interest rates. But, you probably won't have to pay points or other loan fees. And you may not have to qualify as strictly as you would for an institutional lender. A seller may accept a borrower with slightly blemished credit, with a lower down payment, even with less income (less ability to repay) than an institutional lender would, simply to get the house sold.

Tip

It is worth paying more for a property in which the seller will carry the first. The benefits in quicker and easier qualifying as well as lower costs more than justify a higher price.

Assuming the Seller's Mortgage

Yet another type of financing may be to assume the seller's existing mortgage(s). This subject is dealt with in other areas of this book, but here, let's consider the advantages to you as a home buyer.

Most mortgages, as noted earlier, are not assumable. When the properties are sold, they must be paid off.

However, in some cases, particularly with FHA-insured or VA-guaranteed mortgages, you may be able to assume them. If that's the case, you should give the matter considerable thought, since these loans may be far more favorable than anything else out there. If they were placed on the property years ago, they may have a lower interest rate than the current market rate. Also, when it's time for you to resell, these mortgages can be a bonus to the next seller.

The problem is usually that the existing assumable first mortgage is too low. For example, let's say the sellers bought the property 15 years ago, and got an FHA mortgage for $60,000. There is currently an unpaid balance of $55,000, but the property is now selling for $120,000. In order to assume this mortgage, you would need to come up with an additional $65,000, a lot more than most borrowers can handle.

$120,000 Purchase Price

```
┌─────────────────┐
│                 │
│   Difference    │
│   ($65,000)     │
│                 │
│                 │
├─────────────────┤
│                 │
│   Assumable     │
│     First       │
│   ($55,000)     │
│                 │
└─────────────────┘
```

There are several solutions to this dilemma. The seller may be willing to give you a second for most of the difference. Or the seller may be willing to wrap the first in an all-inclusive second. See the earlier discussion of wraps in this chapter.

Yet another solution is to get an institutional second. If the seller wants all cash out, you could, instead of getting a new first mortgage, keep the existing low-interest-rate assumable first and get a new second from a bank or S&L. Lenders are more than willing to make such mortgages today. By combining an institutional second with an assumable first, you may end up with a better deal than simply getting a new first mortgage.

Tip

The key to deciding whether it's better to get a new first or keep the existing assumable first and get a new institutional second is the combined interest rate and payment. You first have to calculate what interest rate you'd be paying on the combined first and second and then compare it to a single first mortgage. Here's an easy example:

Existing first	$50,000 at 8 percent
New second	$50,000 at 12 percent
Combined interest rate	10 percent

In the above example, the combined rate would effectively be 10 percent—you're paying 8 percent on half the money and 12 percent on the other half, so the average is 10. You would now compare this with the market rate. If the current market rate is 11 percent, you've got a good deal. If, for example, it's 9 percent, you don't.

Current mortgage market rate	11% — good deal
Your combined rate	10%
Current mortgage market rate	9% — bad deal

Making the calculation, however, is often much more difficult. The reason is that the amounts of the first and second are almost always different. You have to then assign a percentage of the total borrowed to each mortgage and then calculate an average interest rate based on that percentage. If you have trouble with this, drop into a lender and ask one of the loan officers to make the calculation for you. They can do it in seconds.

Trap

The interest rate isn't the only consideration. You may also want to consider the payment. The existing first may have "aged." That means that it's an old mortgage that perhaps has been on the property for many years. As a result, a substantial amount of each monthly payment may be going toward principal, rather than nearly all going toward interest, as is the case with a fresh mortgage.

As a result, your combined monthly payments with an existing assumable first and a new institutional second may be higher than with a single new first, even though the combined interest rate could be lower! An example will illustrate the point.

```
┌─────────────────────────┐
│   Assumable First       │
│   ($50,000 @ 8%)        │        Combined Monthly Payment = $1096
│   $548 Monthly          │        Combined Interest Rate = 10%
├─────────────────────────┤
│   New Second            │
│   ($50,000 @ 12%)       │
│   $514 Monthly          │
└─────────────────────────┘
0 — — — — — — — — — — —1
```

```
┌─────────────────────────┐
│   New First             │        Single Monthly Payment = $952
│   ($100,000 @ 11%)      │        Single Interest Rate = 11%
│   $952 Monthly          │
└─────────────────────────┘
```

Notice that in the above example, the monthly payment on a single new first mortgage for 11 percent is nearly $150 less than for a combined existing assumable first and new second with an effective rate of 10 percent! How can the payments for an 11 percent mortgage be less than that for a 10 percent mortgage?

The answer has to do with the aging of the first. I assumed that the original balance of the first was $75,000. It was on that figure that the payments were based. Once that mortgage gets more than 20 years old, however, the balance quickly goes down until now, at the time it is assumed, it has a balance of $50,000.

The problem is that when you assume the mortgage, you are making payments on an old original balance of $75,000, not a current existing balance of $50,000. This is not to say that you're losing any money. Quite the contrary, a substantial portion of each payment, as noted earlier, is going to pay down that principal.

However, if you need a lower mortgage payment, then you'll suffer. In short, regardless of how favorable a combined interest rate may be, you must also consider the combined monthly payment when compared to a single new first mortgage. Sometimes, depending on the age of the existing assumable first, the payments will simply be too high. You'll be better off paying a higher interest rate and getting lower monthly payments.

How to Negotiate with the Seller

We've discussed a variety of options that you may want to consider when having the seller help with the financing. One last matter needs to be discussed, and that has to do with the actual negotiation process. How do you negotiate with the seller to get what you want?

There's a three-step process that I use which may be helpful to you.

Step 1. Identify what you want

You can't get it if you don't know what it is. Whether it's a reduced down payment, lower interest rate, or lower payments, determine up front, before you make your offer, what your goal is.

Step 2. Give in order to get

You normally won't get it all. You won't get a good price *and* favorable terms. Therefore, once you decide what you want as indicated above, determine what you're willing to give the seller in return. For example, if you want a low-interest- or no-interest-rate second, give the seller his or her price. If you want a good price, come in for all cash (cash down to a new first mortgage).

Step 3. Try to be flexible

Make your best offer and see what the seller does. You can never know what a seller will do. Very frequently the seller will counter, often in a way that may surprise you. Try to be flexible. Try to adjust terms and price so that both you and the seller get what you want. When that happens, you'll have a deal. Beware of giving the seller everything he or she wants just to get the house. You may pay the price for a bad deal for years to come.

The bottom line is remembering that everything in real estate is negotiable, most importantly including terms. Many sellers simply can't or won't consider helping with the financing. But it usually won't hurt to ask in terms of an offer. (It can hurt if you make an offer asking for favorable terms and lose out to another buyer who comes in with all cash.)

The real trick is getting the right balance between terms, price, and mortgage amount.

8
Making Balloon Payments Work

Their Bad Reputation
May Be Undeserved

Introduction

A "balloon" in real estate finance is nothing more than one payment of a mortgage (usually the last) which is bigger than any of the others. The balloon payment has been talked about so much (often erroneously) in the general press that it has achieved legendary proportions. It is for this reason that a short separate chapter explaining it and its pros and cons is in order.

What's Wrong With the
Balloon Payment?

There is nothing wrong with balloon payments, as long as you, the borrower, understand them and know when they are coming. The problem with balloons in the past—and what has led to much of their bad press— is that they came as a surprise to some borrowers.

A person might buy a home with the seller carrying back a second mortgage for 3 years. At the end of that period of time, the second might come due in a single balloon payment, often for the total amount originally borrowed (if the loan was interest only, as it commonly is)! If the buyer had not anticipated this and had not made plans to refinance or sell, that borrower might end up losing the property.

In the general press, this rare occurrence was blown out of proportion, particularly in the early eighties, by reporters with no experience in real estate. They made the balloon payment seem like a subversive plot.

In truth, the balloon payment is nothing more than a financial device which can be of benefit to the borrower. It's simply a matter of understanding when and how to use it.

Trap

Be aware that many mortgages with balloon payments *do not explicitly state the fact* that a balloon is involved. Rather, the mortgage might be written in such a way that it only specifies interest and term. It leaves it up to you to figure out whether or not a balloon payment will be due.

Common sense helps here. If you have a mortgage for $10,000 at 12 percent interest, your payment is $100 a month, and it's due in 5 years, is it a balloon payment mortgage or not?

The answer is to figure out how much principal will be paid down over the course of the 5 years. In this case you'll be paying a total of $100 a month, or $1200 a year, in interest.

However, 12 percent of $10,000 is $1200. That means that you'll be paying *interest only*. Given this fact, at the end of 5 years, you'll owe exactly what you borrowed. You'll have a balloon payment of $10,000.

To be sure, ask the lender to give you a breakdown of principal and interest for *each payment* over the course of the mortgage term. Here you'll clearly be able to see if the last payment (or any other) is larger.

Balloon
Payment

Regular payments

Any Mortgage Can
Have a Balloon

It's important to understand that any mortgage can have a balloon payment. It's simply the way it's written. Many first mortgages today are written with balloons. For example, one of the most popular mortgages as of this writing is the 30/10. In this mortgage, the payments are amortized over 30 years. However, the entire mortgage is due in 10 years. In other words, there is a balloon of the entire unpaid balance at payment number 121.

The purpose of this mortgage is to insulate the lender against interest rate volatility. The advantage to the borrower is that it gives a lower initial interest rate. However, the borrower must be aware that at year 10, he or she is going to have to refinance or pay off the mortgage. (In practice, this type of mortgage usually also involves some sort of conversion to then-current market interest rates.)

Why It's Good for the Borrower

The balloon mortgage generally allows you to get a lower interest rate and/or to make a lower monthly payment. Here's an example.

Many second mortgages are written with balloon payments. If you are borrowing $10,000 from the seller at 12 percent interest for 5 years, your fully amortized (amortized means to pay back in equal installments) mortgage would carry payments of $332 principle and interest a month. Pay that amount each month and at the end of 3 years, the mortgage is paid off.

However, perhaps you cannot afford to make that high a payment, particularly since you'll probably also be paying on a first mortgage plus taxes and insurance. So instead, you opt for an "interest-only" second mortgage. Here the payments, as noted earlier, are only $100 a month, a savings of $232 monthly. However, because you are paying interest only, at the end of the term, you still owe the entire balance as a balloon. The trade-off has been lower payments for a balloon.

Of course, there's nothing to say that the mortgage has to be interest only to have a balloon payment. You could be making a higher payment, but not enough to pay off all the principal, say $200 a month in our example, and still end up with a sizable balloon payment at the end.

Tip

Many people do not fear a balloon payment because they anticipate that by the time it comes due, they can refinance. They anticipate that as time goes by, they will have a higher income and that inflation will have made the actual amount due on the mortgage worth less in buying power. Historically, this bet has paid off. However, should the country experience a deflation, it might not have such a happy outcome.

The Seller's Incentive

The balloon payment is one of the biggest reasons that a seller may be willing to help the buyer with the financing of a purchase (see Chapter 8). Most sellers will balk at giving a buyer a long-term second mortgage. However, if the mortgage is short-term, particularly if the seller is going to get interest paid monthly with all or most of the principal repaid at the end of the term, it's a different story. Most sellers look gleefully at this kind of financing, and if they don't need all their cash out to buy another property, they may opt for it.

Paying Off the Balloon

There are lots of ways of handling a balloon payment. Here are several:

1. Sell the property and pay off the balloon.
2. Refinance for enough to pay off both the existing note and the balloon second.
3. Make higher payments during the term of the balloon so the mortgage pays off without ballooning.
4. Get the lender-seller to rewrite the balloon mortgage for an additional period of time. As inducements, offer:
   a. A higher interest rate.
   b. To pay off a portion of the principal immediately.
   c. To share equity in the property with the seller.

Tip

The only real problem with a balloon mortgage comes about when you, the borrower, fail to prepare for it. If you know it's coming, you should be able to deal with it.

If you want the seller-lender to refinance the balloon, start early, 6 to 12 months before it's due. Don't wait until the last moment. Otherwise, if the seller-lender doesn't come through, you could be stuck.

9

Convertible Mortgages and Piggybacks

Is Tailoring a Mortgage to Your Needs Worth the Price?

Introduction

A convertible mortgage is something like a convertible car; it has two different modes. With a convertible car you can have the top up and, thus, drive it as a conventional automobile. However, you can also lower the roof and have a sporty open-air vehicle. A convertible mortgage also has two modes. In one mode it is a staid conventional type of loan. In the other it's sporty and has adjustable-rate features.

The convertible can blend adjustable and fixed features. You can get the big advantage of the adjustable-rate mortgage, a lower initial interest rate, but you can also achieve increased stability over the life of the mortgage. For the lender, the convertible is a compromise. It doesn't lock the lender into a long-term fixed rate, which could be catastrophic if interest rates rise. On the other hand, it doesn't give the lender quite as much protection against volatility as the straight adjustable-rate mortgage.

Convertibles are some of the better mortgages available for borrowers. However, you have to shop carefully since they come in all sizes and shapes, and some can be quite ugly.

How a Convertible Mortgage Works

A convertible mortgage is really like two mortgages packaged together. In one popular form, you start out with an adjustable rate. Then after a period of years, you are given the option of converting to a fixed-rate mortgage at a predetermined interest rate.

In another form, you begin with a fixed interest rate, often at or slightly below market, then after a period of years, you can convert to an adjustable (or another fixed rate), usually slightly above then-current market conditions.

If the convertible sounds complicated, don't worry. It really isn't. It is, in fact, often a great mortgage and one which you should spend some time investigating.

Convertibles that start fixed and end up adjustable are usually good bets. Those that start as adjustables and end up fixed are often losers for you, the borrower.

30 Due in 7

One of the most popular convertible mortgages as of this writing is called a "30 due in 7" (or 10, or 5) years. Here's how it works.

Mortgage-Hunting Scenario

Kelly wanted to buy a home for $200,000. She was determined to get a fixed-rate mortgage because she liked its stability, but because she was borderline in qualifying, she needed the lowest possible interest rate.

When she went to her mortgage broker he suggested a "30 due in 7." Naturally Kelly asked him to explain.

He noted that it was quite simple. The mortgage consisted of four features:

1. The initial rate was fixed at ½ percent below market for 7 years.
2. The payments were amortized over 30 years.
3. The mortgage was due in 7 years. In other words, in reality it had only a 7-year term.
4. At the end of 7 years the borrower could automatically convert (without additional qualifying) to an adjustable-rate mortgage which was included in the package.

Note some of the important features of this type of mortgage. First, the rate is below market, and it is fixed. The borrower doesn't have to worry about any fluctuations in the monthly payments.

Next, the payments themselves are amortized over 30 years. This means that a 30-year schedule is used to calculate the monthly payment, giving the borrower the lowest possible payments.

Third, even though the amount of the monthly payment is based on a 30-year term, the loan is due in 7. In other words, it has a balloon at payment number 85. Since, as explained in earlier chapters, almost all of the payments in the first years go to interest, this means that for all practical purposes, this is an interest-only loan.

Finally, at the end of 7 years, the loan automatically converts to an adjustable-rate mortgage. However, at that point you have the option of refinancing elsewhere or selling the property and paying it off.

Trap

The adjustable that this type of mortgage converts to is usually pretty ugly. It often calls for adjustments to be made every month and is frequently set up so that the effective interest rate you pay is between ½ and 1 percent higher than then-current market rates.

The whole point of this conversion adjustable is to provide an escape hatch in case you, the borrower, need one. (Perhaps you can't sell or qualify for a refinance at the time.) If you can't refinance anywhere else, then you can fall back on the conversion. But the conversion itself is made sufficiently unattractive to discourage you from relying on it.

Beware of any type of first mortgage that has a short-term due date (such as 7 years) without the conversion privilege. You never know what can happen in 7 years. You might be ill or out of work and unable to qualify for a new mortgage. The conversion, at least temporarily, might save you from losing the property.

Tip

This type of convertible loan offers you several big bonuses. The first is that the initial rate is often for slightly below market rates. You get a lower initial interest rate and, hence, lower payments.

Also, the rate is fixed for the initial period, typically 5, 7, or 10 years. As a consequence, you don't have to worry about the payment fluctuations you will find with an adjustable-rate mortgage.

Other Forms for the Convertible Mortgage

The 30 due in 7 has a variety of clones. There is, for example, the 30 due in 10 years. The additional 3 years gives you, the borrower, some extra breathing room. Since most people will sell their homes before 10 years are up, this can be considered, for all practical purposes, a permanent loan.

On the other hand, the 30 due in 10 often carries market interest rates. In other words, if the market rate is 10 percent, that's what you'll get on this loan, while the due in 7 may have a rate of 1/2 percent below market.

Similarly there is a 30 due in 5. This often gives you another eighth of a point benefit in interest rates. However, the very short due date can be a trap. Five years isn't very long. Due in 5 years almost guarantees that you'll have to convert or refinance.

Piggybacks

Generally speaking, all of the 30 due in 5-, 7-, or 10-year mortgages with low interest rates are for conforming loans, which can be sold on the secondary market ($191,250 maximum as of this writing). If you want a bigger loan, a "jumbo," you'll have to pay a higher rate of interest.

While conforming mortgages carry the lowest possible interest rates (8.5 percent as of this writing—the rates change almost daily), jumbos, or loans over $191,250, carry much higher rates (10 percent as of this writing.) For someone who wants to borrow just a bit over the conforming maximum, say $250,000, this can mean a significant jump in mortgage interest rate.

To overcome this problem, some lenders have created the "piggy" or "superpiggy." This is actually a blended mortgage.

A piggy is a double mortgage. It consists of a standard conforming 30 due in 5, 7, or 10 years for the maximum $191,250. But it also includes from the same lender a second mortgage. The first is at the lower conforming rate. The second is at a higher rate, usually about half a point higher than a standard jumbo, since it is, after all, a second mortgage. The blended rate, however, is usually lower than for a jumbo.

You, as borrower, benefit from a combined interest rate of the first and second that is lower than if you simply obtained a jumbo loan for the whole amount. Up to about $250,000, you usually save half to three-quarters of a point in interest.

The cost of these piggies (the second mortgage is placed piggyback fashion on top of the first) is no different from other mortgages in terms of points and fees. And the second is structured to be the same 30 due in 5, 7, or 10 years as the first. Further, you make only a single payment to the lender, who then applies the money to the appropriate mortgage.

These piggies or superpiggies provide all the benefits (and draw-backs) of the standard 30 due in 5, 7, or 10 years, plus they offer a slightly reduced interest rate. If you are looking for a jumbo mortgage, be sure to ask your lender about these. They could save you interest and hundreds of dollars in monthly payments.

Tip

Piggies or jumbo piggies are the ideal mortgage for someone who plans to get some money within a year or so that can be applied to the home. For example, I recently purchased a home using a jumbo piggy. However, I had not yet sold another home in a distant area. It took me about 5 months to complete the sale of the second home. When that was done, I took the money I received, and with the lender's permission, paid off the second mortgage part of the piggy, thus effectively dropping my interest rate to that of the conforming loan. (*Note:* Many lenders will not permit a split payoff such as this. Check with the lender *before* securing the mortgage.)

I accomplished the same thing as a refinance, without any refinancing costs at all.

PIGGYBACK MORTGAGE

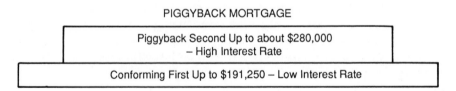

Adjustable Convertibles

A different form of the convertible and one which has been used since about 1988 involves an adjustable-rate mortgage which later converts to a fixed-rate mortgage for the remaining term. (This is the opposite of what we've just been discussing.)

In the adjustable convertible you start out with an adjustable-rate mortgage. However, at some point in time, you are given the opportunity to convert to a fixed rate, if you so choose. The option is yours. You can either stick with the adjustable or convert to a fixed. This type of mortgage also has four separate features:

1. You begin with an adjustable rate, often around 2 points below market.

2. The adjustment periods can vary but are usually either every month, every 6 months, or every year. The initial interest rate varies, depending on the adjustment period chosen. The shorter the period, the lower the rate. For example, if you opt for the monthly adjustment, the initial rate might be 6 percent. If you opt for the 6-month adjustment, the initial rate might be 7 percent. If you opt for the yearly adjustment, the initial rate might be 8 percent.

3. The steps are usually 2 percent with a 5 or 6 percent cap. In other words, the maximum the interest rate can go up or down is 2 percent per adjustment period. The maximum the interest rate can go up or down for the life of the mortgage is 5 or 6 percent.

4. You usually have only a specified window period during which you can convert to a fixed-rate mortgage. For example, you may be able to convert anytime during the third to fifth year. Or you may convert at year 7. Converting is usually not costly. There may be points or fractions of points to pay. Usually, though, you only pay a flat fee, perhaps a few hundred dollars. In some cases you may have to pay some charges such as escrow or title fees. Usually the total fees, however, are far less than if you went out and refinanced with a new mortgage.

Trap

The real cost of the adjustable convertible comes from the fact that you probably will end up with a higher-than-market interest rate on the fixed loan, plus you'll end up with an adjustable which also, over the course of its life, has a higher-than-market rate.

Tip

The value of this type of convertible loan comes from your ability to convert it to a fixed rate at some time in the future. If the conversion window happens to be during a period of lower interest rates, you can get into a fixed mortgage for very little in costs.

Comparing the Adjustable
Convertible

Compare the adjustable features of this mortgage to other adjustable-rate mortgages. Do you have to pay a higher initial rate? What about the margin? Is it higher? If the adjustable features of this mortgage are no different than for any other adjustable mortgage at the time, you will certainly want to seriously consider taking it.

On the other hand, if you have to pay additional to get it, you may want to reconsider. You will want to weigh the up-front costs against any possible benefits of the conversion. Remember that the major benefit is usually lower costs than a refinance. However, this is offset by an often higher-than-market (by usually about ½ percent) interest rate on the converted fixed-rate mortgage.

Trap

Remember that when you convert in this type of mortgage, you don't get a fixed-interest mortgage set at today's market rates. Rather, the basis of the interest rate on the fixed portion is over the *then*-prevailing rates. They might be high or low.

Also, you can't choose when to convert. You can only do it during the conversion window which is specified by the mortgage. If that conversion window happens to fall during a period of high interest rates, you're stuck!

When Does Conversion
Pay Off?

One big question on adjustable convertible mortgages is when does it pay to convert them? When your conversion window appears, how do you decide if the timing is right to convert?

The answer has to do with then current interest rates. If interest rates are high during your conversion window, then my advice is to sit tight with the adjustable, even if it means losing the conversion privilege. When rates fall, you can refinance, hopefully at a significant savings of interest.

On the other hand, if rates are low during the conversion window, then by all means convert, even if you have to accept a half point above market. Let's take an example.

Mortgage-Hunting Scenario

Harry obtained an adjustable convertible. The initial interest rate was 7 percent, moving quickly up to 9.5 percent. The window for conversion was between year 3 and year 5.

For the first four years of the mortgage, interest rates hovered around 10 percent and Harry didn't convert. However, there was some inflationary pressure at year 5 and rates went up to 11 percent. If Harry converted in year 5, he would get a fixed-rate mortgage for one half percent above market or, in this case, 11½ percent. His total conversion costs would be only $500.

However, if he waited, hoping for interest rates to come down, he might be able to refinance in year 6 or later at a lower fixed rate. By waiting, he might get a far better mortgage.

Waiting, however, is offset by the costs of refinancing, which can be as much as 5 percent of the mortgage balance. Harry would have to weigh the chances interest rates might fall against the costs of losing the conversion window and paying the additional costs of refinancing outside the mortgage.

Tip

Harry really doesn't have all that much to lose by sticking with the adjustable. His cap on the adjustable mortgage was only 12 percent, so he's currently only 1 percent away from the top. It's unlikely his mortgage interest rate would go much higher.

Additionally, if rates fall, his adjustable will likewise fall. If he converts, he's stuck at a high fixed rate. If he does nothing and rates fall, he'll end up with a lower interest rate and lower payments!

Is a Convertible for You?

Whether its a 30/10 or an adjustable convertible, it's important not to overlook this type of mortgage. The convertible can offer an opportunity, depending on your borrowing needs.

To make the decision, you need to compare the convertibles to other fixed-rate and adjustable mortgages that are available. You should pay attention to overall costs, interest rates, and monthly payments.

Trap

Beware of adjustable convertibles in which you must pay an additional fee up front at the time you get the mortgage for the privilege of converting later on. Unless that conversion option is covered with gold, you're probably throwing good money away by paying for it at the time you secure the mortgage.

Most important, don't simply get suckered in by looking at a low initial interest rate. Time passes quickly and that low teaser rate will soon disappear. Look down the road. Will this mortgage be as appealing in 2 years? In 3? In 5?

Convertible mortgages are available during most noninflationary periods. You can get them from mortgage brokers and bankers as well as some institutional lenders such as banks and S&Ls.

10
"No-Doc" and "Low-Doc" Mortgages

Cutting the Time It Takes to Qualify— But at What Cost?

Introduction

"Low-doc" and "no-doc" refer to "low-documentation" and "no-documentation." To understand what this is and its advantages, you first have to remember that whenever you apply for a mortgage, you are going to have to prove that you qualify. As discussed earlier, this takes the form of providing proof of sufficient income and good enough credit to demonstrate your intention to repay.

In the past, credit was easily determined through a simple credit report. However, in order to demonstrate sufficient income, you often had to come up with all or most of the following:

A recent paystub

Federal tax returns for the last 2 to 3 years

Written verification of employment going back 3 to 5 years

Written verification of money on deposit in banks or elsewhere (to show you had the down payment)

Written proof of outside income, such as alimony

Written proof of rental income and expenses

Other documents

It's easily seen that the number of documents required has been great. And in some cases, obtaining the documents has been difficult. Further, the load of required documentation often slowed down the lending process significantly.

Self-Employed: Heavily Impacted

The problem with documentation was particularly difficult for self-employed individuals. Self-employed people are automatically suspect by lenders. The reason, quite simply, is that it is difficult to document their true income.

With a salaried individual, a paystub or a letter from an employer will usually suffice. But how do you document how much a entrepreneur really makes?

The answer has traditionally been 2 to 3 years of federal tax returns. These returns show on Schedule C the income and expenses of the self-employed person as well as the bottom-line take-home pay.

The trouble here is threefold. First, self-employed individuals are reticent to show others, even lenders, their most private matters, including their tax returns.

Second, many self-employed individuals actually take home a great deal more than their tax returns show. This is not to say they are cheating (although some may), but rather that many items, such as depreciation or home expenses, appear primarily on paper, not in reality.

Finally, it is not beyond the realm of speculation that some unscrupulous self-employed individuals might create fake federal tax returns which would show their income to be considerably higher than it really was. How would the lender know the fake from the true? The lender has no real way to contact the IRS to confirm the tax return submitted.

Trap

Don't be tempted to submit a false tax return to a lender. While the lender may accept it initially and even issue a mortgage based on it, that tax return stays with your mortgage file forever. If you ever default on the mortgage, the tax return will be dragged up and you may have to get proof from the IRS that it was authentic. Not being able to do so could be considered fraud in applying for a federally regulated mortgage and could result in severe criminal penalties.

Thus, the self-employed individual both has difficulty in complying with documentation requirements as well as being not fully trusted even when he or she presents signed forms. And even the salaried individual has to put up with time-consuming and bothersome searches for documentation.

Enter the No-Document Loan

As a result of this, some lenders began issuing no-document mortgages (also called "nonconforming" loans). These loans simply did not require any documentation at all. There were no verifications from employers or banks, no 2 or 3 years of tax returns. In some cases there weren't even any credit reports!

There was simply a statement that the borrower signed which said, upon penalty of perjury, that he or she made as much money as was claimed. Based on that statement, a mortgage was issued.

Of course, there was a catch . . . several catches. The three big ones were:

1. That this mortgage often carried a higher interest rate, often 1 or 2 points higher than market.
2. The borrower often was required to put down 25 percent instead of the usual 10 or 20 percent.
3. Finally, there were often more points to pay than for a documented mortgage.

Nevertheless, especially for the self-employed individuals who had trouble showing as much income as they actually made, this type of mortgage was a godsend. It gave them the opportunity to get a mortgage to buy a home simply on their signature.

Today the no-document mortgage is more difficult but not impossible to find. To obtain one, seek out a mortgage broker. That is your best source.

Tip

Don't go for a no-document mortgage unless it's your last chance. A documented mortgage will usually provide a lower interest rate, lower costs, and a lower down payment.

Even if you are self-employed and cannot show on tax returns as much income as you feel you make, you may still be able to get a documented mortgage. Contact a mortgage *banker.* These companies fund their own mortgages and may be able to help.

Also, if you bank with a particular S&L or bank, contact them. For a good depositor, they may be willing to make exceptions.

Mortgage-Hunting Scenario

I have a friend who was recently in this situation. He went to his local small bank, where he did over $2 million a year in business, and asked for a $300,000 home loan. When he couldn't come up with the required documentation, the bank turned him down. Whereupon, he notified the bank president that he was turning the bank down by taking his business elsewhere.

Talk about a turnaround! His mortgage was funded within the week.

Low-Documentation Mortgages: All Things Being Equal, the Only Way to Fly

Low-documentation (lo-doc) mortgages differ from no-docs in several important ways. First off, there is some documentation required. For self-employed individuals, this usually does include at least the last 2 years of federal tax returns. However, for salaried people, a couple of W-2 forms or several recent paystubs and a credit report may suffice.

Also, to verify payment of mortgages that you, the borrower, may already have, canceled checks made out to the lender may be all that's needed. There may not need to be any verification of payments made from your current mortgage lender.

Finally, instead of getting verifications of deposit from your bank, you may only need to bring in your check register or savings deposit book.

Advantage of Lo-Docs

The big advantage of the low-documentation mortgage is that it allows you to get a mortgage far more quickly. In the old days, with verification and other requirements, a typical loan took up to 45 days to process. Now, with a lo-doc application, the entire procedure can take only a week. (*Note:* It may take 3 weeks or more before the money for the mortgage is actually funded, but this is a function of the lender's ability to provide funds, not of the application process.)

Tip

Lo-doc mortgages, as opposed to no-docs, do not normally demand any kind of interest rate penalty. There's also no additional closing costs and no bigger down payment required. (They may, however, require a CLTV, whereas otherwise it would only be an LTV—check back to Chapter 3.) There is simply less paperwork. They are less available than in the past, but if you can find a lo-doc lender, it is probably to your advantage to deal with it.

Finding Lo-Doc Lenders

Some lenders today operate on the lo-doc method while others require the traditional documentation. Determining which is which, however, can be difficult for the average borrower.

At one time, it appeared that all lenders might switch to lo-doc mortgages. But then came the big S&L fallout of the early nineties and the discovery that some borrowers had falsified the few documents they were required to turn in. As a result, many lenders either went back to the old system or had never left it in the first place.

Tip

Use a lo-doc mortgage when you want to save time. If you need to get a mortgage fast so that you can make a quick purchase, this may be the ideal loan for you.

Almost any kind of lender today may offer a lo-doc mortgage. Contact a bank, S&L, credit union, or mortgage banker. The important thing to remember is that lo-doc does not mean the mortgage is in any way different from a traditional mortgage (whether it be fixed, ARM, or some other kind). What's different is the quantity and quality of documentation required, as shown in Figure 10-1.

Notice that the big difference between the traditional-documentation and the low-documentation mortgage is that the former requires written (and time-consuming) verification from outside sources. On the other hand, the lo-doc only requires that you come in with documentation that you should already have on hand. You don't have to contact your employer, bank, or current mortgage lender. You can do it all yourself.

Given the choice between traditional and lo-doc (and assuming there are no penalties for lo-doc), it's the only way to go.

Traditional	*Lo-Doc*
Two years of tax returns	W-2 forms or paystubs
Written and signed verification of employment mailed directly to lender by your employer	Paystub showing monthly and year-to-date earnings
Written and signed verification of mortgage mailed directly to lender by your current lender	Credit report or year-end mortgage statement or canceled checks
Written and signed verification of deposit mailed directly to lender by your bank.	Check register and/or savings account book

Figure 10-1. Differences between traditional and lo-doc mortgages.

11

Buy-Downs

Getting Monthly Payments Down
Can Help You Qualify

Introduction

The buy-down is not so much a particular kind of mortgage as it is a tool
which can be used with any kind of mortgage (with the lender's cooper-
ation) to lower your initial monthly payments.

In a buy-down you end up with a lower interest rate for the first years
of the mortgage. A typical buy-down is a 3/2/1 (Figure 11-1). Here the
first year your interest rate is 3 percent below market, the second year it
is 2 percent below, and the last year it is 1 percent lower. Your monthly
payments are correspondingly lower as well.

	Interest rate, %	Monthly Payment, $
Year 1	8	734
Year 2	9	805
Year 3	10	878
Years 4–30	11	952

Figure 11-1. 3/2/1 Buy-Down Example: $100,000 @ 11 percent for 30 years.

Who Pays for Buy-Downs?

It's important to understand that in a buy-down, there is no money actually saved. The lender still collects the full interest rate. The only difference is that instead of it being paid monthly, it is paid in advance in the form of points.

In order to get a buy-down, someone must pay a willing lender additional points up front. The more points paid up front, the bigger the buy-down. (The actual number of points required to lower the interest rate 1 percent per year will vary with market conditions. Check with your lender.)

The most common example of a buy-down occurs when you are buying a brand-new home from a builder. The builder may advertise, for example, "5 percent interest for the first 5 years!" That, of course, is an extremely shocking advertisement in an era when 8 or 9 percent mortgages are exceptionally low. It is almost guaranteed to get buyers flocking to the builder trying to buy those properties. But how does the builder really offer such a low-interest-rate mortgage? Is that builder somehow tied into an exceptionally altruistic lender?

Tip

There are no altruistic lenders!

What the builder does is go to a lender and negotiate a mortgage for the buyers. The builder gives the lender a certain number of points up front, perhaps 10 or 20. In addition, the lender may require an adjustable or higher-than-market mortgage on a fixed interest rate after the first 5 years.

In any event, the builder has paid the lender to lower the interest rate. The actual interest rate on the mortgage may be 9 percent. But the builder has "bought down" the rate on the first 5 years to 5 percent.

Of course, the money has to come from someplace. Consequently, you, as the buyer of the home, can expect to pay a higher price. (Of course in a cold market, the builder may be taking a sizable amount of the cost out of its would-be profits.)

Tip

What's important to understand is that the buy-down does not mean that the mortgage costs less. It only means that someone has paid the lender to lower the interest rate. When you add in the amount paid, you end up with the current market rate. (*Note:* Don't try calculating this straight across. You have to take into account the future cost of today's dollars—a complex calculation—in order to determine exactly how much must be paid to get a buy-down.)

Trap

Money is money to the builder. If you would rather have a lower price and a current rate mortgage, almost any builder will convert the buy-down to a lower sales price. Be sure that you calculate what is best for your particular situation. You may find that you'd rather have a lower price than a lower interest rate mortgage.

Requirements for a Buy-Down

There are only two requirements for a buy-down—someone to pay the up-front money and a willing lender. You yourself as a borrower, for example, can get a buy-down if you're willing to pay the points up front for it.

Tip

A buy-down is a negotiating point. It can be used in any purchase of real estate, not just with a builder. For example, you may be purchasing a home, and you may not be able to make high payments, initially.

You may submit an offer to sellers requesting that they buy down the mortgage a point or two for a couple of years. If the seller is willing and you can find an agreeable lender (which should not be too difficult), you can end up with a much lower initial interest rate and payment. However, as an inducement, you should be prepared to pay a higher price for the property. (*Note:* The price can't go higher than the appraised value.)

You, yourself, can even buy down a mortgage. You can pay additional money up front in order to get the mortgage payment down low. Of course, this is not nearly as desirable as having the seller or builder pay it. Although, in the end it all usually comes out the same—your own—pocket!

Trap

Don't be confused between a buy-down and an ARM (adjustable-rate mortgage). They are two totally different beasts (although they can be combined, as when an ARM is bought down). In a buy-down someone pays cash up front for a lower interest rate and a correspondingly lower monthly payment. In an ARM, the interest rate adjusts up or down, depending on market conditions. It may initially be lower since the lender is offering a "teaser" to hook you onto the loan.

Types of Buy-Downs

The types of buy-downs are limited only by your imagination. We have already looked at the 3/2/1, as well as one in which the interest rate is kept artificially low for a period of years. You can tailor a buy-down to suit your particular needs. You can have a 1/1/1/1 (1 percent lower for four years) or a 2/3/1 (2 percent lower the first year, then 3 percent, then 1 percent). All you need to do is to get a lender to go along.

Lenders are limited only by their ability to resell the mortgage in the secondary market (and by their own conservativeness). If you are a truly qualified buyer, a creative lender should be able to calculate out the points needed to buy-down any amount for any mortgage.

Tip

If you have trouble qualifying, a buy-down may be just the thing for you. Depending on the lender, you may be able to qualify at the buy-down rate, whereas the true mortgage rate would trip you up.

Who Offers Buy-Downs?

Any lender may offer a buy-down. It could be an S&L, a bank, a credit union, a mortgage banker, or even an individual seller. A mortgage banker may be your best source, since the people who run these companies deal with many lenders and often have their fingertips on who is likely to be the most creative.

You'll never know if this option is for you unless you ask.

12

Lines of Credit and Swing Loans

Expensive Money for Your Short-Term Needs

Here is a good alternative to mortgage money which, unfortunately, few people consider. Its drawback is that it is the most expensive type of home borrowing. Its advantage is that it provides instant short-term cash. In this chapter, let's look at how to establish lines of credit and when to use them to your home-borrowing advantage.

What Is a Line of Credit?

A line of credit is probably the oldest form of organized borrowing known. In the European tradition, it was called a "letter of credit." This was a letter from a bank to "whomever it may concern" which identified the bearer as being creditworthy and guaranteed any borrowing he or she might make from another source. Letters of credit were used extensively by businesspeople involved in foreign trade.

The most common type of lines of credit that we have today are credit cards, the ubiquitous "plastic." MasterCard, Visa, American Express, and a few others offer lines from $300 to tens of thousands of dollars simply by presenting a plastic card. The last time you bought something with your credit card, you were using your line of credit.

Trap

It is possible to buy a home using only credit card money! I know of one individual, who shall remain unnamed, who a few years ago managed to get nearly 30 different credit cards. She then drew down her credit line on all of them and used the money to purchase a home! She went in with an all-cash deal to close in 7 days and got a terrific bargain. Then she refinanced to a regular mortgage and paid back her credit lines, most within the 30-day no-charge period!

It was a daring stunt and one which she probably could not pull off today. Today, all credit card companies report their lines to credit agencies. If you have more than three cards, you will find it increasingly difficult to get additional ones. As soon as you begin drawing down credit on any two or three lines, the others may pull back. In short, the credit card companies are on the alert for people who try to use the cards for purposes other than those for which they were issued.

Home-Equity Credit Lines

There are other types of credit lines which you can get today specifically tailored to real estate. Most especially this includes home-equity lines. A home-equity line of credit is essentially a second mortgage—with a twist. Normally when you get an institutional second mortgage (as opposed to having the seller lend it to you, as explained in Chapter 7), you are given cash in exchange for a trust deed placed on your property.

With a line of credit, the same trust deed is placed on the property. However, instead of getting the cash, the bank or savings and loan keeps it until you specifically request it. (You might be given a checkbook. You write checks to draw down on your line.)

You don't pay any interest on the line until you actually take out the money. Then you pay the bank's rate, which is typically 2 to 3 percent higher than the current mortgage market rate.

Here are the features of an equity line of credit:

1. A second mortgage is placed on your existing property.

2. You are given a maximum credit line, usually up to 70 to 80 percent of the value of the property.

3. No interest is charged until you actually withdraw the money, which can be at any time in the future at your discretion.

4. You pay a significantly higher interest rate than with a regular mortgage.

Mortgage-Hunting Scenario

A friend recently placed a credit line on a piece of rental real estate that he owns. Going through the transaction can be helpful in understanding how the process works.

The property was valued at $280,000. It had an existing first mortgage of $120,000. The bank was willing to lend up to 70 percent of the value. Here's how the line looked:

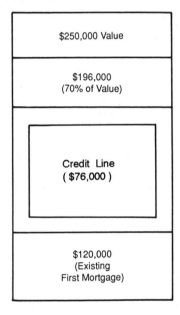

He filled out the usual loan applications for a second mortgage (essentially the same as for a first). A low-document procedure was used (see Chapter 10) so that all that was really needed was to provide a few documents and a credit report.

Then the lender went ahead and placed a second mortgage for $76,000 on the property. The interest rate on this second was adjustable. It was tied to the bank's cost of funds and moved up and down monthly. As ARMS go, it was really ugly. However, it was not intended to be a permanent home mortgage. Rather, it was intended for short-term borrowing.

Tip

In the short term, the amount of interest you pay is not as critical as in the long term. Short term is usually a year or less. Since you'll be paying

the money back quickly, what you are looking for is flexibility. It is often
worth paying 2 or 3 points above market to have that flexibility.

At the time, the bank was offering an introductory special. The
bank absorbed all fees in placing the loan on the property, including
the appraisal, credit report, title insurance, points, and escrow. In essence, he paid nothing. (There would be, however, a $60 annual pro-
cessing fee starting with the second year.)

He was given an innocuous looking checkbook and told that
there was a $76,000 line of credit behind it. At any time he wanted,
he could write a check up to the limit and the bank would honor it.
He would only pay interest on the money he borrowed. He could
pay it back at any time and lower the drawdown on the credit line.

Of course, there were some long-term requirements. For example,
the credit line was good for only 10 years. After that, any money he
had drawn down would revert to a standard adjustable-rate mortgage repayable over the subsequent 15 years. In other words, he
couldn't draw down on the credit line any more after 10 years.

Trap

In the past, there were wide abuses by lenders in home-equity lines of
credit, the worst of which allowed the lender to change any of the conditions of the contract, except for the interest rate, at any time according
to its whim!

Today, because of federal regulations which were passed in 1989, and
which restricted abuses of home-equity credit lines by banks, these
"abuse" clauses are no longer allowed. There are, however, still a number of clauses included in these lines which can work against you. The
most dangerous of these is a clause which allows the bank to close down
your line of credit at any time at its discretion.

What this means is that if the bank, at any time, decides that your cred-
itworthiness has changed, it may refuse to honor your credit! You could
write a check on your preestablished line and the bank might not honor
it.

What would make the bank question your credit?

The bank regularly monitors your credit. Any adverse reports of non-
payment or late payment show up. The bank also monitors other credit
borrowings that you have. If you borrow excessively elsewhere, it may
close down your credit here.

The danger is that you might lose your credit line at a time when you
especially need it. You may be counting on it for a purchase, may even
commit yourself to that purchase only to find the money no longer
available.

Tip
_____

I recommend that if you're going to need to use your credit line, you draw down on it *before* your need is critical. For example, you may plan to make a purchase. Draw down the credit line before you formally sign for the purchase. That way you'll be sure the money is there when you need it.

Use It for a Down Payment

Now, my friend had a line of credit of $76,000. What did he do with it? He used it as a down payment on another home!

He drew down $50,000 and purchased another property for $250,000. He borrowed $200,000 (80 percent mortgage) on the second property and drew down $50,000 on his equity line from the first property. Thus, he had financed 100 percent of the purchase price.

Using a Credit Line as a Swing Loan

The above example gives the most common use for a credit line in real estate. You use it to take money out of one property which you then put down on another property.

Why would you want to do this?

The reason most people do it is because, for one reason or another, they can't sell their present home but they want to buy another one. Maybe the market is cold and there are no buyers. Or perhaps the property is sold, but the sale is going to take several months. Or there could be any of a dozen other reasons.

The point is that you need the money out now, but later on you're going to be able to sell the property. When the property is sold, you pay back the money borrowed from the home-equity line of credit.

This is technically known as a *swing loan.* It allows you to swing a deal between two properties—or to swing a loan.

Problems With Swing Loans

Most swing loans, however, are not structured as described here. Most swing loans are obtained for borrowers as part of the sale of their old home and purchase of a new one. As a result, the borrower is under tremendous pressure to quickly get some money out of the old house and usually doesn't have time to properly search out the best loan.

As a consequence, the swing loan often is for a very high interest rate, often 5 points or more above market; is for a very limited time, perhaps a year or less; and is for just the amount of money that the seller–new buyer needs to complete the transaction.

On the other hand, the home-equity line of credit, as described in this chapter, offers much greater flexibility. You can have the money just when you need it. You can have more or less. And you usually pay less for it.

Tip

If you are planning to purchase a new home and are concerned that you might not be able to sell your old one first, my suggestion is that you immediately arrange a home-equity line of credit on your existing home, particularly if you can do this with no cost to you.

If you never use the mortgage, it won't have cost you a penny to get it. On the other hand, if you need it to close another transaction, the money will be there, ready to go without any hassle.

Trap

Be aware that home-equity lines of credit are not panaceas. If you are the sort who tends to squander cash, they can be a terrible trap. For some, having the ability to get money automatically means spending it.

In our examples, we've talked about using home-equity lines to cover the down payment of new homes. However, the money is yours to do with as you want. If you decide to purchase a new car with it, no one will stop you. You can use it to pay for a cruise or to buy the most fantastic stereo system in the world.

Just remember, however, that it's your equity you're using up and that it has to be repaid, at a *high* interest rate. Short term, it makes sense. But if you end up having to repay long-term, it tends to make very little sense.

Finally, keep in mind that while a mortgage that you get to purchase a home is almost always tax-deductible (up to a million dollars), when you borrow on a home-equity loan, there are certain limits, often up to $100,000. Don't assume you can automatically deduct all the interest. Check with your accountant first, and read Chapter 19 on tax consequences.

Where Do You Get a Home-Equity Loan?

There are a wide variety of sources for home-equity financing. They include the following:

Banks

Banks are often the lenders of choice here. Recently they have led the way in offering "cost-free" lines. A bank is particularly well equipped to offer a line of credit since it is constantly dealing with enormous cash flows.

S&Ls and Savings Banks

Like banks, these offer home-equity lines of credit. However, most S&Ls have been in so much cash trouble of late that their programs have been inconsistent and sometimes costly to the borrower. I would use these only as a second choice after first considering banks.

Commercial Finance Companies

These are companies which have long specialized in home-equity lines of credit. My own experience with these organizations, however, is that they charge higher interest rates, have more costs, and are definitely more disagreeable to work with. I personally stay away from them whenever possible.

Credit Unions

This is an excellent resource. Often their rates are the most competitive. However, you must normally be a member of the credit union to apply for and receive a credit line. Additionally, credit unions rarely waive the costs of getting the line of credit. Thus, you'll probably have to come up with money to cover an appraisal, credit report, escrow, title insurance, and documentation fees. (There are rarely any points for this type of financing.) In short, it could cost you several thousand dollars before you even borrow a penny.

Mortgage Bankers

These organizations are just now getting into home-equity lines of credit and as of this writing have relatively little to offer.

The Bottom Line on Home-Equity Lines of Credit

It's important to remember that in almost all cases, a home-equity line of credit, whether you use it as a swing loan or for some other purpose, is an ARM—an adjustable-rate mortgage. That means the interest rate you pay, and your monthly payments, are going to fluctuate with market conditions.

Over the short term, it shouldn't be a problem. However, for long-term borrowing you're probably better off getting a new first or a conventional second mortgage on your property.

13

Refinancing

How to Get a Second Chance at a Good Deal

We have covered refinancing in various other places in this book, most notably in Chapters 7 and 12, on second mortgages and home-equity lines of credit. Nevertheless, it is something that so many borrowers are concerned about that it deserves its own separate coverage.

Refinancing normally does not involve selling or buying your home. It means that you go out and secure a new mortgage—first, second, or combination—and pay off your existing mortgage(s). Your goals along the way may include any or all of the following:

Getting money out of your property

Going for a lower-interest-rate mortgage

Switching to a fixed-rate from an adjustable-rate loan

Lowering your payments

Tip

On single-family owner-occupied (less than four-unit) properties, most lenders will only lend 80 percent LTV (loan-to-value) for no cash out to you (straight refinance) or 75 percent LTV if you get some cash out.

Also, if you want to refinance less than 18 months after you purchased the property, the lenders will go back to the original purchase price, not a new appraisal. This could hurt you if prices have appreciated. (Of course, if they've really shot up, then you could argue with the lender for a new appraisal. If prices have really dropped down, a lender may insist on it!)

The Refinancing Decision

The decision over whether or not to refinance involves a variety of factors including the following:

1. The interest rate of the existing mortgage
2. The current market interest rates
3. The cost of financing
4. How long you plan to hold before selling
5. Your current credit and income status

In this chapter we'll look at a wide variety of refinancing options which will affect your decision. However, there are a couple of rules of thumb that may prove initially helpful. These are rules which must be taken with a big grain of salt. They may not apply in your particular case. However, they apply in enough cases that they are certainly worth mentioning. Please do not "stake the farm" on them. Just use them as a way to quickly "guesstimate" whether or not you need to refinance.

To justify the costs of refinancing,

- The new interest rate should generally be at least 2 percent lower than the old interest rate.
- You should not pay more than 2 points when you refinance.
- You should plan on staying in your home for an additional 3 years.

Remember, these rules are essentially "made to be broken." However, as rules of thumb they can quickly give you some guidelines to get started.

The Costs of Refinancing

For many people who have not refinanced property before, the costs can come as a major surprise. They are high, typically about 3 to 5 percent, depending on the size of the refinance.

The reason for the high cost of refinancing is that when you refinance, you essentially go through the same legal process as selling your house. However, when you sell, the costs of the transaction are usually split between the buyer and seller. When you refinance, you have to pay all those costs yourself. Of course, you often get a reduced rate. Nevertheless, the costs remain high. They include the following:

Points on the new mortgage

Escrow (fees are usually reduced)

Title insurance (fees are usually reduced)

Appraisal

Credit report

Termite report

Document preparation fees

Document recording fees

Other costs

Trap

Most modern mortgages do not have a prepayment clause. This simply means that you can pay off your existing mortgage at any time without penalty.

However, some older mortgages do have this clause in them. Be sure you check your existing mortgage to see if it contains a prepayment clause. (Any lender should be able to glance through the documents and tell you.) If you have a prepayment clause, it could cost you additional money to pay off your existing mortgage earlier than when it is due.

Let's see just how much these refinancing costs really are. We'll assume that you're getting a new $100,000 mortgage for 30 years (fixed rate, although the charges probably won't be much different for an adjustable). You will be paying 1½ points plus $200 for documentation fees. In a typical refinance, you could expect to see the following costs:

Typical Refinance Costs—$100,000 Mortgage

Points	$1500
Escrow	500
Title insurance	600
Appraisal	350
Credit report	40

Termite report	75
Termite clearance	750 (repair termite damage)
Document prep fees	200
Document recording	50
Other fees	350
Total costs	$4415

In our example, the costs of the refinance are roughly 4.5 percent of the loan amount, pretty close to the rough average of 5 percent.

Tip

Most lenders will allow you to finance the mortgage costs. For example, in this case the lender might agree to a mortgage of $104,415. In other words, your costs of refinancing are added to the loan amount. If you need all the money you are getting out of the property, this can be a godsend. Be sure to ask the lender about "financing the costs."

Trap

If you finance the costs, you may not be able to deduct the points. Check Chapter 19 on taxation, and with your accountant.

How to Lower Your Refinancing Costs

Remember that everything in real estate is negotiable, including the costs of refinancing a mortgage. While you can ask the escrow company and the title insurance company to lower their fees (many do have lower fees for refinances), you won't really save a bundle there.

Tip

The fees for escrow services and title insurance are not the same everywhere. Shop around and you'll find as much as a 15 percent difference between companies!

Credit report costs are pretty much standard, and the appraiser is picked by the lender; hence you can't really negotiate down the price.

Termite reports are likewise pretty much standardized in costs. What one termite report costs, so will another.

Trap

Termite *clearances* can vary enormously in cost. A clearance is what a termite company gives to you to present to the lender saying your property is free of infestation. It typically involves two categories, remedying existing damage and taking preventive steps to avoid future damage. Most lenders don't care about the second category. They normally only require the correction of existing damage. I always recommend only doing the mandatory work. (My theory is that no one can accurately predict future damage.)

Many borrowers get one report that gives them a figure for correcting damage and accept it. That could be a mistake. There's nothing to prevent you from going out and asking a different company to give you a different report.

I was once refinancing a property in southern California and got a termite report that said I had $7000 of corrective work that needed to be done. Most of it involved a back deck that had been put up years earlier and that butted right up to the foundation and ground, instead of being separated from it, thus allowing termites access to the wood.

I simply went out and took down the deck, then called for a new termite report. The second report, since the deck was gone, found no corrective work needing to be done and there was no $7000 to pay! (I later had the deck rebuilt at a cost of around $3000, a lot less than it would have cost for the termite repairs.)

The biggest area of negotiation with regard to lowering the costs of refinancing, however, comes from dealing directly with the lender. The lender can lower or even entirely eliminate your refinance costs!

The lender of the new mortgage can agree to:

Pay for the appraisal and credit report

Not require a termite report or clearance

Pay for title insurance and escrow charges

Pay for all document fees

Waive the cost of points

In short, a lender may be willing to waive or pick up all of the costs of your refinance. Since this can save you upwards of 5 percent of the amount borrowed, it can amount to a great deal of money.

How Do You Get a Lender to Pick Up the Costs?

The way is to find out what kind of mortgages lenders are currently pushing and to go for those. For example, as this is written, many lenders are pushing home-equity loans (discussed in detail in Chapter 12). These mortgages are typically seconds. They allow you to draw cash out of your property without changing the first.

To entice you into getting one of their home-equity mortgages, these lenders are offering to waive all costs. There are no points to pay, no fees, no title insurance and escrow charges . . . nothing! You simply apply for the mortgage, qualify, and soon it's there.

Tip

Contrary to popular belief, home-equity mortgages are also available for single-family rental properties. If you own a rental, you can probably get a home-equity second on it just as easily as if you were living there. The only difference is that the interest rate may be slightly higher, one-quarter to one-half percent, and the loan-to-value ratio may be lower, 70 percent instead of 80 percent.

Trap

A home-equity loan is not for all people and all situations. Typically, it will not give you enough money to pay off your existing first, although you may use it to pay off existing seconds, thirds, etc., and consolidate other high-interest loans.

Also, most home-equity loans, as discussed earlier, are really revolving lines of credit with your home put up as security. This means you will pay about 2 percent more than the current market rate for mortgages. Thus your payments will tend to be higher.

Tip

Be sure to first check with your existing lender. It may be willing to waive or reduce the points if you simply want to refinance the same amount of money at a now lower (market) interest rate. Also, if the existing lender charges you points, it will typically charge them only on the amount borrowed over and above the existing loan. This, too, could dramatically lower your costs.

Deciding What Kind of Refinance to Do

Refinance means to pay off your existing mortgage and get a new one. However, a better alternative for you may be not to refinance, but get a new second. How do you know which will be best for you? The answer depends on your situation. Here's a chart to help you make the right decision.

If you want . . .		Get . . .
Lower payments	→	Refinance
Money out	→	Home-equity second or refinance to bigger first
Stable payments	→	Refinance to new fixed-rate first

The right kind of new mortgage for you will typically be a combination of payments and cash out.

Trap

Investors will have problems refinancing a new first mortgage. Lenders of first mortgages will typically give owner-occupants the same deal on a refinance as they will when obtaining a purchase-money first. That means a loan-to-value ratio of 75 to 80 percent. If your house appraises at $150,000, for example, the mortgage can be as high as $120,000.

If, however, it's a rental property, then it's a different story. The loan-to-value ratio may be lower, especially if you want cash out. In fact, many lenders will simple refuse to refinance for more than your existing loans (first, second, third, etc.) plus costs of refinance.

How to Know How Much You'll Save on a Refinance

We've talked about what to look for when refinancing. But how does one determine just what the savings will be between a new mortgage and an old? Let's take each element separately:

Monthly Payment Savings

The amount you save in monthly payments is tied to four factors: the interest rate difference between the old and new mortgages, the age of the existing mortgage, the amortization, and whether or not you pull out any cash.

Reducing the Interest Rate

Generally speaking, each time you lower the interest rate 1 percent (up to 11 percent interest), you will reduce your monthly payments by around 9 percent. For example, if you borrow $100,000 at 10 percent (for 30 years), your monthly payments for principal and interest are $878. On the other hand, the same $100,000 borrowed at 9 percent reduces those payments to $805. Generally, speaking if you have to pay the full costs of a refinance, or roughly 5 percent of the amount borrowed, it will take you 3 years at a 2 percent mortgage interest rate reduction to recoup the costs. But then, of course, your savings will start adding up.

The Age of the Existing Mortgage

As explained in Chapter 3, because of the way mortgages are mathematically structured, you pay far more in interest in the first years than in the

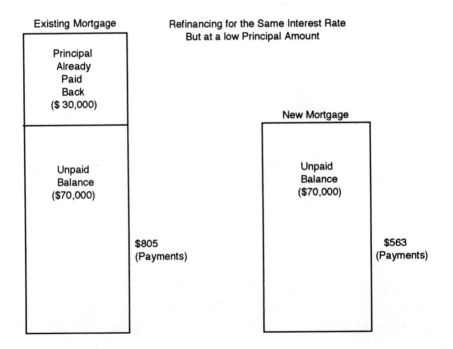

last. In the last years of a mortgage, a far higher portion of your payment goes toward principle or "equity return."

If you refinance an aged mortgage for a new one, you may reduce your payments significantly without any reduction in interest rate. For example, you may have a mortgage with an original balance of $100,000 on which you are paying $805 a month at 9 percent interest. However, that mortgage is 20 years old and you only owe $70,000 on it. You now refinance for a new mortgage of $70,000, still at 9 percent. But, because you are able to reduce the mortgage amount refinanced ($70,000 instead of $100,000), your payments now are only $563 a month, a savings of $292 monthly, while keeping the same interest rate. (Reduce the interest rate at the same time and your payments will fall even more dramatically!)

Trap

The reason the above plan works is that you are taking the money from each payment of the existing mortgage that would ordinarily go toward principle reduction (or equity return) and putting it in your pocket. As a result, with the new mortgage, you are paying virtually nothing but interest.

Pulling Out Cash

If you just refinance for the existing amount you owe (plus costs) and go to a lower interest rate or a lower balance or a combination, you will very likely get lower payments. However, as soon as you pull cash out, you are increasing the amount you owe; hence your payments will be adversely affected. Depending on the other factors, your payments could simply go down less, stay the same, or even go up.

In the example on the next page, the borrower went from a 10 percent mortgage down to an 8 percent loan. But, in the process, $20,000 of equity was taken out in the form of cash. As a result, the payments actually increased.

Calculating the Time Factor

Another consideration is just how long it will take to recoup the costs of refinancing. At the onset, we said that you should plan on staying in your home for at least another 3 years for refinancing to make any kind of sense. However, the actual time is going to be different for each case. It also depends on how you make the calculation.

If you are simply going from a higher to a lower interest rate mortgage, the easiest way is to simply determine the costs of refinancing and

```
                                    ┌─────────────┐
                                    │             │
                                    │   New       │
                                    │  Mortgage   │
                                    │   at 8%     │
                                    │ for $70,000 │   $514
                                    │  ($20,000   │ (Payments)
                                    │  Taken Out) │
              ┌──────────────┐      │             │
              │              │      │             │
              │    Old       │      │             │
              │  Mortgage    │      │             │
              │   at 10%     │ $439 │             │
              │ for $50,000  │(Payments)          │
              │              │      │             │
              │              │      │             │
              └──────────────┘      └─────────────┘
```

then compare them to the difference in monthly payments. For example, you borrow $100,000 at 9 percent to pay off an existing $100,000 at 11 percent. We'll say that you pay $5000 in costs out of pocket up front. How long will you need to stay in the property to justify the refinance?

Calculation Based on Monthly Payment Savings

$100,000 for 30 years @ 11% = $952

$100,000 for 30 years @ 9% =   805

Monthly savings $147

Calculation for Time: $\frac{\$5000 \text{ (costs)}}{\$147 \text{ (savings)}} = 34$ months

You will have to live in the house for 34 months before you will break even and justify the costs of the refinance. Any shorter time than that, and the refinance was not financially justified. Any longer and your savings begin to add up at a rate of $147 a month (for this example).

Trap

The above example assumes that both mortgages were new. If one was aged (over 15 years), the calculation would of necessity be different because, as noted earlier, a significant portion of the payment would be going to principle reduction, rather than just to interest.

Tip

The time to payback of the costs is directly affected not only by the interest rate differential between the old and the new mortgage but by the points charged as well. That's why I suggest reconsidering if you have to pay more than 2 points. Each additional point significantly lengthens the time it takes to pay back the mortgage. Just adding one additional point (to 3 points) can increase the payback period by a year or more!

When to Refinance

Another area of concern is the best time to refinance. The answer has to do with your reason for refinancing.

If you are seeking to lower payments, then by all means wait for a drop in interest rates. The interest rates on mortgages are cyclical. While the cycles vary greatly, we have been in a 10-year cycle for roughly the past two decades, as the following chart graphically depicts.

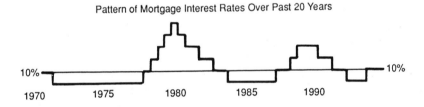

Pattern of Mortgage Interest Rates Over Past 20 Years

We can assume that in all likelihood, the pattern will continue, if not exactly, then approximately. All that this means is that if interest rates are currently high, the chances are that in the not-so-distant future, they will come down. Similarly, if interest rates are currently low, you can expect them to go up. (*Note:* Do not count on the pattern repeating at the intervals noted here—this is just an approximation and the pattern could change, depending on a wide variety of events that affect interest rates.)

Tip

A good rule of thumb to follow is to go for a fixed-rate mortgage when interest rates are low and go for an adjustable rate when they are high, planning to refinance to a fixed rate once they drop.

On the other hand, if you are seeking to get cash out of your property, then it is not necessary to wait for a drop in interest rate. Your primary concern should be that you refinance at a time when you can afford the monthly payments. Once that criterion is met, the level of interest rates is actually irrelevant.

True, it would be nicer to be able to refinance when rates were low. But even if they are not low, your demands for funds will more than likely determine when you refinance.

Tip

If you want to get cash out, but don't need all of the cash at once, you may want to consider a home-equity line of credit. As explained in Chapter 12, this is essentially just an adjustable-rate second mortgage. However, it works like a revolving line of credit. You can take out as much as you need, up to the maximum of the loan. You can also repay as you need. However, the monthly payment is usually based on a 30-year amortization of just the amount borrowed.

Trap

If you are refinancing to do some building on your house, do not start construction until you have the loan in hand. Because of the danger of mechanic's liens, lenders will not make loans often months after all construction has ceased on a property.

Making the Refinance Decision

If you are considering refinancing and you've read this far, then you know what you need to know. Now, you have to go out there and get the current information on mortgage rates and terms as well as gather the information on your current mortgage. Before you make the decision, here's the information you should put together.

Information to Gather

1. Get the current interest rate, monthly payment, and remaining balance of your existing mortgage(s). Your lender can usually provide the current remaining balance and normally will due so at least once

a year in January for tax purposes. You can call the lender if you can't find the most recent summary of your mortgage.

2. Check with at least one bank, one S&L, and one mortgage banker to find out what's available for refinancing. Ask about fixed-rate, adjustable-rate, and equity loans and lines of credit. Emphasize that you are interested in *refinancing*.

Refinance Worksheet

Current monthly payment	$ _____
New monthly payment	$ _____
Savings	$ _____
Current interest rate	_____ %
New interest rate	_____ %
Differential	_____ %
New mortgage amount	$ _____
Remaining balance	$ _____
Equity Removal	$ _____

Costs to Refinance:

Points	$ _____
Appraisal	$ _____
Credit report	$ _____
Escrow	$ _____
Title insurance	$ _____
Termite clearance	$ _____
Document fees	$ _____
Other costs	$ _____
Total Costs	$ _____

$$\frac{\text{Total costs}}{\text{Monthly savings}} = \text{Months to recoup}$$

3. Find out what the costs of refinancing are. Be sure you remember to include:
   - Points
   - Escrow, attorney, and title fees
   - Termite clearances
   - Document preparation and recording charges
   - Appraisal and credit report costs
4. Calculate the total costs to refinance and then determine how long it will take to pay back those costs. (Divide the savings in monthly payments by the costs.)
5. Take into account any "age" factor of your existing mortgage. Remember, if you refinance an old mortgage, you won't be putting very much back into principle anymore.
6. Check with the three rules of thumb:
   - Can you repay in less than 3 years (will you be living in the house that long?)
   - Is the new interest rate at least 2 percent lower than the existing interest rate?
   - Are you paying 2 points or less to get the new mortgage?
7. Check to see if a lender in your community is advertising for "no fees, no points" financing. It could be a very worthwhile trip to talk to them.

Refinancing to Avoid Financial Problems

We have already touched on this in the section on balloon mortgages. But it is worth some additional time to illustrate several points.

Unfortunately, you may find yourself in financial trouble. You may have lost your job or have a health problem or there may be some other calamity that has befallen you. As a result, you find that you need cash. But you need it at the very time that you can't qualify for it (because of your problem).

Is there any hope in refinancing?

Trap

Don't beat a dead horse. You may find that your situation really is hopeless. You have $2500-a-month payments and you've been laid off. Yes, you can try to finance and use that money to make your monthly payments. But you may be better off to simply sell the house and get into one with lower payments. Unless you see your financial problems as truly temporary (resolving within 6 months or less), consider bailing out before refinancing. It could make much more sense.

Refinancing once you are already in financial trouble is difficult. The old maxim is quite true—lenders are only willing to give you money when you don't need it.

Ideally you will have had the foresight to place a home-equity line of credit on your property. Thus, when financial problems arise (and long before the lender learns of them), you can borrow on your already established line of credit. There are no forms to fill out, no documents to sign, and no need to give proof that you can afford to get the loan . . . you already have it.

On the other hand, if you didn't have such financial foresight, it's a different story. Now you have to go, hat in hand, to a lender and try to refinance.

Your best bet is to consider a lender (discussed earlier) who makes nonconforming loans and who really doesn't care a whit about you. This lender only cares that your property will appraise out at a 65 percent loan-to-value ratio. But be prepared to pay a higher-than-market interest rate, perhaps 2 points or more higher.

Refinancing to Avoid Foreclosure

One alternative when faced with imminent foreclosure is to ask your lender if it will refinance the existing mortgage. If you have a lot of equity in the property and if you can demonstrate that your problem is short-term, the lender may agree.

Offer to pay a higher interest rate or to extend the term of the mortgage to get lower payments. Offer to switch to an adjustable-rate mortgage with negative amortization to get the payments lower.

14

Graduated-Payment Mortgages

Trading Higher Future Payments for Lower Payments Now

Recent studies have indicated that well over 85 percent of home purchases in this country are made by people who already own a home. What this means is that most home buyers are, in reality, "moving up." They are simply exchanging one home for another, usually of higher value.

Past home buyers are able to do this for two reasons. First, they are able to transfer their often sizable equities into the new property. This gives them a big down payment. Second, second-time homeowners frequently are individuals or families who are into their more productive years and have relatively high incomes. They can afford the high payments required of home buyers today.

But where does that leave the individuals or young couples who are the first-time home buyers? How do they, often with limited incomes and little down payment, break into the housing market?

The answer that was specifically designed for them by the lending industry is the graduated-payment mortgage (GPM). When combined with a low-down-payment feature, it offers reduced monthly payments in the early years of the mortgage. Then, as the borrower's income presumably grows, the monthly payments increase.

Low monthly payments when the buyer has a small income and then, gradually, higher monthly payments as the buyer's income increases—

it's one method of solving the finance problem for housing. *Note:* A GPM can be combined with most other mortgages, fixed or adjustable.

How the GPM Works

While the GPM's basic operation is quite simple to state—low payments at first, higher payments to make up for it later on—the actual operation of the mortgage is better seen from an example.

We'll take a variety of a GPM that's been around for a few years. It is the FHA-HUD plan. This particular mortgage was intended for use as part of an FHA loan. It incorporates the low-down-payment feature of the FHA with the reduced-payment feature of the GPM. The mortgage is for $35,000. The down payment on the property to obtain this mortgage was only $1250. Since this first example is taken from the mid-1970s, the interest rate is only 8½ percent for 30 years (Table 14-1).*

The chart lists years from 1 through 11+. It also indicates the "level payment." The level payment is the amount that would be paid each

Table 14-1 Level Payment Schedule vs. GPM for a $35,000, 30-Year Loan at 8½ Percent

(U.S. Dept. of Housing and Urban Development)*

Year	Level-payment loan	GPM Plans				
		1	2	3	4	5
1	$269	$245	$223	$203	$243	$223
2	269	251	234	218	248	230
3	269	257	245	234	254	237
4	269	264	258	252	258	233
5	269	270	271	271	263	251
6	269	277	284	291	269	258
7	269	277	284	291	274	266
8	269	277	284	291	280	274
9	269	277	284	291	285	282
10	269	277	284	291	291	291
11+	269	277	284	291	297	300

*From *How to Buy a House at a Reasonable Price*, by Robert Irwin, Copyright © 1979 by McGraw-Hill. Used with permission of McGraw-Hill, Inc. (This same mortgage is still available today, although at current interest rates.)

month—if all the monthly payments were equal—in order to fully amortize the mortgage over a 30-year period. A payment of $269 per month will accomplish this.

Next to the level-payment schedule are five separate GPM payment schedules. Each has different features.

Plan 1—Cutting the Payments

This plan offers a rate of graduation of 2½ percent for a graduation term of 5 years. This simply means that the monthly payment increases *no more* than 2½ percent per month. If we were to take 2½ percent of the first year's monthly payment of $245, we would find it is approximately $6. We then add that $6 to the $245 and we get the second year's payment of $251.

First year's payment	$ 245
Rate of graduation	× 0.025
Increase after 1 year	6
First year's payment	+ 245
Second year's payment	$ 251

The graduation period is 5 years. After that time, there is a level payment high enough to *fully amortize* the mortgage.

Under Plan 1, note that the savings are not that substantial. At year 1, the year of greatest savings, only $24 a month is saved under the plan.

The savings are listed below.

Year	Savings on monthly payment
1	$24
2	18
3	12
4	5
5	−1
6+	−8

Although there's a nominal savings initially, there is also a nominal loss in terms of higher monthly payments for the last 25 years of the mortgage.

This plan might be helpful for someone who was just trying to squeeze into a home and could barely make it.

Plan 2—Cutting the
Payments Lower

The term for this plan is the same term as that for Plan 1, 5 years. But Plan 2 doubles the graduation rate. It has a rate of 5 percent. Here's what the monthly savings now look like.

Year	Savings
1	$46
2	35
3	24
4	11
5	-3
6+	-15

Under Plan 2, the savings, at least in the first 2 years of the mortgage, are substantial. In year 1, the savings are 17 percent of the monthly payment.

In year 2, they are 13 percent. That's enough to make a buyer stop and consider. If you can cut your payments by 17 percent the first year and 13 percent the second, maybe it's worthwhile having that extra-heavy high payment for the last 25 years of the mortgage. After all, many buyers figure that, after 5 years, they will sell the property anyhow.

Plan 3—A Radical
Payment Reduction

This plan carries the whole process even further. With the same term, 5 years, it increases the graduation rate to 7½ percent. The results are dramatic:

Year	Savings
1	$66
2	51
3	24
4	17
5	-2
6+	-22

The percent savings the first year here is about 25 percent. You can cut your monthly payments by one-quarter under this plan. And they will stay lower than under a standard fixed-rate plan until year 5. After year

6, the payments will only be $22 higher than they would have been under a traditional mortgage.

It's easy to see why many people prefer this particular plan. They figure that by year 5 their income will have increased significantly and inflation will have reduced the value of the dollar to the point where they can easily afford the higher payments later.

Plans 4 and 5—Increasing the Term

Plan 4 goes back to a lower graduation rate—2 percent. But the graduation period is extended to 10 years.

What should be apparent when you look at Plan 4 is that extending the term works against the borrower more than it works for him or her. While it's true that initially the monthly payment is marginally lower, ultimately it grows significantly higher. This plan is roughly comparable to Plan 1. Yet Plan 1, which had a first-year payment within $2 a month of this plan, ended up after year 5 with a monthly payment that was $14 lower than the final monthly payment on this plan.

This discussion is not intended to confuse, but merely to illustrate once again that extending the life of the graduation, like extending the life of a mortgage, does not significantly lower the monthly payment after the first critical years.

Plan 5 again has a 10-year term, this time with a 3 percent rate of graduation.

2 percent GPM rate—10-year term	
Year	Savings
1	$26
2	21
3	16
4	11
5	6
6	0
7	−5
8	−11
9	−16
10	−20
11+	−26

The FHA-HUD GPM plan has been in existence since about 1977.

Other similar plans were adopted by the Federal Home Loan Bank Board for use by savings and loan associations in 1978 and 1979.

Combining the GPM With an Adjustable-Rate Mortgage

Today it is possible to combine the low initial mortgage payments of a GPM with an ARM. When this is done, the borrower typically gets very low initial payments for a set period of time. Here are the features of the GPM-ARM:

1. The mortgage typically has a graduation period between 3 and 10 years, with 5 years being the most common. What this means is that after 5 years, for example, the payments must be raised to the level where the loan is being fully amortized.
2. The maximum graduation varies between institutions, but the most common appears to be 7.5 percent. What this means is that the monthly payment is never allowed to rise by more than 7.5 percent of the previous year's monthly payment.
3. The adjustment period is commonly 1 year.

Advantages

The principal advantages of the ARM-GPM are lower initial payments *and* the fact that the borrower supposedly knows in advance exactly how much the payment is going to increase each period during the graduation time. (This is different from the straight ARM, where this is not known.)

Disadvantages

This principal disadvantage of the ARM-GPM is negative amortization. This almost invariably occurs because the payment schedule is set up so that the payment does not cover the full amount of the interest. The interest not paid accumulates and is added to the mortgage amount. Thus, as with all negative amortization, we end up owing more than we borrowed.

Limits to Negative Amortization

One of the features of the ARM-GPM not found in the fixed-rate GPM is the possibility that a lender at some future time could "recast" the loan *before* the end of the graduation period.

To understand how this could happen, we must remember that the ARM-GPM is still tied to an index. If that index should rise dramatically, then the negative amortization would also increase. Most lenders, however, will not allow the negative amortization to grow to more than 125 percent of the original loan amount. (The lender isn't just being nice here. It's just that 125 percent of an 80 percent loan means that the negative amortization has eaten up the buyer's entire original down payment and equity! The property, based on the original appraisal, isn't worth more than 125 percent of the original loan amount.)

If at any time the negative reaches 125 percent, the lender may "recast" the loan. This means that the loan payments will immediately be boosted up to whatever level is necessary to fully amortize (pay back) the outstanding amount.

Hidden Danger of Recasting

This presents the single greatest danger of the ARM-GPM. If interest rates skyrocket after you take out a loan and your negative amortization increases to the limit, the lender may simply recast the loan as noted above. At that point you could have monthly payment shock as your payments move up very significantly, perhaps enough to force you into default.

ARM-GPMs offer benefits. But lurking in those benefits are also significant dangers.

Who Benefits Most From a GPM?

As noted at the beginning and indicated by the discussion of the mortgage itself, the GPM is primarily designed for buyers who anticipate having increases in their income. (While the big eye-catching feature of this mortgage is the lower initial monthly payments, it must be remembered that the monthly payments increase each year until they are substantially higher than they would have been had this been a standard loan, either fixed-rate or ARM.)

Typically, the GPM works best for a young couple or an individual in the 25 to 35 age group. This is because advancement, including increasing salary, is usually fastest in this age group.

The GPM is not recommended for those on fixed incomes or for those whose incomes are likely to remain stable or decline. Typically, this means that the GPM would be a high-risk mortgage for the individual or family in the 50-plus age group.

Advantages of the GPM

The big advantage of the GPM has already been fairly well discussed—the lower initial payments. But, perhaps it's worth remembering that this lower monthly payment has an additional bonus.

First, for the same value of house price and mortgage, the monthly payment may be reduced, thus easing the financial burden on the borrower.

Second, instead of reducing the monthly payment, the use of a GPM may mean a borrower can get a higher mortgage and a higher-priced house. For example, let's say that you've been looking at homes in the $100,000 price range. You anticipate putting $10,000 down and will thus end up with a $90,000 mortgage. At 14 percent interest, your monthly payments will be $1066 plus taxes and insurance.

You're fairly well off financially and you figure you can just make the payments. Your lender agrees that you would qualify for the mortgage. Under the conventional approach you would look for a home at no more than $100,000 in price.

But, now let's say that you can qualify for a GPM. Under the GPM, your first year's payment will still be roughly $1066. However, this represents a 25 percent reduction from the standard mortgage payment, because of the graduated feature. For $1066 at 14 percent, you no longer are limited to a $90,000 mortgage. You can actually now afford a $120,000 mortgage and a house which costs $130,000 or more!

What I've done is not complicated, and it is well worth spending an additional moment to understand it. The emphasis thus far has been on using the GPM to *reduce* the monthly payment. What I am suggesting here is that you look at the other side of the coin and see that the reverse works equally well. The GPM can be used to keep a monthly payment (if you know what you can afford) within a budget and increase the mortgage amount and, thereby, the price we can afford to pay.

If you can only afford a $100,000 home under the traditional fixed-rate mortgage and ARM, you probably can afford a $130,000 or bigger home under the GPM. Thus the GPM broadens your horizons considerably.

15

Government Mortgages

Attractive Deals If You Can Survive the Red Tape

During the 1950s and part of the 1960s, the most popular mortgages in real estate were those offered under the Federal Housing Authority (FHA) and the Veterans Administration (VA) programs. In those days, it seemed that when a buyer bought a home, he or she first tried to get one of these mortgages. Only after this proved impossible would the buyer settle for a "conventional," or nongovernment, mortgage.

During the 1970s, however, particularly when housing prices sky-rocketed, the allure of these mortgages diminished. Private mortgage insurance (PMI) was available to provide low-down-payment conventional financing. Additionally, the bureaucratic red tape made FHA-VAs less desirable choices. By the end of the 1970s, fewer than 10 percent of all mortgages were from these government programs.

Then in the 1980s the FHAs and VAs came roaring back. Assumability became important, and these loans were all assumable. In addition the maximum loan amounts were raised, making them even more attractive. Today, they are considered among the best loans a borrower can get.

FHA Mortgages

The FHA does not usually lend money to borrowers. Under the most commonly used programs, the FHA isn't even in the mortgage lending business. Instead, it insures mortgages. The borrower gets a loan from a lender, for instance, an S&L. If it's an FHA loan, the government insures payment of the mortgage to the lender. If the borrower doesn't make the payments, the FHA steps in and pays off the lender. With an FHA loan, the lender can't lose.

There are a number of FHA programs. They have included the following:

Title II

203(b).   Financing of one- to four-family dwellings

203(b).   Special financing for veterans

207.   Financing rental housing and mobile home parks

221(d).   Financing low-cost one- to four-family dwellings for displaced or moderate-income families

222.   Financing one-family homes for service personnel

234(f).   Financing condominium units

234(d).   Financing condo projects and condo conversion projects

235.   Assistance to low-income families to make home purchase by subsidizing mortgage interest payments

Title I

(b).   Financing purchase of a mobile home unit

Many of these programs have been cut or at least severely pruned as federal budget cutting has proceeded in Washington. But the basic program, 203(b), still helps finance home mortgages.

Advantages of FHA Loans

1. *They may be assumable.* At one time, all FHA loans were fully assumable by any buyer. That meant that any time you wanted to sell your property, all you had to do was turn your existing (often low-interest) FHA loan over to the buyer. After 1987, however, the FHA imposed stricter rules. Now buyers must qualify, including credit reports and income verifications. When the buyer does qualify, however, he or she still can take over the existing interest rate mortgage.

   Additionally, the seller may continue to be liable under certain circumstances. For mortgages issued after December of 1986, liability may extend for 5 years. For those issued after December of 1989, liability may extend for 10 years or more.

2. *There are no prepayment penalties.* An FHA mortgage may be paid off in full at any time without penalty.

3. *Not only does the buyer have to qualify for the FHA mortgage, but the property has to qualify as well.* This means something more than the house simply being appraised for enough money to warrant the mortgage. It means that the house has to qualify structurally. Sometimes on FHA mortgages, the seller will be required to bring any substandard construction up to current building codes. Any damage, such as that done by wind, water, termites, fungus, erosion, and so forth, might also have to be corrected. When a buyer purchases a home under an FHA program, he or she has virtually a government stamp of approval on it.

Disadvantages of the FHA Loan

There are some disadvantages (not many) to the FHA mortgage. These include:

1. *Maximum loan amount is $90,000 currently.* That's all right for some parts of the country, but for the west coast, east coast, and areas in between where residential property prices are high, it's frequently just too low for the FHA to be a useful source of financing.

2. *The borrower must occupy the property to get the low down payment.* If you want to pay under 5 percent down, then you must be an owner-occupant. You can still get the FHA financing as a nonoccupant investor, *but* you're required to put 15 percent down.

3. *The borrower must pay a mortgage insurance premium.* The premium is a substantial amount.

Qualifying for FHA Mortgages

The qualification procedure for an FHA mortgage is not quite the same as the one for a conventional loan. The FHA uses a different and somewhat more complex procedure. It looks something like this:

1. Total housing expenses are calculated. They must not be more than 38 percent of net income.
   Net income is defined as gross income less federal income tax, and housing expenses are principal, interest, taxes, insurance, utilities. If

the borrower meets the above requirement, he or she goes on to the second step in the qualification process.

2. Housing expenses are *added* to the following: alimony paid, child support payments, long-term debt.

   From this figure is *subtracted:* a portion of income tax deductions (federal and state); social security income; alimony received.

   The resulting figure is termed the borrower's "fixed payments." The ratio of fixed payments to net income can be no more than 53 percent to 55 percent. (Of course, good credit history, proof of employment, and verification of deposit are also required.)

If you think this is complicated, you're right! However, an easy rule of thumb to follow is that if you qualify under a 10-percent-down conventional mortgage, then chances are that you probably will also qualify for an FHA mortgage.

It's also important to note that there is a great deal of gray area in the FHA qualifications. Each application is individually reviewed, and it is possible to present special evidence to avoid a negative decision.

Mortgage Premium

The mortgage insurance premium (MIP) for residential property is currently 0.325 percent (subject to frequent change) of the original loan amount. Normally that money must be paid up front at the time the loan is made. (In the past it would have been paid monthly as a slight increase in payment.)

Down Payment

As noted, the down payment is 5 percent or less for owner-occupied property or 15 percent for investor-purchased. In the past, this down payment had to be in cash. Recently, however, the FHA has allowed it to be handled through secondary financing.

It works like this: If you want to buy a piece of property using an FHA mortgage, you can either put 15 percent cash down *or* you can put up a second mortgage *on a different piece of property.*

Note that the second mortgage *cannot be on the property being financed.* Rather, it has to be on some other property. For example, you may own a lot or another house. You can give the seller of the property you are currently buying a second mortgage on your other house. It may be a bit complicated, but it does work.

The FHA is part of HUD (the Department of Housing and Urban Development), with offices in all major cities and main offices in Washington, D.C.

VA Mortgages

The VA program is similar to the FHA program in that it is administered by the government. However, that's where the similarities tend to end. For new VA mortgages, the borrower has to have one vital ingredient. He or she has to be a veteran and have qualifying duty as noted below.

The biggest advantage the VA loan program has over the FHA is that in many cases there is *no down payment.* The borrower doesn't have to put up anything to make the purchase (with, of course, the exception of closing costs).

Literally millions of veterans have used the VA program. Some have gone back and used it many times. (Soon we'll see how.)

How the VA Program Works

Like an FHA mortgage, the VA loan is obtained from a lender such as a bank or an S&L. However, while the FHA insures the lender against loss, the VA "guarantees" a portion of the loan. It currently guarantees the top $46,000 of the amount borrowed. If the veteran defaults, the VA will pay the first $46,000 of the debt.

Since that usually represents any loss a lender is likely to sustain, it virtually removes the lender from any risk. In actual practice, when a borrower defaults, the VA, like the FHA, buys the entire mortgage back from the lender and then tries to resell the property. (These are called VA, or FHA, "repos.") Unlike the FHA, however, the VA, if it sustains any loss on the resale of the property, can come after the borrower, a veteran, to try to recoup its loss.

Down Payment

The maximum VA mortgage as of this writing is $184,000. The down payment is negotiated between the lender and the veteran. The VA charges a funding fee to the veteran depending on the amount put down. The fee schedule is as follows:

Less than 5% down	1.87 (% of loan balance)
5% to 10% down	1.375
Over 10% down	1.125

The funding fee is paid by the veteran to the VA. Points are paid by the seller.

Entitlement

The $46,000 that the VA guarantees is called the veteran's "entitlement." When the program was first started, the entitlement was only $2000. However, housing prices have gone up, and so has the entitlement.

Reusing Entitlement

The veteran's entitlement usually remains with the vet for life. This means that if the veteran sells the property *and the VA loan is paid off,* he or she may reapply for and receive back the entitlement; he or she would then be able to get another VA loan.

Using Remaining Entitlement

Because the entitlement amount has risen, there are many veterans who bought homes years ago when the entitlement was lower and who still are eligible for a portion of their entitlement. For example, if a vet bought a home in the 1950s, when the entitlement was $5000, he or she may today be able to claim the difference between the entitlement used ($5000) and the current maximum ($46,000), or $41,000.

Qualifying for a VA Loan

Unlike the FHA or even conventional lenders, the VA does not have a hard-and-fast formula that it uses to qualify a veteran. Rather, it has criteria. The criteria are

1. A history of good credit
2. Sufficient income to make the payments and support the veteran's family
3. Enough money in the bank to handle at least 6 months' worth of payments

The VA has been extremely flexible in the past regarding mortgages to vets. I have seen cases where a vet who was turned down went directly to the VA and won a reversal on the strength of a promise to make payments. A large part of the VA program has been aimed as helping veterans get a home and get started.

Eligibility Requirements

The eligibility requirements for VA loans seem to be always changing. To be sure what the current requirements are, you should check with your nearest VA office. As of this writing, vets need to have one of the following:

1. *90 days' active service* during World War II, the Korean War, or the Vietnam War
2. *180 days' continuous active service* during peacetime, providing the entire time was served prior to September 7, 1980
3. *24 months' active duty* (or the enlistment period) served after September 7, 1980

Spouses of veterans may also be eligible if the husband or wife was an MIA (missing in action) or died of a service-related injury.

Children of veterans and people who received dishonorable discharges from the military do not qualify.

If you qualify and want a VA loan, you must obtain a Certificate of Eligibility (CE) from a VA office.

VA Appraisals

When a veteran applies for a mortgage, the VA appraises the property and then issues a Certificate of Reasonable Value (CRV). Sales contracts which specify that the borrower is obtaining a VA loan must also specify that if the property does not appraise for the sale price (the CRV doesn't equal the sale price), the veteran may withdraw from the sale, *or,* the veteran may opt to pay more than the CRV. However, the loan amount will still be based on the CRV, not the final sale price.

Automatics

Because of the long delays which have occurred in the past in funding VA loans, the VA has designated certain lenders to handle automatic funding. What this means is that the lender qualifies the veteran, makes the loan, and closes the deal. Then the lender secures the loan guarantee from the VA. Most large S&Ls, banks, and mortgage bankers are approved for automatics.

Owner-Occupancy Requirement

The VA has long required that the veteran plan to occupy the property. If the property is larger than a home (a duplex for example), the vet must plan to occupy one unit on the property. There are no age requirements for either VA or FHA loans.

Impound Accounts

Both VA and FHA mortgages require that the borrower establish an impound account (also called a trust fund account). This simply means that the borrower must pay for the taxes and insurance on the property on a monthly basis (i.e., must pay one-twelfth of the yearly total each month). The monthly payment goes into a lender's special impound account, and the lender pays the fees at the appropriate times each year.

16
SAM, PLAM, and Options

Mortgages for Special Circumstances

There are literally dozens of varieties of the mortgages we have already covered. And there are some specialty mortgages that have unique characteristics (not the least of which is an alphabet soup of names). We'll cover three of the latter in this chapter. The following mortgages may be just the ticket to a home for you, if you fit the profile at which they aim.

SAM (Shared Appreciation Mortgage)

This remains an experimental type of mortgage that has been used only infrequently. It was first offered in the south by a major lender in the early 1980s and has since been offered sporadically in various locations around the country. You would need to check with a mortgage banker to see if any lenders are currently offering it in your area.

The basic concept behind a SAM is that in exchange for giving you, the borrower, a much lower interest rate, the lender participates in the anticipated appreciation of the property. The most commonly used formula has been that the lender will offer a one-third reduction in interest from the market rate in exchange for one-third of all future appreciation of the property.

For the borrower, this formula can mean the difference between getting into a property and not. For example, if you were trying to get a $100,000 mortgage and the current market interest rate was 9 percent, your payments would be $805 a month. But with a SAM, the interest rate might be reduced to just 6 percent a month and your payments would be under $600 a month.

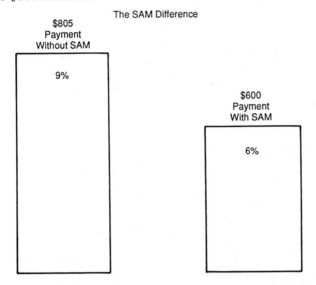

The SAM Difference

$805
Payment
Without SAM

9%

$600
Payment
With SAM

6%

With the SAM, the interest is reduced by one-third for the life of the mortgage. The trade-off is that when you sell the property, you give one-third of the appreciation to the lender.

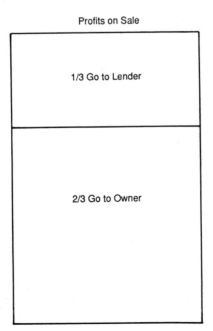

Profits on Sale

1/3 Go to Lender

2/3 Go to Owner

Obviously the SAM was far more popular with lenders before the recent downturn in real estate prices. Even so, some lenders continued to make SAM loans believing that the long-term outlook for residential real estate remains quite healthy.

Tip

Go for a SAM when you need a lower interest rate to get into a property and when you anticipate that it will be many years before real estate prices appreciate. Avoid a SAM when rates are already low and the market is hot.

SAM Problems for Borrowers

The SAMs, when available, are not foolproof and they do create some difficulties. Here are a few.

1. *When do you sell?* Most lenders of SAMs do not want you to sell until there has been sufficient appreciation to warrant the issuing of the mortgage. Given current market conditions, that could be 5 to 7 years. A clause to the effect that you will not sell before that time may be written into the mortgage. But what if you have to sell before the appointed time? You may have to pay a penalty to the lender.

2. *What if there is some major problem with the property?* For example, what happens if there's an earthquake and 30 percent of the home is destroyed? Should you pay for all repairs knowing you'll only get two-thirds back when you sell?

Some SAMs contain a clause that allows you to add any necessary repairs onto the original cost of the home so that you get paid back first before the lender gets any money. However, usually you must get the lender's signed approval before making such repairs.

3. *What about the maintenance of the property?* If the lender is going to get one-third of the appreciation, shouldn't it put up some money for maintenance such as periodic painting? What about the fixing up that needs to be done prior to selling?

Some SAM lenders have a small allowance for fix-up prior to selling. Few allow for any other maintenance.

SAM Problems for Lenders

In addition to all of the problems just cited, there's one additional big problem that has made many lenders hesitate when it comes to SAMs, the threat of "red-lining."

Red-lining refers to a practice of some lenders in the 1970s to refuse mortgages to certain areas of a city, most notably ghetto, blighted, or depressed areas. The term came from the fact that these lenders would put a red line around those areas on a map of the city and refuse to lend money there.

Of course, the inability of owners in that area to secure financing for sales and refinancing only contributed to the further decay of the area. They complained, and as a consequence, red-lining was outlawed. Today large lenders are still hesitant to make loans in blighted areas, but will do so if pressed. However, when it comes to a SAM, there's a special problem.

In making the calculation for a SAM, the lender has to factor in the current interest rate, prepayment assumptions, taxes, and, perhaps most important, anticipated inflation. The SAM only works for a lender if housing prices go up.

As a consequence, SAM lenders only want mortgages in neighborhoods which show the greatest likelihood of appreciation. Does this mean, however, that if a lender makes a SAM in a good neighborhood, it can be accused of red-lining for refusing to make a SAM in a blighted neighborhood?

The threat of such accusations, and the legal problems that could follow, have greatly reduced the number of SAMs that lenders have been willing to make. Typically, only a lender whose geographical area includes only good neighborhoods will entertain the idea of SAMs.

PLAM (Price-Level-Adjusted Mortgage)

The problem with a SAM (as discussed above) from a lender's perspective is that the lender could lose. If housing did not appreciate, the lender might have made a below-market-interest-rate mortgage that it could not recoup.

Lenders are loath to lose. Hence, they came up with a different kind of mortgage that virtually guarantees they won't lose. It's called a PLAM. A PLAM is a kind of combination SAM and ARM. (Some say it combines the worst features of both, for the borrower.)

Under the PLAM both the interest rate and the principal borrowed are tied to a a true measure of inflation, the Consumer Price Index (CPI), for example. Like an ARM, as the CPI goes up, so too do the payments. However, unlike an ARM where just the interest rate goes up, with a PLAM the amount you owe likewise can increase!

_____

PLAMs offer the lowest interest rate and lowest initial payments of any mortgages on the market today. Often you can get an interest rate fully one-third lower than the market for the life of the mortgage.

Here's the reasoning behind a PLAM. Lenders are concerned about inflation, about the decreased value of money they lend out. As a consequence, they must make certain assumptions before they offer any mortgage. These assumptions include

1. How long before the mortgage is paid back (typically 5 to 7 years)
2. What the inflation rate will be during that time
3. How high an interest rate they must charge both to receive a profit and to avoid being penalized by inflation

As a result, lenders typically charge 2 to 5 points higher than what is currently justified by market conditions when they make a mortgage. The sad truth is that if you get a mortgage for 10 percent interest, the lender has built in a 2 to 5 percent cushion to account for the factors noted above. If the lender did not have to worry about inflation, it could probably offer you a 7 percent or lower mortgage. A PLAM does this.

Under a PLAM, your mortgage payment will increase as inflation (not higher interest rates) increases. In the most commonly used form of a PLAM it will increase in this way. As inflation reduces the buying power of the principal you borrowed, the principal is increased. As a result, you owe more than when you started and as a consequence, although the interest rate may remain constant, the payment goes up.

_____

As noted, the PLAM offers the lowest possible initial payments, typically far lower than available for any ARM. This is the tease which draws people to this type of mortgage. In some cases the monthly payment can be half of what is charged for a mortgage at market interest rates!

Let's take an example. You want to borrow $100,000 on a home and the market interest rate is 10 percent. Your monthly payments, amortized over 30 years, would be $878. On the other hand, a PLAM may offer a 6 percent interest rate. Your monthly payments would be only $600 a month, a third less.

Comparing a PLAM

The *initial* mortgage payment is far lower with a PLAM than with a conventional mortgage or even with an ARM.

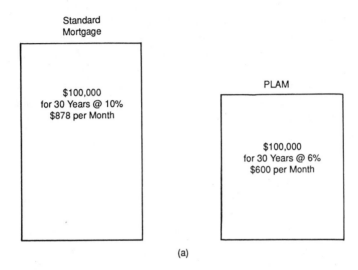

(a)

The amount borrowed can increase with a PLAM as inflation increases.

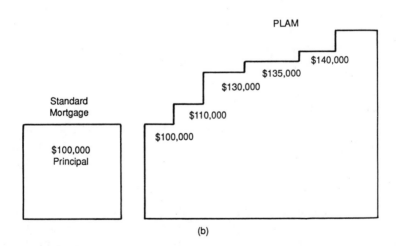

(b)

Typically with a PLAM, the increases to mortgage balance (principle) and, correspondingly to monthly payments, are done on a yearly basis.

If inflation is small, then the increase is small. On the other hand, if inflation is high, then the increase is correspondingly high.

Tip

Monthly payments typically do not increase significantly during the early years of a PLAM. For example, if you borrowed $100,000 at 6 percent, and if inflation for the first year was 5 percent, your mortgage balance would increase to $105,000 and your payments would increase by only about $30 a month. In a favorable-case scenario (relatively low inflation), you could go 5 to 10 years before you'd reach a level where your payments were equal to what you would have paid if you had borrowed at a market mortgage rate.

Trap

Your principal balance will increase each year according to inflation. The increases can be significant. The real problem is that inflation can go up at the same time as your house's value can go down. This happened during the real estate recession of the early 1990s. You could see all of your down payment eaten up by an increased loan balance. You could end up owing more than the house is worth, even if prices only stayed constant!

The PLAM is the ultimate negative amortization mortgage. In exchange for the tease of low initial rates, it means that, in most cases, you will never get most of the appreciation your house may show. Rather, that appreciation will go to the lender. You exchange low payments for little to no equity increase.

Option Mortgage

This mortgage was actually developed by Shearson Lehman Mortgage Company. It has waxed and waned in popularity over the years. Today it is available in some marketplaces; not so in others from a variety of lenders.

The basic thought behind the option mortgage is that borrowers seek low interest rates. What this means is that even though you may be willing to pay a higher interest rate initially, if during the time you have the mortgage the interest rates fall, you'll pay off the existing mortgage and get a new one at a lower rate.

For the borrower this presents a problem. Namely, interest rates typically will bounce up and down within 5 years. High rates today will probably give way to low(er) rates within 5 years. As a result, within 5 years you, the borrower, are likely to refinance out of the high-interest-rate mortgage and into a low-interest-rate one.

For the lender, this means the hassle of processing the money a second time, finding a second borrower, potentially having the money on hand not collecting interest until that second borrower is found, and losing a high-interest-rate mortgage. Why not, some lenders have argued, simply make it easier for the first borrower to flip the loan over to a lower market rate?

The *option reduction* does this. Typically, you will be able to refinance with the same lender for a total cost of $100 plus a quarter percent of the remaining balance to a lower rate. The catch is, you must do it between the second and fifth year of the mortgage, as represented in the chart below. (This guarantees the lender at least one full year of the higher rate, plus after 5 years, no more option to reduce the interest rate.)

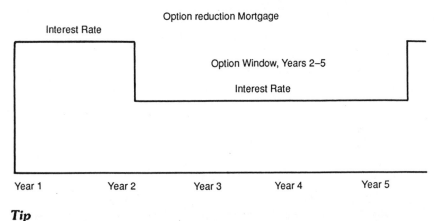

Tip

If an option reduction choice is available to you at no additional cost (no extra points or interest), you should go for it. It gives you the option of scaling down to a lower interest rate sometime in the future at very little cost.

If you have to pay additional points or interest for the option reduction, you should consider. Is the market interest rate currently high? If it is, then an option reduction may still be worthwhile, since when it turns down, you will want to refinance.

Trap

If interest rates are currently low, it makes little sense to pay for an option reduction. In the future, rates are likely to be higher than they are at present, meaning that it's unlikely you'll want to refinance.

17

Reverse Annuity Mortgages

Access to Equity for the Retired Set

The RAM (reverse annuity mortgage) takes money out of your home and gives it back to you on a monthly basis. It was conceived to help older citizens get their equity out and still have a home to live in.

The RAM has had a spotted past. It was first conceived on the east coast, but only a couple of lenders tried it, with mixed results. Then a few lenders in the south tried it with better results, but the savings and loan debacle of the late 1980s made it impractical to use. More recently it is seeing a comeback in different parts of the country sponsored by the FHA as the Home Equity Conversion Mortgage (HECM). (Mortgages really are an alphabet soup of letters!)

The way a basic RAM works is relatively simple. It assumes that a borrower owns a house free and clear, or close to it. The lender sends out an appraiser who determines current value. Then the lender agrees to a loan-to-value ratio, typically 80 percent.

The owner-borrower can now receive 80 percent of the value. However, he or she only receives it in the form of a monthly payment, typically about as much as would have been paid in if the whole amount had been borrowed.

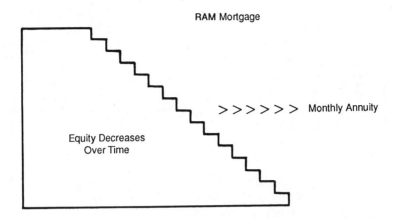

As each monthly payment is made, the principal and interest on it are subtracted from the equity in the house. Thus, the mortgage amount increases. The monthly payments continue until all of the equity is used up (typically 5 to 10 years). At that time the lender goes out and reappraises the property and, if it has appreciated, a new RAM is created for the increased equity.

Tip

The RAM is useful if you as a borrower are only going to need it for a relatively few years. It will provide a steady nonchanging income *and* you will be able to continue living in your home.

Trap

If you outlive the RAM, and your house doesn't appreciate in value, you could find that the monthly payments stop. At the present time, many state laws prevent lenders from evicting you, however. Usually, you can continue to stay in the house, but might receive no payments.

Additionally, the payments you get are constant. Their buying power diminishes, however, with inflation. Thus, after 5 years the value of those monthly payments will be less. While initially they might be sufficient to cover your needs, over time they could become too low to pay for your expenses.

The FHA HECM

Begun in 1989, this plan provides for a RAM to be made by a private lender but insured by the FHA. There are several options available.

The Tenure Option. The "tenure" option gives you the lowest level of payment but guarantees that payment as long as you live.

Tip

Use the tenure plan if you are quite young and healthy when you start. But keep in mind that the payments are low and, with inflation, their buying power will decrease.

The Annuity Version. The annuity version is similar to the basic RAM. It provides income for a set period of time, typically 10 years. The shorter the term, the higher the payments.

Tip

If you are older, you may want to consider a shorter-term annuity. It will give you higher payments, but when the term runs out, the payments will stop.

The Line of Credit. This allows you to draw as much or as little money as you need when you need it. It expires when you've drawn down the full amount of your equity plus interest accrued.

Tip

The line of credit is most useful if you've got other income and only want the money from your equity to supplement it.

To qualify for an FHA HECM, you must be at least 62 years old and your home must be free and clear (or your mortgage must be very low). To set up the mortgage, you'll have to pay typical closing costs, points, and an FHA premium. These will be added to the mortgage amount, so no cash up front is needed. The advantage of the HECM to the lender is the guarantee. It allows the lender to feel secure that, one way or another, the money will be repaid.

To learn more about the HECM, you need to contact an FHA office. They are located in most major cities, and their headquarters is in Washington, D.C. They can tell you if any lenders participate in the program in your area.

From Another Age

The reverse annuity mortgage is really an offshoot of an old tradition that was practiced in Europe for hundreds of years. By this tradition, when a couple grew older, they would sometimes approach a wealthy individual and offer to pledge their home if this person would, in turn, look out for them in their older age. Often the wealthy person was a relative and the procedure worked quite well. The older couple was provided with food, caring, and some small amount of money. When they died, their house went to the wealthy individual.

But, it is instructive to learn that it did not always work out as planned. On some occasions, the wealthy individual did not really care for the older couple and, if they lived too long (by their benefactor's standards), they might find a bit of arsenic in their food! After all, the only thing keeping the house from the benefactor was their lives.

As a result, in some areas such arrangements were outlawed for years. However, RAMs are seeing a resurgence. Nevertheless, it is well worth remembering that they work best when the borrowers don't live too long. A long-lived borrower may see payments stop and, in the worst case, the house being lost as well.

18

Mortgage Insurance Rip-Offs

Read the Fine Print and Know the Following

Introduction

Mortgage insurance is increasingly becoming a part of the mortgage process, particularly as housing prices go up and people have less and less cash available for a down payment. Basically, mortgage insurance guarantees a portion of the mortgage to the lender in the event that the borrower defaults.

There are two types of mortgage insurance—government and private. Government mortgage insurance is required on all FHA mortgages. Private is generally required whenever the loan-to-value ratio exceeds 80 percent. (For example, a 90 percent mortgage normally requires mortgage insurance.)

Tip

I say "normally is required" with conventional loans because a few portfolio lenders have been making 90 percent loans without private mortgage insurance. This, however, is a rarity and often means paying more points or a higher-than-market interest rate. You might as well pay the insurance.

There is no problem, per se, with mortgage insurance. It is the lubricant that allows lenders to make bigger loans. For you, the borrower, it often allows you get into a property that you could not otherwise afford.

The problems occur later on down the road. Let's consider the conventional mortgage first.

Conventional Loans With Private Mortgage Insurance (PMI)

As noted earlier, whenever the loan-to-value ratio exceeds 80 percent, in theory the lender is supposed to get private mortgage insurance (PMI). This insures the lender against loss for the difference between roughly 75 percent of the loan value and the appraised value. If the lender, for example, loaned you 90 percent of the property's value, the PMI would insure the top 10 to 15 percent of the mortgage.

For the privilege of insuring itself, the lender charges you the premium, typically between one-fourth to one-half percent of the loan amount tacked onto the loan.

Tip

The private mortgage insurance does not insure you. It insures the lender. Why, you may ask, should you then be charged for it?

The answer is simple. Without the insurance, most lenders won't make higher than 80 percent loans. If you want the loan, you have to pay for the insurance.

How Long Must You Pay?

A little-known aspect of the PMI rule is that it is only required for as long as the loan-to-value remains above 80 percent. For example, if your original loan was for 90 percent and you've been paying for 10 years, you've probably paid down enough to lower the original loan amount below 80 percent. At that point, there's no further need of the insurance.

The Rip-Off

The problems arise out of the fact that as of this writing, lenders are not required to tell borrowers that they need not pay the PMI after their loan balance drops below the original 80 percent loan-to-value ratio. Rather, the lenders simply keep collecting the money.

If it were just a bookkeeping oversight, then one could simply say ho-hum, call the lender, get it straightened out, and continue. But most lenders are not fools. They know the rules and you can be sure that as soon as your mortgage drops below the 80 percent loan-to-value ratio, they will cancel the insurance.

What that means is that in many cases the lenders cancel the insurance, but keep collecting the premium from you. In short, they pull in another quarter to half percent interest for themselves!

Tip

If it's been more than 18 months after the purchase, you will need a new appraisal to get the PMI removed. But the cost of the appraisal is only a few hundred dollars and it may save you thousands in insurance payments.

Removing the PMI can give you an immediate benefit. If you're paying ½ percent on a $100,000 loan, that's $500 a year. That's a substantial savings.

Increasingly, borrowers are becoming aware of this rip-off. They have called lenders, demanding that the PMI be removed once they've paid down the loan.

Interestingly, almost all mortgages are written in such a way that the lender has the *option* but not the obligation of removing the PMI. Many lenders simply won't do it. If you demand it, they will stall, ignore you, or simply say no. They like collecting that free half percent or so of interest!

As a result of this rip-off, legislation is being introduced in many states that would *require* lenders to cancel the PMI premium charged to borrowers on mortgages as soon as they canceled the insurance. This would do away with the practice of lenders hanging on to your money when they had no ethical reason to keep it.

Check with a lender to see what the status of legislation is in your state. You may find the lender is required to eliminate your PMI and reduce your mortgage payment!

The Rip-off Remains

Most current legislation, however, does not address the real problem with PMI. Namely, PMI does not take into account appreciated values of property. For example, you buy a home for $100,000 with a 90 percent, or $90,000, mortgage. Because the loan-to-value ratio is above 80 percent, you are required to pay the additional ½ percent or so of PMI.

However, within 6 months, your house jumps in value to $125,000. You still, however, only owe $90,000. However, the current loan-to-value is now 72 percent, well below the 80 percent required.

If, however, you call up the lender and ask about having the PMI removed, you could get a stonewalled answer. You could be told that it's the original loan-to-value ratio that counts, not the current one.

Tip

___

To see how specious this argument is, consider the same property after 5 years. Let's say it's now valued at $200,000. The current loan-to-value ratio is 45 percent. But, because you haven't paid the loan down to below 80 percent of the *original* loan-to-value, the PMI isn't removed!

In all fairness to lenders and private mortgage insurers, it must be pointed out that in a falling market as we've had for the past few years, linking the PMI to the original price-to-value ratio makes some sense.

However, in most markets, to my way of thinking it's simply a rip-off of you, the borrower, requiring you to pay for insurance that the lender, after property values increase, does not need.

Trap

___

In order to prove to the lender that your house has appreciated, you will need a new appraisal. The lender, however, can still refuse to accept the new appraisal and remove the PMI.

I hope that new legislation will address this issue further. Until then, however, when a lender says with a straight face that it is required to charge you for the next 10 years or so for private mortgage insurance, try to keep from laughing.

Life Insurance

At one time some lenders were requiring borrowers to take out life insurance with their new mortgage. That quickly stopped. Today, no lender can require you take out life insurance for the value of the new mortgage. But many will try to push this option. If they do, resist. It's simply not worth it.

Trap

Mortgage life insurance is nothing more than simple term insurance. It's built on your age. There are two problems with it.

First, it's usually more expensive than regular term insurance bought directly from an insurance company. Second, the beneficiary is not your wife or your children, but the lender! If you die, the lender gets paid off.

Unless you consider the lender more important to you than spouse and children, don't get this insurance. If you want insurance, get it from an insurance agent, not from a mortgage lender.

FHA Mortgage Insurance

The FHA has always charged a premium for the mortgage insurance it offers. That premium has been around ½ percent, and for more than 40 years it was collected with each monthly payment (just like private mortgage insurance). However, in the mid-1980s the FHA made a historic change. Instead of collecting the premium monthly, it began demanding that borrowers pay the premium for the entire 30 years of the mortgage up front, at the time the money was borrowed.

Common sense says that there's something wrong here. When you buy insurance of any kind from life insurance to health to auto you don't normally pay for a lifetime's insurance up front. You pay annually as you use up the insurance. (There are, of course, single-premium policies where there is only one big payment up front. But often these are purchased for investment or tax advantages over their insurance benefits.)

The truth is that collecting the premium up front for FHA insurance can be a rip-off of the borrower, although few borrowers understand why when they pay it. We'll see the details in a moment, but first it's helpful to understand why the FHA made the change.

The FHA has always had to take back some property it insured through foreclosure. The process is fairly straightforward. The borrower can't pay, the lender forecloses, then sells the house to the FHA, which becomes the owner.

However, during the late 1970s and early 1980s another feature of FHA loans made them a target for unscrupulous investors—their assumability. FHA loans had always been 100 percent assumable. That means that if you obtained an FHA mortgage when you bought the property, anyone could take over the mortgage when you sold. There was no qualifying, not even a credit report.

Unscrupulous investors began going out and taking over properties with high FHA loans on them, often paying the owners a few thousand for their equity. Then, these investors would turn around and sell these homes at inflated prices to home buyers, often carrying back large seconds. In the superheated real estate market of the late 1970s, this was easily done. However, the new buyers were often unable to make payments and defaulted. When this happened, everyone walked away leaving the FHA to pick up the remains. Often the foreclosure never even showed up on anyone's credit report!

By the mid-1980s this had been done so many times that, coupled with the real estate slowdown of that period, the FHA was in financial trouble. The ½ percent in insurance fees that it was pulling in was insufficient to keep it afloat, given all the foreclosures it had.

So the FHA had to make a decision. It could either ask the federal government for more money, something it had not done since it was founded during the Great Depression. Or, it could demand that buyers pay that insurance premium in one lump sum up front. It chose the latter, and in so doing came into a windfall of money which it then used to help clean up its stockpile of foreclosed homes.

Tip

The FHA also restricted the assumability of its mortgages. For mortgages issued after December of 1986, the buyer must qualify with a credit report. Also, the seller remains liable for the mortgage for 5 years after the sale. For mortgages issued after 1989, the seller remains liable for the mortgage, for practical purposes, for the life of the loan. The days of free-and-easy assumability on new FHA loans is over.

This was great for the FHA, but terrible for the borrower. The reason is twofold. First, you have to come up with the premium up front. Since the premium ends up being around five percent of the sales price, it's a big chunk of money.

But the real rip-off comes when you sell. Few, if any, buyers are willing to pay you back that premium. In other words, you pay the premium for 30 years up front. But when you sell, perhaps in 5 years, you get none of it back. Because you paid up front, you lose the remaining years of insurance, in this case the last 25 years.

No Correcting the Problem

Unlike problems with PMI, there are no solutions on the horizon with FHA. In fact there are only more problems. While collecting the insurance premium up front seemed like a good idea at the time, it has some severe repercussions later on. The FHA gets the lump-sum money and then spends it on current operating costs. But as time goes by it needs still more money. However, more money isn't available because there are no more insurance premiums to be collected. The only new money comes from new mortgages, which have been declining as the advantages of FHA loans have declined.

As a result, the FHA finds itself increasingly in a cash-short bind, while those who borrow increasingly resent having to pay for 30 years' worth of insurance on a mortgage when they'll only benefit from a small portion of that term.

Of course, it could be argued that you can demand that a new buyer pay for the unused portion of the insurance. Perhaps in a hot market that would work. But in the recent cold market, most sellers are delighted to get a buyer at any price, not withstanding a demand that the buyer pay an additional insurance fee.

19
Tax Considerations

How You Play the Tax Angle Can Make or Break Your Mortgage

Introduction

There are at least three important tax considerations with regard to mortgages. These are

The deductibility of points

The deductibility of interest

How a mortgage affects gain or loss on sale

In this chapter we'll look into each of these and consider a few others besides. But before proceeding, it's important to first understand the nature of tax laws.

The tax laws are always evolving. What is true as I write this, for example, may be different by the time you read it, depending on court interpretations, IRS rulings, and new laws passed by the government. Therefore, while a serious effort has been made to see that the following material is as up-to-date and accurate as possible, you should not rely on it exclusively. When making any decisions involving taxation, you should first check with a competent professional such as a tax attorney or an accountant.

Deductibility of Points

Points, as you'll recall, are a form of prepaid interest that you may be required to pay to the lender in order to secure a mortgage. These are paid up front when you get the loan. The question inevitably arises: Are these points deductible from my income taxes?

The answer is yes, generally speaking, but not usually all at once. Let's clarify.

If the points represent prepaid interest, then you can deduct them. However, you must deduct them over the life of the mortgage. If the mortgage is for 30 years, then the deduction for points must be spread out over that period of time. For example:

2 Points on a $120,000, 30-Year Mortgage
are Deductable at $80 a Year

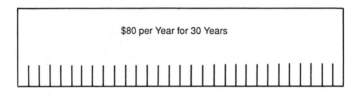

$80 per Year for 30 Years

Most borrowers, however, would not find this particularly useful since we all want deductions in the year we have the expense. How sweet it would be to be able to deduct the $5000 we paid in points (or however much) in the year we paid it.

Deducting Points in the Year Paid

There is an exception to the above rule that allows you to deduct points in the year you pay them, providing you meet certain criteria. These criteria include

1. *You pay the points out of your own funds.* The points are not paid out of the money loaned by the lender.

Tip
___

Many borrowers have taken to writing a separate check to the lender to cover the cost of the points. In this way they have a paper record of having paid for them separate from funds advanced by the lender.

2. *The mortgage must be for your principal residence.* It must be used for buying or improving that residence.

Trap

You cannot deduct points in the year paid on a mortgage for a second residence, even though interest on that mortgage may be deductible. You may deduct the points over the life of the mortgage.

3. *The amount of points charged must be customary for the area.*

Trap

If you buy down a mortgage, as described in an earlier chapter by paying additional points up front, the government may determine that the points you paid were in excess of what is customary for your area and disallow the deduction in the year paid.

4. *The points must represent interest.* They cannot be the fees paid for appraisals, credit reports, or the origination fees charged for FHA loans or special fees charged for VA loans.

Tip

Note that the above rules apply to property that is your principal residence. If you are purchasing or refinancing a rental property, different rules apply. In these cases, you may deduct the points only over the life of the mortgage. However, you may also be able to deduct your other costs and fees as a business expense. Check with your accountant.

Your principal residence is generally the place where you spend most of your time. Although the rules here are foggy, the government has become increasingly strict in determining what constitutes a principal residence. Unless you spend more than 50 percent of your time there, it might be hard to prove that a house was your principal residence.

5. *The deductions are applicable only if the points do not exceed the maximum interest deduction allowable on a residence.* See the discussion to follow.

Deducting points paid on a home mortgage is one of the biggest areas of confusion when it comes to paying taxes for home owners. The good news is that if you handle it correctly, you probably can deduct most of the points. The bad news is that you probably do need a tax consultant to look at your particular situation to determine what may be deductible and what may not.

Interest Deductions

At one time, all the interest paid on any mortgage was fully deductible. (At one time, in fact, you could prepay interest years in advance and then deduct in the year paid!)

All that has changed, however, under the guise of tax reform. Tax reform has severely limited the amount of interest on a home mortgage that you may deduct from your taxes.

Tip

Home mortgage interest deductibility was originally started to help Americans buy their own homes. It is a great tradition which allowed more individuals in this country to own property than virtually any other country on the planet.

However, in recent years the federal government through overspending has gotten itself into such a financial bind that the only way out is to increase revenues. The logical move would be to raise taxes. To do this, however, would be admitting that those running the government had erred. Consequently, for more than a decade politicians have ridden the banner of "no new taxes."

The piper must be paid, however. Consequently, instead of directly raising taxes, deductions have been reduced. The only remaining significant deduction for most Americans is the deductibility of interest and taxes on the home, and those in government, frightened of a general tax increase, have been whittling away at these. In the future, unless there is a call to arms by home owners, we can expect to see interest and property tax deductions reduced even further.

Today, the amount of interest you can deduct on a home that you own is limited.

1. The deduction applies only to your principal residence and to a second home. If it's a second home, you must use it part of the year.

2. The maximum mortgage amount can be $1 million, provided that the mortgage was used to purchase, build, or improve your home.

Tip

Any mortgage debt taken out prior to October 13, 1987, is grandfathered in. For example, if you took out a mortgage for $3 million prior to that date, the interest on all of it is deductible.

Trap

After October 13, 1987, the maximum mortgage amount on which interest is deductible is $1 million, *including any mortgages grandfathered in.*

3. If you take out a mortgage (refinance) on your home for purposes other than to improve, build, or add on, you are limited to $100,000 of debt on which interest may be deducted.

It's important to understand how this rule works. For example, you may purchase a home with a mortgage of $150,000. Under the rule, all of the interest on this mortgage is deductible. However, after you buy the property, you decide to add to the house and secure a mortgage for $250,000 more. If the money is used to build or improve the property, all the interest on the second mortgage is likewise deductible.

On the other hand, if you took out a second on the same property for $250,000 and used the money to start a business of your own, only the interest on the first $100,000 of the debt would be deductible.

Trap

If you take out a mortgage against your home and then buy bonds that are tax-free or otherwise receive tax-free income, the interest on the mortgage may not be deductible.

As can be seen from the above examples and explanations, while home interest is generally deductible, it isn't necessarily so. That being the case, you should consult with an accountant on the tax ramifications before taking out any mortgage.

Note: I've been discussing interest on residences and second homes. Different rules apply if you are dealing with rental property. Check with your accountant.

Taxes When You Sell or Refinance Your Property

Many people wonder how a mortgage affects them when they sell or refinance their property. The answer is that is can affect them greatly . . . or not at all. It depends on when the mortgage was taken out and what their gain, if any, is on the sale. Let's take some examples.

When You Refinance

Let's say that 10 years ago you purchased a home for $100,000. You obtained an $80,000 mortgage as part of the purchase price. Since that time the value of your home went up to $250,000. You decided to refinance and took out an additional $100,000 in another mortgage. Do you have any taxes to pay?

The answer is no. When you refinance, you do not increase your tax liability. True, you are reducing your equity in the property. But, because you are personally liable for the mortgage and have not sold the property, you do not change the tax basis of the property.

It is for this reason that many times people will refinance instead of sell, particularly with investment properties.

When You Sell

Sales, however, can produce different results. You owe taxes on any gain on the sale. Gain is calculated as the difference between your adjusted basis and your net selling price.

Let's say you bought the home for $100,000 and that's your basis in the property. (We'll overlook adjustments to the basis such as improvements.) You later sold for $350,000. (Again, we'll overlook adjustments to the sales price such as commission and other costs.) Your net gain is $250,000. This is the amount on which you would owe taxes.

However, if the home were your principal residence, you could defer all that gain by buying a new principal residence within 2 years before or after the sale of the old one.

Tip

You can defer a portion of the gain even if you buy a residence for less than what you sold your old home for. The calculation is fairly complicated; check with your accountant.

Trap

The deferral of gain on sale does not apply either to a second residence or to rental property. It only applies to your principal residence.

Let's say, however, that you wanted to retire and not purchase such an expensive house. Instead, you purchased a house for only $80,000. If that were the case, then you would owe taxes on the $250,000 in gain.

The tax law provides for a once-in-a-lifetime $125,000 exclusion if you are over 55 and are selling your principal residence. In other words, you may avoid paying taxes on up to $125,000 of your gain. The rules for qualifying are fairly strict. Again, check with your accountant.

Thus far, I've been considering taxes alone. But now, let's factor in a refinanced mortgage. Say that you had an $80,000 mortgage on the property when you bought it and borrowed (refinanced) another $100,000 later on for a total debt of $180,000. When you sold for $350,000 (overlooking costs), you netted out $170,000.

However, your gain still was $250,000. Remember that gain is determined by subtracting adjusted basis from net sales price (see the chart below). It does not take into account refinancing. As a result, this means that you must pay tax on $250,000 of gain, even though you only received $170,000 at the time of the sale!

Tax Liability vs Equity

$350,000
Sales Price

$350,000
Sales Price

$170,000
Net
Equity

$250,000
Taxable
Gain

$180,000
in
Mortgages

$100,000
Tax Basis

The apparent aberration is caused by the fact that you pulled out some of your equity earlier when you refinanced. The point here is that although there is no immediate tax liability when you refinance, later on when you sell, that refinance can come back to haunt you.

Mortgage Interest versus Personal Interest

It is worthwhile noting that beginning in 1991, all personal interest is nondeductible. That means that interest on your car loan, credit cards, department stores charges, and so forth are not deductible.

On the other hand, mortgage interest, up to the limits noted earlier, is deductible. Essentially that means that if you borrow $20,000 in personal debt, there is no tax deduction for the interest. However, if you borrow $20,000 on a home-equity loan, even if the money is over and above your cost of acquiring the property (up to the $100,000 limit discussed earlier), the money may be tax-deductible.

For this reason, many people today are opting for the home-equity loan over other types of personal finance for their financing needs.

Trap

Keep in mind that I am only talking about the deductibility of mortgages on your principal residence. Mortgages on a second home may not apply. Different rules will also apply for rental property.

Tip

Be careful of home-equity mortgages that are sold on the basis of their tax deductibility. Oftentimes the "friendly" lender really doesn't closely examine your personal finances to discover whether or not such a mortgage would benefit you, particularly.

It may turn out that for one reason or another, you cannot afford a home-equity mortgage. Or, if you're planning to sell, you may need the equity to pay taxes on gain, as noted above.

A home-equity mortgage is a good means of financing, if you are aware of your needs and the consequences of taking it out. It is not, however, a panacea.

Other Tax Considerations

There are a few other topics of concern regarding mortgages and taxes.

Late Payments on Your Mortgage

These generally can be deducted, if they constitute interest. On the other hand, if they are for a specific service that the lender performs, such as sending out late-payment notices, they probably are not deductible.

Negative Amortization

Here, your payment is not sufficient to cover all the interest. The unpaid interest is, therefore, added to principal. Can you deduct it?

Generally speaking you can't deduct interest unless you pay it. By converting it to principal, it stops being interest. You can, however, deduct the extra interest incurred because of the additional principal.

Imputed Interest

This is generally a problem for a seller-lender, but it is worth noting. If a seller gives a buyer a second or other mortgage for less than the current interest rate, the government may contend that the lower interest rate was actually an inducement to purchase and as such is taxable. Hence the government may "impute" or add interest, for tax purposes, to the mortgage, even though the seller never receives it! For example, the seller may take back a 5 percent second. But the government may contend that the market interest rate was 10 percent and may impute an additional 5 percent, for tax purposes, to the mortgage. A similar effect could happen to the buyer.

Imputed interest is a complex subject. Check with your accountant before giving or receiving a below-market interest rate.

The subject of taxes and mortgages is enormous and treacherous. What appears to make good sense on the surface may have nothing at all to do with the way the laws are interpreted or applied.

Therefore, as noted in the beginning, you are urged to consult your tax professional before you make any move involving real estate, including refinancing or purchasing with a mortgage. It may very well be that by just structuring the deal slightly differently, you can save yourself an enormous amount of taxes later on.

20
Paying Off
Your Mortgage
Early

The Benefits Depend
on Your Circumstances

Introduction

There are a few lucky people who are in a position to pay off their mortgage early. If you're one of them, typically you've had the mortgage on the property for a fairly long time and it's close to maturity. Perhaps it has 5 or 10 years to go out of 30. Now, you're wondering if it makes sense to pay it off early. Are there advantages? Disadvantages? In this chapter we'll consider some of the ramifications of early payoff.

The decision to pay off an existing mortgage should not be taken lightly, particularly if you are retired and living on a fixed income. Don't rely simply on the information in this chapter. Consult with a trusted adviser. You don't want to make a mistake and put your future into jeopardy.

Trap

Continuing to keep an existing mortgage means that you have less and less interest to deduct from your taxes. Remember, as a mortgage ages, particularly after year 10, the amount of the payment that goes to interest begins to fall dramatically.

Equity Return

I've mentioned it before, but it's particularly applicable here. The return of equity from a mortgage is much greater in its later years than in its earlier ones (see Table 20-1).

When your mortgage gets to its final years, most of each monthly payment goes to principal, less and less to interest. Thus, what you are doing in those last years is rapidly paying off the mortgage and rapidly adding to your equity in the property.

Many people feel that this period of rapid equity return is the golden period of the mortgage. It's that rare time when you get the benefits instead of the mortgage company.

Nevertheless, the question must be asked, could you make better use of that money that you are paying out each month? For example, let's say your monthly payments on the mortgage are $750 a month, of which $500 is going to equity and $250 is going to interest.

For practical purposes you can think of the $500 as "money in the bank." It's going toward your equity or your savings in the home.

But, can you afford to save $500 a month? Perhaps you are struggling to make other payments. Perhaps you are on a fixed income and you desperately need all the cash you can get hold of. Might it not be better to pay off that mortgage and avoid having to pay out $750 a month?

Paying Off the Mortgage

There are two alternatives here—refinancing and paying off the mortgage. I've already considered refinancing in an earlier chapter. Here I'll consider a payoff.

Oftentimes people who find themselves in the position described above have some savings in the bank. They ask themselves, wouldn't it be better to take out those savings and pay off the mortgage, thus avoiding that big monthly payment?

It depends, I believe, on two factors. The first is the interest rate. If the interest rate on the mortgage is *higher* than the interest rate on the money in savings, it definitely makes economic sense.

Consider. Let's say the outstanding balance on the mortgage is $10,000 and the interest rate is 10 percent. That means that the current year you are spending roughly $1000 in interest on that mortgage.

On the other hand, let's say that you also have $10,000 in the bank earning 7 percent interest. Your money that year earns $700.

Table 20-1 Equity Return of 30-Year Mortgage

Monthly Payment of $1028 on a $100,000 Mortgage at 12 Percent

Month	Balance	Interest	Equity return
1	$99,971.30	$1000.00	$28.62
12	99,636.30	996.69	31.93
24	99,226.30	992.63	35.99
36	98,764.10	988.05	40.57
48	98,243.30	982.89	45.73
60	97,656.40	977.08	51.54
72	96,995.30	970.54	58.08
84	96,250.30	963.16	65.46
96	95,411.00	954.85	73.77
108	94,465.10	945.49	83.13
120	93,399.30	934.93	93.69
132	92,198.50	923.05	105.57
144	90,845.80	909.65	118.97
156	89,320.30	894.55	134.74
168	87,602.00	877.54	151.08
180	85,665.80	858.37	170.25
192	83,484.10	836.76	191.86
204	81,025.60	812.42	216.20
216	78,255.60	785.00	243.62
228	75,133.90	754.09	274.53
240	71,616.30	719.26	309.36
252	67,652.60	680.02	348.60
264	63,186.70	635.80	392.83
276	58,154.80	585.98	442.64
288	52,484.70	529.84	498.78
300	46,095.60	466.58	562.04
312	38,896.10	395.30	633.32
324	30,783.50	314.98	713.64
336	21,642.10	224.47	804.15
348	11,341.40	112.48	906.14

Final payment = $756.38

Total interest = $270,016

Total payments = $370,016

Comparison of Mortgage with Savings

Mortgage interest	− $1000
Savings interest	+ $ 700
Net loss	$ 300

The net result of keeping $10,000 in the bank at 7 percent and paying out 10 percent on a mortgage with a $10,000 balance is a loss of $300 a year. In short, simply by paying off the mortgage, you can pick up an additional $300 a year in income.

Of course, the amount to be gained will vary according to the amount of the mortgage and the difference in interest rates. But, I think the point should be clear. Economically, without any other considerations, it makes sense here to pay off the mortgage.

There are, however, other considerations. The first is taxes.

Tax Considerations

Mortgage interest is generally deductible on your income taxes if you itemize. Depending on your tax bracket, the deduction can be worth a considerable amount of money, as much as 30 percent of the interest in federal taxes plus whatever the rate is for your state and local (if any) income taxes.

In our above example, let's factor in someone who is in a combined federal and state tax bracket of roughly 40 percent (a California resident, for example). The interest of $1000, because it's on your home, is deductible. (There are limitations to interest deductions—see Chapter 19 on taxation.)

If your deductions are worth 40 percent to you, that means that the interest you pay is offset by the $400 that you save in taxes. Another way to think of it is that the government is paying 40 percent of every dollar in interest for you. In the case of the $1000 annual interest cost, the government is paying $400 (by subtracting this amount from taxes you would otherwise owe). Now the figures work out differently.

Comparison of Mortgage with Savings, Adding Taxes

Mortgage interest	− $1000
Tax savings	+ 400
Net interest cost	$ 600

Now let's consider savings. Your savings produce $700. However, that interest income is taxable. If you're still in the combined 40 percent tax bracket, that means that you'll end up paying $280 in taxes on it.

Savings interest	+ $700
Taxes	− 280
Net interest received	$420

When we now add together the net interest received on savings from the net interest paid out on the mortgage, the figures are slightly different.

Net mortgage interest	$600
Net savings interest	− 420
Net loss	$180

After taxes, your loss has been greatly reduced. Do you still want to pay off the mortgage from savings? You would save roughly $180 a year if you did so. But, that also means you wouldn't have any more savings.

Trap

The above example only holds for someone in the top tax bracket. The lower your tax bracket, the less that tax savings is worth. It may turn out, from an economic perspective, that it's still better to pay off the mortgage.

Tip

Many people in lower income brackets don't itemize on their returns. If you don't itemize, then you can't claim the interest deduction, so it's worth nothing to you. You must still, however, pay taxes on the income received from savings! In this case the economics suggest it makes far more sense to pay off the mortgage.

The Value of Cash

There's another consideration that's well worth making, particularly for those on limited incomes. How important is it to you to have cash in the bank?

If you need a cash reserve to pay for medical or other unforeseen expenses, then you may be placing yourself in jeopardy by paying off your mortgage early. You may, in fact, be jumping from the frying pan into the fire.

The reason is that it's easy to get hold of cash in a savings account. Just go to the bank and withdraw it. It's hard to get cash out from equity in your home. You have to refinance or sell, and both offer problems.

You may not be able to refinance just when you most need the money because at that time, a lender may not feel you are creditworthy or otherwise qualified. Consider, you may have gotten the mortgage on the property years ago when you had a much higher income.

Today, your lower income may cause a lender to doubt your ability to repay, particularly if you are in dire straights at the moment and need the money for a medical or other emergency.

Savings vs. Borrowing

$10,000
in
Savings

Easy
to Get
Out

$10,000 in Home Equity

Difficult to Get Out

Consider Refinancing

Of course, the payments may simply be too high for you with your present income. If that's the case, then consider refinancing *before* you're in dire straights and while you still have the cash in the bank.

Remember, if it's an old mortgage, the chances are that most of your payment is going to principal, not to interest. By refinancing for just the amount you owe plus costs of the refinancing, you can often cut your payment in half, sometimes in a third, sometimes even more.

Further, you may even be able to refinance with the existing lender, who will be happy to cut your payments down in order to get a return of more interest and less principal.

Be Careful

As I mentioned at the beginning, the decision to pay off an existing mortgage should not be taken lightly, particularly if you are retired and living on a fixed income. Don't rely simply on the information in this chapter. Consult with a trusted advisor. You don't want to make a mistake and put your future into jeopardy.

21
Settlement Costs

**Making Sure You
Get a Fair Shake**

Introduction

Whenever you obtain a mortgage from an institutional lender such as a bank or savings and loan (as opposed to having it come from the seller), there are going to be loan costs. Some of these are reasonable, some are not. In this chapter we'll attempt to tell the former apart from the latter.

RESPA

In 1974 Congress passed the Real Estate Settlement Procedures Act (RESPA). This act grew out of the many abuses that some lenders had perpetrated on home buyers and borrowers.

RESPA requires specific disclosures from lenders. It also prohibits lenders from getting kickbacks from other parties to a transaction.

Tip

You should be aware that under RESPA, it is illegal for the seller to require you, the buyer-borrower, as a condition of the sale, to purchase insurance from any specific title insurance company. If the seller violates

220

this, he or she could be liable for as much as three times the cost of the title insurance.

Trap

RESPA requires that lenders disclose to you the various costs. It does not, however, regulate those costs. You have to be aware of what's reasonable and what's not.

RESPA kicks in at several critical junctures during the mortgage process. Your first contact with it will be when you fill out an application for a home mortgage with a lender.

The lender is required by RESPA to provide you with a "good faith estimate" of the cost involved in closing the deal, that is, the settlement costs. This estimate must be delivered or mailed to you within 3 working days of receiving your loan application.

Good-Faith Estimate

The good-faith estimate should include all of the costs which can be estimated by the lender. These include points and other fees, but do not include prorations for taxes and insurance, which cannot be calculated until the close of escrow. The estimate should include the annual percentage rate (APR), which is the true interest rate you will be paying for the mortgage.

Tip

The APR will usually be different from the quoted rate for the mortgage. Don't be misled by this. There may be nothing wrong.

There are two reasons for this. The first is that the APR must take into account many costs and all interest, including points, which are considered prepaid interest. Hence, the APR tends to be higher than the interest rate on which your loan amortization is based.

Second, with ARMs, the APR takes into account the overall expected interest rate of the mortgage, not just the teaser rate you may have been quoted. Hence, it may once again be higher.

Be sure that in addition to the APR, the estimate also shows the rate you have been quoted and that if you have an ARM, it spells out the details of the teaser, the steps, the adjustments, and the caps.

Trap

The emphasis here is on "good faith." As long as the lender gives you a statement with the majority of expected costs, it has probably fulfilled its obligation. This does not mean, however, that the lender's statement will be entirely accurate or that every single cost will be on it. Most times any increases or additional costs are minor. However, some lenders do tend to exaggerate their fees downward.

The whole point of the good-faith estimate is to allow you some time to shop around. Since it is given so soon after you make the application, you should have time to reject that lender and find another, should you choose to do so. The lender is obligated to hold roughly to the terms listed in the good-faith estimate when the final documents are drawn.

Settlement Statement

It is difficult for the lender to know the exact costs until the close of escrow. But, it is possible to know them at the close of escrow when you are given a settlement statement.

Tip

One of the worst feelings is to walk into an escrow company to sign documents only to discover that the mortgage isn't as it should be. You can avoid this problem.

You can demand that the lender, or the person handling the closing, show you the HUD-1 settlement statement, which the lender must use and which lists all closing costs. *You can make this demand one business day before closing.*

Granted, one business day is not a whole lot of time. But if there is something significantly wrong, it does give you time to alert your agent or attorney and, if necessary, to hold up the close of escrow.

Trap

By the time it comes to close escrow, you are probably contractually obligated to go through with the deal. That means that you are probably obligated to pay your closing costs (unless for some reason the seller reneges on the deal or the title can't be cleared) as shown on the settlement statement.

At this point it may be too late to argue about a cost that you think is unfair. That should be done when you are given your good-faith estimate.

What you can argue about, however, is a cost that appears on your settlement statement that did not appear on your good-faith estimate (exclusive of prorations). If you think there is an unjustified cost here, let the lender, agents, attorneys, and everyone else know.

You can be sure that every attempt will be made to explain the cost to you, and it may turn out to be perfectly justified. Or it may turn out to be a mistake. Or it could be something else.

Typical Mortgage Settlement Costs

Here, then, are your typical mortgage settlement costs. Keep in mind that we have not covered other possible costs such as title insurance, escrow, your attorney's fee, or real estate agent's commission.

Appraisal Fee

The lender sends out an appraiser to give a written estimate of the property's value. This estimated value is what the mortgage is based upon.

The cost of the appraisal will vary enormously. It might be as inexpensive as $175 and as costly as $350 or more, depending on the value of the property. However, since the lender picks the appraiser and sets the charge, your only two choices are to pay it or get a different lender.

Tip

An appraisal is a necessary part of the mortgage lending process, and you will be told that it is customary for the borrower to pay for it. That's true, too. However, there is nothing to keep the lender from absorbing this cost, if it wants to. In a tight market with lots of lenders and few borrowers, some lenders will offer free appraisals. It's something to shop for.

Assumption Fee

If you are assuming an existing mortgage, the lender will probably charge a fee for handling the paperwork. This fee is usually around $100.

Attorney's Fees

If you have an attorney, you can expect to be charged a fee. However, if the lender has an attorney, you may be also charged a separate fee.

There is no reason you should have to pay for the lender's attorney. This should be a typical cost of doing business for the lender. You may want to challenge this fee if it did not appear on your original good-faith estimate.

Credit Report Fee

The lender charges for a credit report. This fee usually is under $50 for a "standard factual." (See Chapter 4 for more details.) It is a normal and customary fee. You have to pay it, unless the lender agrees to absorb the cost (see "Appraisal," above).

Discount Points

This is a one-time charge. Each point is equal to 1 percent of the loan.

Points are used to adjust the yield of the mortgage to correspond to market conditions. For example, the market may be at 9 percent. But, you are getting an 8⅞ percent mortgage. For that extra one-eighth, you might be charged a point up front.

Points were originally charged only on FHA mortgages. The reason was that there were federal constraints limiting the maximum interest rate that could be charged. When the FHA rate was below the market rate, points were charged to make up the difference in yield.

There are no such limitations with conventional loans. However, in order to entice borrowers, conventional lenders often lower the interest rate below market and then add points to bring the yield back up. You can verify this is the case by offering to pay a lender a higher interest rate for fewer points. Virtually all lenders will agree.

Trap

In the past, lenders wanted more points because they could declare them as income in the year received. Current tax treatment for lenders, however, requires them to capitalize points over the life of the mortgage. Hence, for the lender today, points and interest are roughly the same.

As a result, some lenders charge points as a way of confusing you, the borrower, as to the actual interest rate you are paying. You think you are getting a low-interest-rate mortgage. But, when the points are added in, you may be paying above market!

Your best bet is to shop around. Find the lowest rate with the lowest points. As a rough means of comparison, each point is worth about ¼ to ⅛ percent of interest.

Document Preparation

The escrow company will usually charge a fee, often under $50, for the preparation of documents such as the deed. However, some lenders will also charge an additional document preparation fee for preparing the deed of trust or mortgage. I have seen these fees range from $35 to $300.

Some lenders don't do their own document preparation. This is particularly the case if you're dealing with a mortgage broker, banker, and secondary pool. Hence, the cost does make sense.

Nevertheless, to my way of thinking if the lender is giving you a mortgage, it should be a cost of business to prepare the mortgage document.

If this fee was not disclosed on your original good-faith estimate, you may want to challenge it.

Fire Insurance

You will be required to provide a fire and hazard insurance policy. Typically you must pay for these policies at least 1 year in advance into escrow.

Impounds

If your mortgage was for more than 80 percent loan-to-value ratio, you will probably be required to impound taxes and insurance. What this means is that the lender will collect a portion of the money for taxes and insurance from you in advance and then pay them when due.

Trap

In the past, lenders have required large impound balances, then have deposited the money until payment was due, collected interest, and not paid that interest to borrowers. Recent legislation has attempted to correct this problem. Nevertheless, you should question your lender on the size of the impounds and upon whether or not you'll receive interest on the money.

Also, be aware that some lenders charge a separate fee for setting up the impound account and yet another fee for administering it. These last two, to my way of thinking, are totally unjustified.

Whenever I get a mortgage for 80 percent loan-to-value or less, I refuse impounds and instead pay my own taxes and insurance. That gives me a lower monthly payment, but does mean that I have to come up with lump-sum monies to pay for taxes and insurance. Also, I don't have to worry about a lender abusing the impound account.

You may want to do the same. But be aware of your saving and budgeting habits. It only works if you're able to save the money on your own to pay taxes and insurance when they come due.

Interest

You will be obligated to pay the interest from the date of the closing to the first monthly payment.

Tip

Unlike rent, interest on a mortgage is paid is arrears. Thus, if you can arrange to have the escrow close on the last day of the month, the next payment won't be due until the first day of the month after next. This means you won't have to pay any interest into escrow and you'll have a whole month before your first payment comes due.

Lender's Title Insurance

Most lenders will require a separate, more comprehensive, and more expensive policy of title insurance. This is frequently required because of underwriting. You'll simply have to pay it.

Mortgage Insurance Premium

For an FHA loan, this has to be paid all in advance into escrow. For private mortgage insurance the amount may be for several months in advance to cover the payment in the event you default on the mortgage.

Origination Fee

This is a charge to cover the lender's administrative costs in processing a loan. It is standard with FHA government-insured loans.

With conventional loans it is often expressed as a few hundred dollars plus points. For example, a particular mortgage might be 2 points plus

$350. The $350 is the origination fee. It goes to pay a mortgage banker or a loan officer for processing the loan.

To my way of thinking there is no justification for this fee. The lender is getting the interest; that should be sufficient. If there are other administrative costs, the final lender should advance these and the interest rate should be adjusted accordingly. However, almost all lenders do squeeze in a few hundred dollars as a way of milking you of additional money when obtaining a mortgage.

Tip

Look at the total costs. If the origination fee is high but the points are low, you may still have a good loan. Similarly if the points are low or the origination fee high, you may have the exact same loan in terms of costs.

What you need to consider are the total costs. The time to be worried is when all of the costs, including origination fee and points, are high.

In addition to the costs listed above, there could be additional charges which may or may not be reasonable. You'll have to use common sense here or check with your real estate attorney.

Challenging Lender Fees

The time to challenge lender's fee is when you first get your good-faith estimate. If you don't like a fee, ask the lender about it. If the explanation isn't adequate, ask that the fee be removed. If the lender refuses, consider finding a different lender.

Trap

Sometimes a lender will offer such a good mortgage that you're willing to put up with all sorts of unreasonable fees. However, sometimes there are so many additional unreasonable fees that the mortgage package overall is unfavorable. Some lenders, in fact, create a package with a low interest rate as a teaser and then make up for it with additional fees. Be wary of this. Check your good-faith estimate closely.

If you find yourself at closing and discover fees that are not reasonable, you can still ask the lender about them, particularly if they were not on the original good-faith estimate. You can always say that you'll refuse to pay. But be aware that by the time you get to settlement, you may be

obligated to close the deal. Holding up the transaction could have legal
consequences for you. Check with your attorney.

Complaints

At any time, you can complain about lender's actions directly to HUD,
which administers RESPA. You should be aware, however, that HUD is
desperately understaffed and it, rather than looking closely at individual
complaints, tends to investigate those lenders who have had a whole bat-
tery of complaints leveled against them.

If you want to complain, write out a statement of the problem and include copies of all supporting documents. Send them to:

U.S. Dept. of Housing and Urban Development Director
Office of Insured Single Family Housing
Attention: RESPA
451 Seventh St. S.W.
Washington, DC 20410

Also check to see if there are any agencies at the state level which likewise supervise lenders. You may have an even better chance of getting
help, there.

In truth, the biggest problem with lender settlement costs tends to be
the fact that they are so difficult to understand and that even the most
common ones can appear unwarranted. Before you rush off in anger to
challenge the lender, read this chapter through again and see if maybe
the fee is perfectly normal. It may simply be another cost involved with
the purchase of a home and with obtaining a new mortgage for it.

Appendix **1**

Amortization Table

Use the following table to determine the monthly mortgage payment (principal and interest) when you already know the loan amount. Just multiply the loan amount by the factor and you'll be given the monthly payment.

	Years					
Interest	3	5	7	10	15	30
7.00	.030877	.019801	.015092	.011610	.008988	.006653
7.25	.030991	.019919	.015215	.011740	.009129	.006822
7.50	.031106	.020037	.015338	.011870	.009270	.006992
7.75	.031221	.020157	.015462	.012001	.009413	.007164
8.00	.031336	.020276	.015586	.012133	.009557	.007338
8.25	.031341	.020396	.015711	.012265	.009701	.007513
8.50	.031567	.020516	.015836	.012399	.009847	.007689
8.75	.041683	.020637	.015962	.012533	.009995	.007867
9.00	.031799	.020758	.016089	.012668	.010143	.008046
9.25	.031916	.020879	.016216	.012802	.010292	.008227
9.50	.032032	.021001	.016344	.012940	.010442	.008409
9.75	.032149	.021124	.016472	.013077	.010594	.008592
10.00	.032267	.021247	.016601	.013215	.010746	.008776
10.25	.032385	.021370	.016730	.013354	.010896	.008961
10.50	.032502	.021494	.016861	.013494	.011054	.009147
10.75	.032621	.021618	.016991	.013634	.011210	.009335
11.00	.032739	.021742	.017122	.013775	.011366	.009523
11.25	.032857	.021867	.017254	.013917	.011523	.009713

Interest	Years					
	3	5	7	10	15	30
11.50	.032976	.021993	.017387	.014060	.011682	.009903
11.75	.033095	.022118	.017520	.014203	.011841	.010094
12.00	.033214	.022244	.017653	.014347	.012002	.010286
12.25	.033334	.022371	.017787	.014492	.012163	.010479
12.50	.033454	.022498	.017921	.014638	.012325	.010673
12.75	.033574	.022625	.018056	.014784	.012488	.010867
13.00	.033694	.022753	.018192	.014931	.012652	.011062
13.25	.033815	.022881	.018328	.015079	.012817	.011258
13.50	.033935	.023010	.018465	.015227	.012983	.011454
13.75	.034056	.023139	.018602	.015377	.013150	.011651
14.00	.034178	.023268	.018740	.015527	.013317	.011849

Appendix **2**
Mortgage Finder

How to Use the Mortgage Finder

The tables in this appendix are probably unlike any you've seen before. They can be used to find the following information.*

1. *To find maximum price you can pay given the maximum monthly payment you can afford.* Read down "Monthly Payment" to the maximum you can afford, then right to "Maximum Price."

2. *To find your total monthly payment for a specific purchase price.* Read down "Maximum Price" column to your purchase price, then left to "Monthly Payment" column to see the monthly payment, including principal, interest, taxes, and insurance.

3. *To find the approximate income needed to qualify for a particular mortgage.* Read down "Maximum Amount" to your mortgage amount, then right to "Income To Qualify" column.

4. *To find approximate maximum price you can afford given your income.*

---

*Special note: These tables assume that the mortgage is fixed rate for 30 years, you are putting 20 percent down, lenders require that no more than 33 percent of income be used for net monthly payment (principal, interest, taxes and insurance) and that taxes and insurance will be 2 percent of the purchase price annually. (In addition, gross monthly payment—net payment plus long-term debt—cannot exceed 36 percent of income.)

If you should put only 10 percent down (instead of 20 percent), many of the figures in these tables will not apply. (The amount of monthly payment for principal and interest for any given loan amount, however, will still remain accurate.)

Additionally on the west coast, particularly California, where property taxes tend to be low, the payment shown may be a bit high. In parts of the midwest and east coast where property taxes tend to be higher, the payment shown may be a bit low.

For these reasons, these tables must only be taken as *approximations.* The actual figures you encounter may be somewhat different.

Read "Income To Qualify" until you find your income, then read left to "Maximum Price."

5. *To find the maximum mortgage amount given the purchase price.* Read down the column marked "Maximum Price" to your price, then over to the left to the column marked "Maximum Amount."

6. *To find the approximate maximum mortgage you can get given your income.* Read down the column marked "Income To Qualify" to your income, then over to the left to "Maximum Amount."

7. *To find the maximum purchase price given a specific mortgage amount.* Read down "Maximum Amount" column, then right to "Maximum Price" column.

8. *To find the principal and interest only monthly payment for a mortgage amount.* Read down "Maximum Amount" column, then right to "Mortgage P & I" column.

7% Interest, 30-Year Term, 20% Down

(2% of purchase price assumed for taxes and insurance; 33% of gross monthly income allowed for mortgage payment)

Monthly payment	Maximum mortgage		Maximum price	Income to qualify	
	Amount	P & I		Monthly	Annual
$349	$40,000	$266	$50,000	$1,048	$12,581
$363	$41,600	$277	$52,000	$1,090	$13,084
$377	$43,200	$287	$54,000	$1,132	$13,587
$391	$44,800	$298	$56,000	$1,174	$14,091
$405	$46,400	$309	$58,000	$1,216	$14,594
$419	$48,000	$319	$60,000	$1,258	$15,097
$433	$49,600	$330	$62,000	$1,300	$15,600
$447	$51,200	$341	$64,000	$1,342	$16,104
$461	$52,800	$351	$66,000	$1,384	$16,607
$475	$54,400	$362	$68,000	$1,426	$17,110
$489	$56,000	$373	$70,000	$1,468	$17,613
$503	$57,600	$383	$72,000	$1,510	$18,116
$517	$59,200	$394	$74,000	$1,552	$18,620
$531	$60,800	$405	$76,000	$1,594	$19,123
$545	$62,400	$415	$78,000	$1,636	$19,626
$559	$64,000	$426	$80,000	$1,677	$20,129
$573	$65,600	$436	$82,000	$1,719	$20,633
$587	$67,200	$447	$84,000	$1,761	$21,136
$601	$68,800	$458	$86,000	$1,803	$21,639
$615	$70,400	$468	$88,000	$1,845	$22,142
$629	$72,000	$479	$90,000	$1,887	$22,646
$643	$73,600	$490	$92,000	$1,929	$23,149
$657	$75,200	$500	$94,000	$1,971	$23,652
$671	$76,800	$511	$96,000	$2,013	$24,155
$685	$78,400	$522	$98,000	$2,055	$24,659
$699	$80,000	$532	$100,000	$2,097	$25,162
$713	$81,600	$543	$102,000	$2,139	$25,665
$727	$83,200	$554	$104,000	$2,181	$26,168
$741	$84,800	$564	$106,000	$2,223	$26,671
$755	$86,400	$575	$108,000	$2,265	$27,175
$769	$88,000	$585	$110,000	$2,306	$27,678
$783	$89,600	$596	$112,000	$2,348	$28,181
$797	$91,200	$607	$114,000	$2,390	$28,684
$811	$92,800	$617	$116,000	$2,432	$29,188
$825	$94,400	$628	$118,000	$2,474	$29,691
$839	$96,000	$639	$120,000	$2,516	$30,194
$853	$97,600	$649	$122,000	$2,558	$30,697
$867	$99,200	$660	$124,000	$2,600	$31,201
$881	$100,800	$671	$126,000	$2,642	$31,704
$895	$102,400	$681	$128,000	$2,684	$32,207
$909	$104,000	$692	$130,000	$2,726	$32,710
$923	$105,600	$703	$132,000	$2,768	$33,214
$937	$107,200	$713	$134,000	$2,810	$33,717

Monthly payment	Maximum mortgage		Maximum price	Income to qualify	
	Amount	P & I		Monthly	Annual
$951	$108,800	$724	$136,000	$2,852	$34,220
$965	$110,400	$735	$138,000	$2,894	$34,723
$979	$112,000	$745	$140,000	$2,936	$35,227
$992	$113,600	$756	$142,000	$2,977	$35,730
$1,006	$115,200	$766	$144,000	$3,019	$36,233
$1,020	$116,800	$777	$146,000	$3,061	$36,736
$1,034	$118,400	$788	$148,000	$3,103	$37,239
$1,048	$120,000	$798	$150,000	$3,145	$37,743
$1,062	$121,600	$809	$152,000	$3,187	$38,246
$1,076	$123,200	$820	$154,000	$3,229	$38,749
$1,090	$124,800	$830	$156,000	$3,271	$39,252
$1,104	$126,400	$841	$158,000	$3,313	$39,756
$1,118	$128,000	$852	$160,000	$3,355	$40,259
$1,132	$129,600	$862	$162,000	$3,397	$40,762
$1,146	$131,200	$873	$164,000	$3,439	$41,265
$1,160	$132,800	$884	$166,000	$3,481	$41,769
$1,174	$134,400	$894	$168,000	$3,523	$42,272
$1,188	$136,000	$905	$170,000	$3,565	$42,775
$1,202	$137,600	$916	$172,000	$3,607	$43,278
$1,216	$139,200	$926	$174,000	$3,648	$43,782
$1,230	$140,800	$937	$176,000	$3,690	$44,285
$1,244	$142,400	$947	$178,000	$3,732	$44,788
$1,258	$144,000	$958	$180,000	$3,774	$45,291
$1,272	$145,600	$969	$182,000	$3,816	$45,794
$1,286	$147,200	$979	$184,000	$3,858	$46,298
$1,300	$148,800	$990	$186,000	$3,900	$46,801
$1,314	$150,400	$1,001	$188,000	$3,942	$47,304
$1,328	$152,000	$1,011	$190,000	$3,984	$47,807
$1,342	$153,600	$1,022	$192,000	$4,026	$48,311
$1,356	$155,200	$1,033	$194,000	$4,068	$48,814
$1,370	$156,800	$1,043	$196,000	$4,110	$49,317
$1,384	$158,400	$1,054	$198,000	$4,152	$49,820
$1,398	$160,000	$1,065	$200,000	$4,194	$50,324

7½% Interest, 30-Year Term, 20% Down

(2% of purchase price assumed for taxes and insurance; 33% of gross monthly income allowed for mortgage payment)

Monthly payment	Maximum mortgage Amount	P & I	Maximum price	Income to qualify Monthly	Annual
$363	$40,000	$280	$50,000	$1,089	$13,069
$378	$41,600	$291	$52,000	$1,133	$13,592
$392	$43,200	$302	$54,000	$1,176	$14,115
$407	$44,800	$313	$56,000	$1,220	$14,638
$421	$46,400	$324	$58,000	$1,263	$15,160
$436	$48,000	$336	$60,000	$1,307	$15,683
$450	$49,600	$347	$62,000	$1,350	$16,206
$465	$51,200	$358	$64,000	$1,394	$16,729
$479	$52,800	$369	$66,000	$1,438	$17,251
$494	$54,400	$380	$68,000	$1,481	$17,774
$508	$56,000	$392	$70,000	$1,525	$18,297
$523	$57,600	$403	$72,000	$1,568	$18,820
$537	$59,200	$414	$74,000	$1,612	$19,342
$552	$60,800	$425	$76,000	$1,655	$19,865
$566	$62,400	$436	$78,000	$1,699	$20,388
$581	$64,000	$448	$80,000	$1,743	$20,911
$595	$65,600	$459	$82,000	$1,786	$21,433
$610	$67,200	$470	$84,000	$1,830	$21,956
$624	$68,800	$481	$86,000	$1,873	$22,479
$639	$70,400	$492	$88,000	$1,917	$23,002
$653	$72,000	$503	$90,000	$1,960	$23,525
$668	$73,600	$515	$92,000	$2,004	$24,047
$683	$75,200	$526	$94,000	$2,048	$24,570
$697	$76,800	$537	$96,000	$2,091	$25,093
$712	$78,400	$548	$98,000	$2,135	$25,616
$726	$80,000	$559	$100,000	$2,178	$26,138
$741	$81,600	$571	$102,000	$2,222	$26,661
$755	$83,200	$582	$104,000	$2,265	$27,184
$770	$84,800	$593	$106,000	$2,309	$27,707
$784	$86,400	$604	$108,000	$2,352	$28,229
$799	$88,000	$615	$110,000	$2,396	$28,752
$813	$89,600	$627	$112,000	$2,440	$29,275
$828	$91,200	$638	$114,000	$2,483	$29,798
$842	$92,800	$649	$116,000	$2,527	$30,321
$857	$94,400	$660	$118,000	$2,570	$30,843
$871	$96,000	$671	$120,000	$2,614	$31,366
$886	$97,600	$682	$122,000	$2,657	$31,889
$900	$99,200	$694	$124,000	$2,701	$32,412
$915	$100,800	$705	$126,000	$2,745	$32,934
$929	$102,400	$716	$128,000	$2,788	$33,457
$944	$104,000	$727	$130,000	$2,832	$33,980
$958	$105,600	$738	$132,000	$2,875	$34,503
$973	$107,200	$750	$134,000	$2,919	$35,025

Monthly payment	Maximum mortgage		Maximum price	Income to qualify	
	Amount	P & I		Monthly	Annual
$987	$108,800	$761	$136,000	$2,962	$35,548
$1,002	$110,400	$772	$138,000	$3,006	$36,071
$1,016	$112,000	$783	$140,000	$3,049	$36,594
$1,031	$113,600	$794	$142,000	$3,093	$37,117
$1,046	$115,200	$806	$144,000	$3,137	$37,639
$1,060	$116,800	$817	$146,000	$3,180	$38,162
$1,075	$118,400	$828	$148,000	$3,224	$38,685
$1,089	$120,000	$839	$150,000	$3,267	$39,208
$1,104	$121,600	$850	$152,000	$3,311	$39,730
$1,118	$123,200	$861	$154,000	$3,354	$40,253
$1,133	$124,800	$873	$156,000	$3,398	$40,776
$1,147	$126,400	$884	$158,000	$3,442	$41,299
$1,162	$128,000	$895	$160,000	$3,485	$41,821
$1,176	$129,600	$906	$162,000	$3,529	$42,344
$1,191	$131,200	$917	$164,000	$3,572	$42,867
$1,205	$132,800	$929	$166,000	$3,616	$43,390
$1,220	$134,400	$940	$168,000	$3,659	$43,913
$1,234	$136,000	$951	$170,000	$3,703	$44,435
$1,249	$137,600	$962	$172,000	$3,747	$44,958
$1,263	$139,200	$973	$174,000	$3,790	$45,481
$1,278	$140,800	$985	$176,000	$3,834	$46,004
$1,292	$142,400	$996	$178,000	$3,877	$46,526
$1,307	$144,000	$1,007	$180,000	$3,921	$47,049
$1,321	$145,600	$1,018	$182,000	$3,964	$47,572
$1,336	$147,200	$1,029	$184,000	$4,008	$48,095
$1,350	$148,800	$1,040	$186,000	$4,051	$48,617
$1,365	$150,400	$1,052	$188,000	$4,095	$49,140
$1,380	$152,000	$1,063	$190,000	$4,139	$49,663
$1,394	$153,600	$1,074	$192,000	$4,182	$50,186
$1,409	$155,200	$1,085	$194,000	$4,226	$50,708
$1,423	$156,800	$1,096	$196,000	$4,269	$51,231
$1,438	$158,400	$1,108	$198,000	$4,313	$51,754
$1,452	$160,000	$1,119	$200,000	$4,356	$52,277

8% Interest, 30-Year Term, 20% Down

(2% of purchase price assumed for taxes and insurance; 33% of gross monthly income allowed for mortgage payment)

Monthly payment	Maximum mortgage Amount	P & I	Maximum price	Income to qualify Monthly	Annual
$377	$40,000	$294	$50,000	$1,131	$13,567
$392	$41,600	$305	$52,000	$1,176	$14,109
$407	$43,200	$317	$54,000	$1,221	$14,652
$422	$44,800	$329	$56,000	$1,266	$15,195
$437	$46,400	$340	$58,000	$1,311	$15,737
$452	$48,000	$352	$60,000	$1,357	$16,280
$467	$49,600	$364	$62,000	$1,402	$16,823
$482	$51,200	$376	$64,000	$1,447	$17,365
$497	$52,800	$387	$66,000	$1,492	$17,908
$513	$54,400	$399	$68,000	$1,538	$18,451
$528	$56,000	$411	$70,000	$1,583	$18,993
$543	$57,600	$423	$72,000	$1,628	$19,536
$558	$59,200	$434	$74,000	$1,673	$20,079
$573	$60,800	$446	$76,000	$1,718	$20,621
$588	$62,400	$458	$78,000	$1,764	$21,164
$603	$64,000	$470	$80,000	$1,809	$21,707
$618	$65,600	$481	$82,000	$1,854	$22,249
$633	$67,200	$493	$84,000	$1,899	$22,792
$648	$68,800	$505	$86,000	$1,945	$23,335
$663	$70,400	$517	$88,000	$1,990	$23,877
$678	$72,000	$528	$90,000	$2,035	$24,420
$693	$73,600	$540	$92,000	$2,080	$24,962
$708	$75,200	$552	$94,000	$2,125	$25,505
$724	$76,800	$564	$96,000	$2,171	$26,048
$739	$78,400	$575	$98,000	$2,216	$26,590
$754	$80,000	$587	$100,000	$2,261	$27,133
$769	$81,600	$599	$102,000	$2,306	$27,676
$784	$83,200	$611	$104,000	$2,352	$28,218
$799	$84,800	$622	$106,000	$2,397	$28,761
$814	$86,400	$634	$108,000	$2,442	$29,304
$829	$88,000	$646	$110,000	$2,487	$29,846
$844	$89,600	$657	$112,000	$2,532	$30,389
$859	$91,200	$669	$114,000	$2,578	$30,932
$874	$92,800	$681	$116,000	$2,623	$31,474
$889	$94,400	$693	$118,000	$2,668	$32,017
$904	$96,000	$704	$120,000	$2,713	$32,560
$920	$97,600	$716	$122,000	$2,759	$33,102
$935	$99,200	$728	$124,000	$2,804	$33,645
$950	$100,800	$740	$126,000	$2,849	$34,188
$965	$102,400	$751	$128,000	$2,894	$34,730
$980	$104,000	$763	$130,000	$2,939	$35,273
$995	$105,600	$775	$132,000	$2,985	$35,816
$1,010	$107,200	$787	$134,000	$3,030	$36,358

Monthly payment	Maximum mortgage		Maximum price	Income to qualify	
	Amount	P & I		Monthly	Annual
$1,025	$108,800	$798	$136,000	$3,075	$36,901
$1,040	$110,400	$810	$138,000	$3,120	$37,444
$1,055	$112,000	$822	$140,000	$3,166	$37,986
$1,070	$113,600	$834	$142,000	$3,211	$38,529
$1,085	$115,200	$845	$144,000	$3,256	$39,072
$1,100	$116,800	$857	$146,000	$3,301	$39,614
$1,115	$118,400	$869	$148,000	$3,346	$40,157
$1,131	$120,000	$881	$150,000	$3,392	$40,700
$1,146	$121,600	$892	$152,000	$3,437	$41,242
$1,161	$123,200	$904	$154,000	$3,482	$41,785
$1,176	$124,800	$916	$156,000	$3,527	$42,328
$1,191	$126,400	$928	$158,000	$3,573	$42,870
$1,206	$128,000	$939	$160,000	$3,618	$43,413
$1,221	$129,600	$951	$162,000	$3,663	$43,956
$1,236	$131,200	$963	$164,000	$3,708	$44,498
$1,251	$132,800	$974	$166,000	$3,753	$45,041
$1,266	$134,400	$986	$168,000	$3,799	$45,584
$1,281	$136,000	$998	$170,000	$3,844	$46,126
$1,296	$137,600	$1,010	$172,000	$3,889	$46,669
$1,311	$139,200	$1,021	$174,000	$3,934	$47,212
$1,327	$140,800	$1,033	$176,000	$3,980	$47,754
$1,342	$142,400	$1,045	$178,000	$4,025	$48,297
$1,357	$144,000	$1,057	$180,000	$4,070	$48,840
$1,372	$145,600	$1,068	$182,000	$4,115	$49,382
$1,387	$147,200	$1,080	$184,000	$4,160	$49,925
$1,402	$148,800	$1,092	$186,000	$4,206	$50,468
$1,417	$150,400	$1,104	$188,000	$4,251	$51,010
$1,432	$152,000	$1,115	$190,000	$4,296	$51,553
$1,447	$153,600	$1,127	$192,000	$4,341	$52,096
$1,462	$155,200	$1,139	$194,000	$4,387	$52,638
$1,477	$156,800	$1,151	$196,000	$4,432	$53,181
$1,492	$158,400	$1,162	$198,000	$4,477	$53,724
$1,507	$160,000	$1,174	$200,000	$4,522	$54,266

8½% Interest, 30-Year Term, 20% Down

(2% of purchase price assumed for taxes and insurance; 33% of gross monthly income allowed for mortgage payment)

Monthly payment	Maximum mortgage		Maximum price	Income to qualify	
	Amount	P & I		Monthly	Annual
$391	$40,000	$308	$50,000	$1,173	$14,073
$407	$41,600	$320	$52,000	$1,220	$14,636
$422	$43,200	$332	$54,000	$1,267	$15,199
$438	$44,800	$344	$56,000	$1,313	$15,761
$453	$46,400	$357	$58,000	$1,360	$16,324
$469	$48,000	$369	$60,000	$1,407	$16,887
$485	$49,600	$381	$62,000	$1,454	$17,450
$500	$51,200	$394	$64,000	$1,501	$18,013
$516	$52,800	$406	$66,000	$1,548	$18,576
$532	$54,400	$418	$68,000	$1,595	$19,139
$547	$56,000	$431	$70,000	$1,642	$19,702
$563	$57,600	$443	$72,000	$1,689	$20,265
$579	$59,200	$455	$74,000	$1,736	$20,828
$594	$60,800	$468	$76,000	$1,783	$21,391
$610	$62,400	$480	$78,000	$1,829	$21,953
$625	$64,000	$492	$80,000	$1,876	$22,516
$641	$65,600	$504	$82,000	$1,923	$23,079
$657	$67,200	$517	$84,000	$1,970	$23,642
$672	$68,800	$529	$86,000	$2,017	$24,205
$688	$70,400	$541	$88,000	$2,064	$24,768
$704	$72,000	$554	$90,000	$2,111	$25,331
$719	$73,600	$566	$92,000	$2,158	$25,894
$735	$75,200	$578	$94,000	$2,205	$26,457
$751	$76,800	$591	$96,000	$2,252	$27,020
$766	$78,400	$603	$98,000	$2,299	$27,583
$782	$80,000	$615	$100,000	$2,345	$28,145
$797	$81,600	$627	$102,000	$2,392	$28,708
$813	$83,200	$640	$104,000	$2,439	$29,271
$829	$84,800	$652	$106,000	$2,486	$29,834
$844	$86,400	$664	$108,000	$2,533	$30,397
$860	$88,000	$677	$110,000	$2,580	$30,960
$876	$89,600	$689	$112,000	$2,627	$31,523
$891	$91,200	$701	$114,000	$2,674	$32,086
$907	$92,800	$714	$116,000	$2,721	$32,649
$923	$94,400	$726	$118,000	$2,768	$33,212
$938	$96,000	$738	$120,000	$2,815	$33,775
$954	$97,600	$750	$122,000	$2,861	$34,337
$969	$99,200	$763	$124,000	$2,908	$34,900
$985	$100,800	$775	$126,000	$2,955	$35,463
$1,001	$102,400	$787	$128,000	$3,002	$36,026
$1,016	$104,000	$800	$130,000	$3,049	$36,589
$1,032	$105,600	$812	$132,000	$3,096	$37,152
$1,048	$107,200	$824	$134,000	$3,143	$37,715

Monthly payment	Maximum mortgage		Maximum price	Income to qualify	
	Amount	P & I		Monthly	Annual
$1,063	$108,800	$837	$136,000	$3,190	$38,278
$1,079	$110,400	$849	$138,000	$3,237	$38,841
$1,095	$112,000	$861	$140,000	$3,284	$39,404
$1,110	$113,600	$874	$142,000	$3,331	$39,967
$1,126	$115,200	$886	$144,000	$3,377	$40,529
$1,141	$116,800	$898	$146,000	$3,424	$41,092
$1,157	$118,400	$910	$148,000	$3,471	$41,655
$1,173	$120,000	$923	$150,000	$3,518	$42,218
$1,188	$121,600	$935	$152,000	$3,565	$42,781
$1,204	$123,200	$947	$154,000	$3,612	$43,344
$1,220	$124,800	$960	$156,000	$3,659	$43,907
$1,235	$126,400	$972	$158,000	$3,706	$44,470
$1,251	$128,000	$984	$160,000	$3,753	$45,033
$1,267	$129,600	$997	$162,000	$3,800	$45,596
$1,282	$131,200	$1,009	$164,000	$3,847	$46,159
$1,298	$132,800	$1,021	$166,000	$3,893	$46,721
$1,313	$134,400	$1,033	$168,000	$3,940	$47,284
$1,329	$136,000	$1,046	$170,000	$3,987	$47,847
$1,345	$137,600	$1,058	$172,000	$4,034	$48,410
$1,360	$139,200	$1,070	$174,000	$4,081	$48,973
$1,376	$140,800	$1,083	$176,000	$4,128	$49,536
$1,392	$142,400	$1,095	$178,000	$4,175	$50,099
$1,407	$144,000	$1,107	$180,000	$4,222	$50,662
$1,423	$145,600	$1,120	$182,000	$4,269	$51,225
$1,439	$147,200	$1,132	$184,000	$4,316	$51,788
$1,454	$148,800	$1,144	$186,000	$4,363	$52,351
$1,470	$150,400	$1,156	$188,000	$4,409	$52,913
$1,485	$152,000	$1,169	$190,000	$4,456	$53,476
$1,501	$153,600	$1,181	$192,000	$4,503	$54,039
$1,517	$155,200	$1,193	$194,000	$4,550	$54,602
$1,532	$156,800	$1,206	$196,000	$4,597	$55,165
$1,548	$158,400	$1,218	$198,000	$4,644	$55,728
$1,564	$160,000	$1,230	$200,000	$4,691	$56,291

9% Interest, 30-Year Term, 20% Down

(2% of purchase price assumed for taxes and insurance; 33% of gross monthly income allowed for mortgage payment)

Monthly payment	Maximum mortgage Amount	P & I	Maximum price	Income to qualify Monthly	Annual
$405	$40,000	$322	$50,000	$1,216	$14,587
$421	$41,600	$335	$52,000	$1,264	$15,170
$438	$43,200	$348	$54,000	$1,313	$15,754
$454	$44,800	$360	$56,000	$1,361	$16,337
$470	$46,400	$373	$58,000	$1,410	$16,921
$486	$48,000	$386	$60,000	$1,459	$17,504
$502	$49,600	$399	$62,000	$1,507	$18,088
$519	$51,200	$412	$64,000	$1,556	$18,671
$535	$52,800	$425	$66,000	$1,605	$19,255
$551	$54,400	$438	$68,000	$1,653	$19,838
$567	$56,000	$451	$70,000	$1,702	$20,422
$583	$57,600	$463	$72,000	$1,750	$21,005
$600	$59,200	$476	$74,000	$1,799	$21,588
$616	$60,800	$489	$76,000	$1,848	$22,172
$632	$62,400	$502	$78,000	$1,896	$22,755
$648	$64,000	$515	$80,000	$1,945	$23,339
$665	$65,600	$528	$82,000	$1,994	$23,922
$681	$67,200	$541	$84,000	$2,042	$24,506
$697	$68,800	$554	$86,000	$2,091	$25,089
$713	$70,400	$566	$88,000	$2,139	$25,673
$729	$72,000	$579	$90,000	$2,188	$26,256
$746	$73,600	$592	$92,000	$2,237	$26,840
$762	$75,200	$605	$94,000	$2,285	$27,423
$778	$76,800	$618	$96,000	$2,334	$28,007
$794	$78,400	$631	$98,000	$2,383	$28,590
$810	$80,000	$644	$100,000	$2,431	$29,174
$827	$81,600	$657	$102,000	$2,480	$29,757
$843	$83,200	$669	$104,000	$2,528	$30,341
$859	$84,800	$682	$106,000	$2,577	$30,924
$875	$86,400	$695	$108,000	$2,626	$31,508
$891	$88,000	$708	$110,000	$2,674	$32,091
$908	$89,600	$721	$112,000	$2,723	$32,674
$924	$91,200	$734	$114,000	$2,771	$33,258
$940	$92,800	$747	$116,000	$2,820	$33,841
$956	$94,400	$760	$118,000	$2,869	$34,425
$972	$96,000	$772	$120,000	$2,917	$35,008
$989	$97,600	$785	$122,000	$2,966	$35,592
$1,005	$99,200	$798	$124,000	$3,015	$36,175
$1,021	$100,800	$811	$126,000	$3,063	$36,759
$1,037	$102,400	$824	$128,000	$3,112	$37,342
$1,053	$104,000	$837	$130,000	$3,160	$37,926
$1,070	$105,600	$850	$132,000	$3,209	$38,509
$1,086	$107,200	$863	$134,000	$3,258	$39,093

Monthly payment	Maximum mortgage		Maximum price	Income to qualify	
	Amount	P & I		Monthly	Annual
$1,102	$108,800	$875	$136,000	$3,306	$39,676
$1,118	$110,400	$888	$138,000	$3,355	$40,260
$1,135	$112,000	$901	$140,000	$3,404	$40,843
$1,151	$113,600	$914	$142,000	$3,452	$41,427
$1,167	$115,200	$927	$144,000	$3,501	$42,010
$1,183	$116,800	$940	$146,000	$3,549	$42,594
$1,199	$118,400	$953	$148,000	$3,598	$43,177
$1,216	$120,000	$966	$150,000	$3,647	$43,760
$1,232	$121,600	$978	$152,000	$3,695	$44,344
$1,248	$123,200	$991	$154,000	$3,744	$44,927
$1,264	$124,800	$1,004	$156,000	$3,793	$45,511
$1,280	$126,400	$1,017	$158,000	$3,841	$46,094
$1,297	$128,000	$1,030	$160,000	$3,890	$46,678
$1,313	$129,600	$1,043	$162,000	$3,938	$47,261
$1,329	$131,200	$1,056	$164,000	$3,987	$47,845
$1,345	$132,800	$1,069	$166,000	$4,036	$48,428
$1,361	$134,400	$1,081	$168,000	$4,084	$49,012
$1,378	$136,000	$1,094	$170,000	$4,133	$49,595
$1,394	$137,600	$1,107	$172,000	$4,182	$50,179
$1,410	$139,200	$1,120	$174,000	$4,230	$50,762
$1,426	$140,800	$1,133	$176,000	$4,279	$51,346
$1,442	$142,400	$1,146	$178,000	$4,327	$51,929
$1,459	$144,000	$1,159	$180,000	$4,376	$52,513
$1,475	$145,600	$1,172	$182,000	$4,425	$53,096
$1,491	$147,200	$1,184	$184,000	$4,473	$53,679
$1,507	$148,800	$1,197	$186,000	$4,522	$54,263
$1,524	$150,400	$1,210	$188,000	$4,571	$54,846
$1,540	$152,000	$1,223	$190,000	$4,619	$55,430
$1,556	$153,600	$1,236	$192,000	$4,668	$56,013
$1,572	$155,200	$1,249	$194,000	$4,716	$56,597
$1,588	$156,800	$1,262	$196,000	$4,765	$57,180
$1,605	$158,400	$1,275	$198,000	$4,814	$57,764
$1,621	$160,000	$1,287	$200,000	$4,862	$58,347

9½% Interest, 30-Year Term, 20% Down

(2% of purchase price assumed for taxes and insurance; 33% of gross monthly income allowed for mortgage payment)

Monthly payment	Maximum mortgage Amount	Maximum mortgage P & I	Maximum price	Income to qualify Monthly	Income to qualify Annual
$420	$40,000	$336	$50,000	$1,259	$15,109
$436	$41,600	$350	$52,000	$1,309	$15,713
$453	$43,200	$363	$54,000	$1,360	$16,317
$470	$44,800	$377	$56,000	$1,410	$16,922
$487	$46,400	$390	$58,000	$1,460	$17,526
$504	$48,000	$404	$60,000	$1,511	$18,130
$520	$49,600	$417	$62,000	$1,561	$18,735
$537	$51,200	$431	$64,000	$1,612	$19,339
$554	$52,800	$444	$66,000	$1,662	$19,943
$571	$54,400	$457	$68,000	$1,712	$20,548
$588	$56,000	$471	$70,000	$1,763	$21,152
$604	$57,600	$484	$72,000	$1,813	$21,756
$621	$59,200	$498	$74,000	$1,863	$22,361
$638	$60,800	$511	$76,000	$1,914	$22,965
$655	$62,400	$525	$78,000	$1,964	$23,569
$671	$64,000	$538	$80,000	$2,014	$24,174
$688	$65,600	$552	$82,000	$2,065	$24,778
$705	$67,200	$565	$84,000	$2,115	$25,382
$722	$68,800	$579	$86,000	$2,166	$25,987
$739	$70,400	$592	$88,000	$2,216	$26,591
$755	$72,000	$605	$90,000	$2,266	$27,195
$772	$73,600	$619	$92,000	$2,317	$27,800
$789	$75,200	$632	$94,000	$2,367	$28,404
$806	$76,800	$646	$96,000	$2,417	$29,008
$823	$78,400	$659	$98,000	$2,468	$29,613
$839	$80,000	$673	$100,000	$2,518	$30,217
$856	$81,600	$686	$102,000	$2,568	$30,821
$873	$83,200	$700	$104,000	$2,619	$31,426
$890	$84,800	$713	$106,000	$2,669	$32,030
$907	$86,400	$727	$108,000	$2,720	$32,634
$923	$88,000	$740	$110,000	$2,770	$33,239
$940	$89,600	$753	$112,000	$2,820	$33,843
$957	$91,200	$767	$114,000	$2,871	$34,447
$974	$92,800	$780	$116,000	$2,921	$35,052
$990	$94,400	$794	$118,000	$2,971	$35,656
$1,007	$96,000	$807	$120,000	$3,022	$36,260
$1,024	$97,600	$821	$122,000	$3,072	$36,865
$1,041	$99,200	$834	$124,000	$3,122	$37,469
$1,058	$100,800	$848	$126,000	$3,173	$38,073
$1,074	$102,400	$861	$128,000	$3,223	$38,678
$1,091	$104,000	$875	$130,000	$3,274	$39,282
$1,108	$105,600	$888	$132,000	$3,324	$39,887
$1,125	$107,200	$901	$134,000	$3,374	$40,491

Monthly payment	Maximum mortgage		Maximum price	Income to qualify	
	Amount	P & I		Monthly	Annual
$1,142	$108,800	$915	$136,000	$3,425	$41,095
$1,158	$110,400	$928	$138,000	$3,475	$41,700
$1,175	$112,000	$942	$140,000	$3,525	$42,304
$1,192	$113,600	$955	$142,000	$3,576	$42,908
$1,209	$115,200	$969	$144,000	$3,626	$43,513
$1,225	$116,800	$982	$146,000	$3,676	$44,117
$1,242	$118,400	$996	$148,000	$3,727	$44,721
$1,259	$120,000	$1,009	$150,000	$3,777	$45,326
$1,276	$121,600	$1,022	$152,000	$3,827	$45,930
$1,293	$123,200	$1,036	$154,000	$3,878	$46,534
$1,309	$124,800	$1,049	$156,000	$3,928	$47,139
$1,326	$126,400	$1,063	$158,000	$3,979	$47,743
$1,343	$128,000	$1,076	$160,000	$4,029	$48,347
$1,360	$129,600	$1,090	$162,000	$4,079	$48,952
$1,377	$131,200	$1,103	$164,000	$4,130	$49,556
$1,393	$132,800	$1,117	$166,000	$4,180	$50,160
$1,410	$134,400	$1,130	$168,000	$4,230	$50,765
$1,427	$136,000	$1,144	$170,000	$4,281	$51,369
$1,444	$137,600	$1,157	$172,000	$4,331	$51,973
$1,460	$139,200	$1,170	$174,000	$4,381	$52,578
$1,477	$140,800	$1,184	$176,000	$4,432	$53,182
$1,494	$142,400	$1,197	$178,000	$4,482	$53,786
$1,511	$144,000	$1,211	$180,000	$4,533	$54,391
$1,528	$145,600	$1,224	$182,000	$4,583	$54,995
$1,544	$147,200	$1,238	$184,000	$4,633	$55,599
$1,561	$148,800	$1,251	$186,000	$4,684	$56,204
$1,578	$150,400	$1,265	$188,000	$4,734	$56,808
$1,595	$152,000	$1,278	$190,000	$4,784	$57,412
$1,612	$153,600	$1,292	$192,000	$4,835	$58,017
$1,628	$155,200	$1,305	$194,000	$4,885	$58,621
$1,645	$156,800	$1,318	$196,000	$4,935	$59,225
$1,662	$158,400	$1,332	$198,000	$4,986	$59,830
$1,679	$160,000	$1,345	$200,000	$5,036	$60,434

10% Interest, 30-Year Term, 20% Down

(2% of purchase price assumed for taxes and insurance; 33% of gross monthly income allowed for mortgage payment)

Monthly payment	Maximum mortgage		Maximum price	Income to qualify	
	Amount	P & I		Monthly	Annual
$434	$40,000	$351	$50,000	$1,303	$15,637
$452	$41,600	$365	$52,000	$1,355	$16,263
$469	$43,200	$379	$54,000	$1,407	$16,888
$486	$44,800	$393	$56,000	$1,459	$17,514
$504	$46,400	$407	$58,000	$1,512	$18,139
$521	$48,000	$421	$60,000	$1,564	$18,765
$539	$49,600	$435	$62,000	$1,616	$19,390
$556	$51,200	$449	$64,000	$1,668	$20,016
$573	$52,800	$463	$66,000	$1,720	$20,641
$591	$54,400	$477	$68,000	$1,772	$21,267
$608	$56,000	$491	$70,000	$1,824	$21,892
$625	$57,600	$505	$72,000	$1,876	$22,517
$643	$59,200	$520	$74,000	$1,929	$23,143
$660	$60,800	$534	$76,000	$1,981	$23,768
$678	$62,400	$548	$78,000	$2,033	$24,394
$695	$64,000	$562	$80,000	$2,085	$25,019
$712	$65,600	$576	$82,000	$2,137	$25,645
$730	$67,200	$590	$84,000	$2,189	$26,270
$747	$68,800	$604	$86,000	$2,241	$26,896
$764	$70,400	$618	$88,000	$2,293	$27,521
$782	$72,000	$632	$90,000	$2,346	$28,147
$799	$73,600	$646	$92,000	$2,398	$28,772
$817	$75,200	$660	$94,000	$2,450	$29,398
$834	$76,800	$674	$96,000	$2,502	$30,023
$851	$78,400	$688	$98,000	$2,554	$30,649
$869	$80,000	$702	$100,000	$2,606	$31,274
$886	$81,600	$716	$102,000	$2,658	$31,900
$903	$83,200	$730	$104,000	$2,710	$32,525
$921	$84,800	$744	$106,000	$2,763	$33,151
$938	$86,400	$758	$108,000	$2,815	$33,776
$956	$88,000	$772	$110,000	$2,867	$34,402
$973	$89,600	$786	$112,000	$2,919	$35,027
$990	$91,200	$800	$114,000	$2,971	$35,653
$1,008	$92,800	$814	$116,000	$3,023	$36,278
$1,025	$94,400	$828	$118,000	$3,075	$36,904
$1,042	$96,000	$842	$120,000	$3,127	$37,529
$1,060	$97,600	$857	$122,000	$3,180	$38,155
$1,077	$99,200	$871	$124,000	$3,232	$38,780
$1,095	$100,800	$885	$126,000	$3,284	$39,406
$1,112	$102,400	$899	$128,000	$3,336	$40,031
$1,129	$104,000	$913	$130,000	$3,388	$40,657
$1,147	$105,600	$927	$132,000	$3,440	$41,282
$1,164	$107,200	$941	$134,000	$3,492	$41,908

| Monthly payment | Maximum mortgage | | Maximum price | Income to qualify | |
---	Amount	P & I	---	Monthly	Annual
$1,181	$108,800	$955	$136,000	$3,544	$42,533
$1,199	$110,400	$969	$138,000	$3,597	$43,159
$1,216	$112,000	$983	$140,000	$3,649	$43,784
$1,234	$113,600	$997	$142,000	$3,701	$44,410
$1,251	$115,200	$1,011	$144,000	$3,753	$45,035
$1,268	$116,800	$1,025	$146,000	$3,805	$45,660
$1,286	$118,400	$1,039	$148,000	$3,857	$46,286
$1,303	$120,000	$1,053	$150,000	$3,909	$46,911
$1,320	$121,600	$1,067	$152,000	$3,961	$47,537
$1,338	$123,200	$1,081	$154,000	$4,014	$48,162
$1,355	$124,800	$1,095	$156,000	$4,066	$48,788
$1,373	$126,400	$1,109	$158,000	$4,118	$49,413
$1,390	$128,000	$1,123	$160,000	$4,170	$50,039
$1,407	$129,600	$1,137	$162,000	$4,222	$50,664
$1,425	$131,200	$1,151	$164,000	$4,274	$51,290
$1,442	$132,800	$1,165	$166,000	$4,326	$51,915
$1,459	$134,400	$1,179	$168,000	$4,378	$52,541
$1,477	$136,000	$1,194	$170,000	$4,431	$53,166
$1,494	$137,600	$1,208	$172,000	$4,483	$53,792
$1,512	$139,200	$1,222	$174,000	$4,535	$54,417
$1,529	$140,800	$1,236	$176,000	$4,587	$55,043
$1,546	$142,400	$1,250	$178,000	$4,639	$55,668
$1,564	$144,000	$1,264	$180,000	$4,691	$56,294
$1,581	$145,600	$1,278	$182,000	$4,743	$56,919
$1,598	$147,200	$1,292	$184,000	$4,795	$57,545
$1,616	$148,800	$1,306	$186,000	$4,848	$58,170
$1,633	$150,400	$1,320	$188,000	$4,900	$58,796
$1,651	$152,000	$1,334	$190,000	$4,952	$59,421
$1,668	$153,600	$1,348	$192,000	$5,004	$60,047
$1,685	$155,200	$1,362	$194,000	$5,056	$60,672
$1,703	$156,800	$1,376	$196,000	$5,108	$61,298
$1,720	$158,400	$1,390	$198,000	$5,160	$61,923
$1,737	$160,000	$1,404	$200,000	$5,212	$62,549

10½% Interest, 30-Year Term, 20% Down

(2% of purchase price assumed for taxes and insurance; 33% of gross monthly income allowed for mortgage payment)

Monthly payment	Maximum mortgage Amount	P & I	Maximum price	Income to qualify Monthly	Annual
$449	$40,000	$366	$50,000	$1,348	$16,172
$467	$41,600	$381	$52,000	$1,402	$16,819
$485	$43,200	$395	$54,000	$1,456	$17,466
$503	$44,800	$410	$56,000	$1,509	$18,113
$521	$46,400	$424	$58,000	$1,563	$18,760
$539	$48,000	$439	$60,000	$1,617	$19,407
$557	$49,600	$454	$62,000	$1,671	$20,054
$575	$51,200	$468	$64,000	$1,725	$20,701
$593	$52,800	$483	$66,000	$1,779	$21,348
$611	$54,400	$498	$68,000	$1,833	$21,994
$629	$56,000	$512	$70,000	$1,887	$22,641
$647	$57,600	$527	$72,000	$1,941	$23,288
$665	$59,200	$542	$74,000	$1,995	$23,935
$683	$60,800	$556	$76,000	$2,049	$24,582
$701	$62,400	$571	$78,000	$2,102	$25,229
$719	$64,000	$585	$80,000	$2,156	$25,876
$737	$65,600	$600	$82,000	$2,210	$26,523
$755	$67,200	$615	$84,000	$2,264	$27,170
$773	$68,800	$629	$86,000	$2,318	$27,817
$791	$70,400	$644	$88,000	$2,372	$28,463
$809	$72,000	$659	$90,000	$2,426	$29,110
$827	$73,600	$673	$92,000	$2,480	$29,757
$845	$75,200	$688	$94,000	$2,534	$30,404
$863	$76,800	$703	$96,000	$2,588	$31,051
$880	$78,400	$717	$98,000	$2,641	$31,698
$898	$80,000	$732	$100,000	$2,695	$32,345
$916	$81,600	$746	$102,000	$2,749	$32,992
$934	$83,200	$761	$104,000	$2,803	$33,639
$952	$84,800	$776	$106,000	$2,857	$34,285
$970	$86,400	$790	$108,000	$2,911	$34,932
$988	$88,000	$805	$110,000	$2,965	$35,579
$1,006	$89,600	$820	$112,000	$3,019	$36,226
$1,024	$91,200	$834	$114,000	$3,073	$36,873
$1,042	$92,800	$849	$116,000	$3,127	$37,520
$1,060	$94,400	$864	$118,000	$3,181	$38,167
$1,078	$96,000	$878	$120,000	$3,234	$38,814
$1,096	$97,600	$893	$122,000	$3,288	$39,461
$1,114	$99,200	$907	$124,000	$3,342	$40,108
$1,132	$100,800	$922	$126,000	$3,396	$40,754
$1,150	$102,400	$937	$128,000	$3,450	$41,401
$1,168	$104,000	$951	$130,000	$3,504	$42,048
$1,186	$105,600	$966	$132,000	$3,558	$42,695
$1,204	$107,200	$981	$134,000	$3,612	$43,342

Monthly payment	Maximum mortgage		Maximum price	Income to qualify	
	Amount	P & I		Monthly	Annual
$1,222	$108,800	$995	$136,000	$3,666	$43,989
$1,240	$110,400	$1,010	$138,000	$3,720	$44,636
$1,258	$112,000	$1,025	$140,000	$3,774	$45,283
$1,276	$113,600	$1,039	$142,000	$3,827	$45,930
$1,294	$115,200	$1,054	$144,000	$3,881	$46,577
$1,312	$116,800	$1,068	$146,000	$3,935	$47,223
$1,330	$118,400	$1,083	$148,000	$3,989	$47,870
$1,348	$120,000	$1,098	$150,000	$4,043	$48,517
$1,366	$121,600	$1,112	$152,000	$4,097	$49,164
$1,384	$123,200	$1,127	$154,000	$4,151	$49,811
$1,402	$124,800	$1,142	$156,000	$4,205	$50,458
$1,420	$126,400	$1,156	$158,000	$4,259	$51,105
$1,438	$128,000	$1,171	$160,000	$4,313	$51,752
$1,456	$129,600	$1,186	$162,000	$4,367	$52,399
$1,473	$131,200	$1,200	$164,000	$4,420	$53,045
$1,491	$132,800	$1,215	$166,000	$4,474	$53,692
$1,509	$134,400	$1,229	$168,000	$4,528	$54,339
$1,527	$136,000	$1,244	$170,000	$4,582	$54,986
$1,545	$137,600	$1,259	$172,000	$4,636	$55,633
$1,563	$139,200	$1,273	$174,000	$4,690	$56,280
$1,581	$140,800	$1,288	$176,000	$4,744	$56,927
$1,599	$142,400	$1,303	$178,000	$4,798	$57,574
$1,617	$144,000	$1,317	$180,000	$4,852	$58,221
$1,635	$145,600	$1,332	$182,000	$4,906	$58,868
$1,653	$147,200	$1,347	$184,000	$4,960	$59,514
$1,671	$148,800	$1,361	$186,000	$5,013	$60,161
$1,689	$150,400	$1,376	$188,000	$5,067	$60,808
$1,707	$152,000	$1,390	$190,000	$5,121	$61,455
$1,725	$153,600	$1,405	$192,000	$5,175	$62,102
$1,743	$155,200	$1,420	$194,000	$5,229	$62,749
$1,761	$156,800	$1,434	$196,000	$5,283	$63,396
$1,779	$158,400	$1,449	$198,000	$5,337	$64,043
$1,797	$160,000	$1,464	$200,000	$5,391	$64,690

11% Interest, 30-Year Term, 20% Down

(2% of purchase price assumed for taxes and insurance; 33% of gross monthly income allowed for mortgage payment)

Monthly payment	Maximum mortgage		Maximum price	Income to qualify	
	Amount	P & I		Monthly	Annual
$464	$40,000	$381	$50,000	$1,393	$16,714
$483	$41,600	$396	$52,000	$1,449	$17,382
$501	$43,200	$411	$54,000	$1,504	$18,051
$520	$44,800	$427	$56,000	$1,560	$18,719
$539	$46,400	$442	$58,000	$1,616	$19,388
$557	$48,000	$457	$60,000	$1,671	$20,056
$576	$49,600	$472	$62,000	$1,727	$20,725
$594	$51,200	$488	$64,000	$1,783	$21,394
$613	$52,800	$503	$66,000	$1,839	$22,062
$631	$54,400	$518	$68,000	$1,894	$22,731
$650	$56,000	$533	$70,000	$1,950	$23,399
$669	$57,600	$549	$72,000	$2,006	$24,068
$687	$59,200	$564	$74,000	$2,061	$24,736
$706	$60,800	$579	$76,000	$2,117	$25,405
$724	$62,400	$594	$78,000	$2,173	$26,073
$743	$64,000	$609	$80,000	$2,228	$26,742
$761	$65,600	$625	$82,000	$2,284	$27,410
$780	$67,200	$640	$84,000	$2,340	$28,079
$799	$68,800	$655	$86,000	$2,396	$28,748
$817	$70,400	$670	$88,000	$2,451	$29,416
$836	$72,000	$686	$90,000	$2,507	$30,085
$854	$73,600	$701	$92,000	$2,563	$30,753
$873	$75,200	$716	$94,000	$2,618	$31,422
$891	$76,800	$731	$96,000	$2,674	$32,090
$910	$78,400	$747	$98,000	$2,730	$32,759
$929	$80,000	$762	$100,000	$2,786	$33,427
$947	$81,600	$777	$102,000	$2,841	$34,096
$966	$83,200	$792	$104,000	$2,897	$34,764
$984	$84,800	$808	$106,000	$2,953	$35,433
$1,003	$86,400	$823	$108,000	$3,008	$36,102
$1,021	$88,000	$838	$110,000	$3,064	$36,770
$1,040	$89,600	$853	$112,000	$3,120	$37,439
$1,059	$91,200	$869	$114,000	$3,176	$38,107
$1,077	$92,800	$884	$116,000	$3,231	$38,776
$1,096	$94,400	$899	$118,000	$3,287	$39,444
$1,114	$96,000	$914	$120,000	$3,343	$40,113
$1,133	$97,600	$929	$122,000	$3,398	$40,781
$1,151	$99,200	$945	$124,000	$3,454	$41,450
$1,170	$100,800	$960	$126,000	$3,510	$42,119
$1,189	$102,400	$975	$128,000	$3,566	$42,787
$1,207	$104,000	$990	$130,000	$3,621	$43,456
$1,226	$105,600	$1,006	$132,000	$3,677	$44,124
$1,244	$107,200	$1,021	$134,000	$3,733	$44,793

249

Monthly payment	Maximum mortgage		Maximum price	Income to qualify	
	Amount	P & I		Monthly	Annual
$1,263	$108,800	$1,036	$136,000	$3,788	$45,461
$1,281	$110,400	$1,051	$138,000	$3,844	$46,130
$1,300	$112,000	$1,067	$140,000	$3,900	$46,798
$1,319	$113,600	$1,082	$142,000	$3,956	$47,467
$1,337	$115,200	$1,097	$144,000	$4,011	$48,135
$1,356	$116,800	$1,112	$146,000	$4,067	$48,804
$1,374	$118,400	$1,128	$148,000	$4,123	$49,473
$1,393	$120,000	$1,143	$150,000	$4,178	$50,141
$1,411	$121,600	$1,158	$152,000	$4,234	$50,810
$1,430	$123,200	$1,173	$154,000	$4,290	$51,478
$1,449	$124,800	$1,189	$156,000	$4,346	$52,147
$1,467	$126,400	$1,204	$158,000	$4,401	$52,815
$1,486	$128,000	$1,219	$160,000	$4,457	$53,484
$1,504	$129,600	$1,234	$162,000	$4,513	$54,152
$1,523	$131,200	$1,249	$164,000	$4,568	$54,821
$1,541	$132,800	$1,265	$166,000	$4,624	$55,489
$1,560	$134,400	$1,280	$168,000	$4,680	$56,158
$1,579	$136,000	$1,295	$170,000	$4,736	$56,827
$1,597	$137,600	$1,310	$172,000	$4,791	$57,495
$1,616	$139,200	$1,326	$174,000	$4,847	$58,164
$1,634	$140,800	$1,341	$176,000	$4,903	$58,832
$1,653	$142,400	$1,356	$178,000	$4,958	$59,501
$1,671	$144,000	$1,371	$180,000	$5,014	$60,169
$1,690	$145,600	$1,387	$182,000	$5,070	$60,838
$1,709	$147,200	$1,402	$184,000	$5,126	$61,506
$1,727	$148,800	$1,417	$186,000	$5,181	$62,175
$1,746	$150,400	$1,432	$188,000	$5,237	$62,843
$1,764	$152,000	$1,448	$190,000	$5,293	$63,512
$1,783	$153,600	$1,463	$192,000	$5,348	$64,181
$1,801	$155,200	$1,478	$194,000	$5,404	$64,849
$1,820	$156,800	$1,493	$196,000	$5,460	$65,518
$1,839	$158,400	$1,509	$198,000	$5,516	$66,186
$1,857	$160,000	$1,524	$200,000	$5,571	$66,855

11½% Interest, 30-Year Term, 20% Down

(2% of purchase price assumed for taxes and insurance; 33% of gross monthly income allowed for mortgage payment)

Monthly payment	Maximum mortgage Amount	P & I	Maximum price	Income to qualify Monthly	Annual
$479	$40,000	$396	$50,000	$1,438	$17,260
$499	$41,600	$412	$52,000	$1,496	$17,951
$518	$43,200	$428	$54,000	$1,553	$18,641
$537	$44,800	$444	$56,000	$1,611	$19,332
$556	$46,400	$459	$58,000	$1,668	$20,022
$575	$48,000	$475	$60,000	$1,726	$20,712
$595	$49,600	$491	$62,000	$1,784	$21,403
$614	$51,200	$507	$64,000	$1,841	$22,093
$633	$52,800	$523	$66,000	$1,899	$22,784
$652	$54,400	$539	$68,000	$1,956	$23,474
$671	$56,000	$555	$70,000	$2,014	$24,164
$690	$57,600	$570	$72,000	$2,071	$24,855
$710	$59,200	$586	$74,000	$2,129	$25,545
$729	$60,800	$602	$76,000	$2,186	$26,236
$748	$62,400	$618	$78,000	$2,244	$26,926
$767	$64,000	$634	$80,000	$2,301	$27,617
$786	$65,600	$650	$82,000	$2,359	$28,307
$805	$67,200	$665	$84,000	$2,416	$28,997
$825	$68,800	$681	$86,000	$2,474	$29,688
$844	$70,400	$697	$88,000	$2,532	$30,378
$863	$72,000	$713	$90,000	$2,589	$31,069
$882	$73,600	$729	$92,000	$2,647	$31,759
$901	$75,200	$745	$94,000	$2,704	$32,449
$921	$76,800	$761	$96,000	$2,762	$33,140
$940	$78,400	$776	$98,000	$2,819	$33,830
$959	$80,000	$792	$100,000	$2,877	$34,521
$978	$81,600	$808	$102,000	$2,934	$35,211
$997	$83,200	$824	$104,000	$2,992	$35,901
$1,016	$84,800	$840	$106,000	$3,049	$36,592
$1,036	$86,400	$856	$108,000	$3,107	$37,282
$1,055	$88,000	$871	$110,000	$3,164	$37,973
$1,074	$89,600	$887	$112,000	$3,222	$38,663
$1,093	$91,200	$903	$114,000	$3,279	$39,354
$1,112	$92,800	$919	$116,000	$3,337	$40,044
$1,132	$94,400	$935	$118,000	$3,395	$40,734
$1,151	$96,000	$951	$120,000	$3,452	$41,425
$1,170	$97,600	$967	$122,000	$3,510	$42,115
$1,189	$99,200	$982	$124,000	$3,567	$42,806
$1,208	$100,800	$998	$126,000	$3,625	$43,496
$1,227	$102,400	$1,014	$128,000	$3,682	$44,186
$1,247	$104,000	$1,030	$130,000	$3,740	$44,877
$1,266	$105,600	$1,046	$132,000	$3,797	$45,567
$1,285	$107,200	$1,062	$134,000	$3,855	$46,258

Monthly payment	Maximum mortgage		Maximum price	Income to qualify	
	Amount	P & I		Monthly	Annual
$1,304	$108,800	$1,077	$136,000	$3,912	$46,948
$1,323	$110,400	$1,093	$138,000	$3,970	$47,638
$1,342	$112,000	$1,109	$140,000	$4,027	$48,329
$1,362	$113,600	$1,125	$142,000	$4,085	$49,019
$1,381	$115,200	$1,141	$144,000	$4,142	$49,710
$1,400	$116,800	$1,157	$146,000	$4,200	$50,400
$1,419	$118,400	$1,173	$148,000	$4,258	$51,091
$1,438	$120,000	$1,188	$150,000	$4,315	$51,781
$1,458	$121,600	$1,204	$152,000	$4,373	$52,471
$1,477	$123,200	$1,220	$154,000	$4,430	$53,162
$1,496	$124,800	$1,236	$156,000	$4,488	$53,852
$1,515	$126,400	$1,252	$158,000	$4,545	$54,543
$1,534	$128,000	$1,268	$160,000	$4,603	$55,233
$1,553	$129,600	$1,283	$162,000	$4,660	$55,923
$1,573	$131,200	$1,299	$164,000	$4,718	$56,614
$1,592	$132,800	$1,315	$166,000	$4,775	$57,304
$1,611	$134,400	$1,331	$168,000	$4,833	$57,995
$1,630	$136,000	$1,347	$170,000	$4,890	$58,685
$1,649	$137,600	$1,363	$172,000	$4,948	$59,376
$1,668	$139,200	$1,378	$174,000	$5,005	$60,066
$1,688	$140,800	$1,394	$176,000	$5,063	$60,756
$1,707	$142,400	$1,410	$178,000	$5,121	$61,447
$1,726	$144,000	$1,426	$180,000	$5,178	$62,137
$1,745	$145,600	$1,442	$182,000	$5,236	$62,828
$1,764	$147,200	$1,458	$184,000	$5,293	$63,518
$1,784	$148,800	$1,474	$186,000	$5,351	$64,208
$1,803	$150,400	$1,489	$188,000	$5,408	$64,899
$1,822	$152,000	$1,505	$190,000	$5,466	$65,589
$1,841	$153,600	$1,521	$192,000	$5,523	$66,280
$1,860	$155,200	$1,537	$194,000	$5,581	$66,970
$1,879	$156,800	$1,553	$196,000	$5,638	$67,660
$1,899	$158,400	$1,569	$198,000	$5,696	$68,351
$1,918	$160,000	$1,584	$200,000	$5,753	$69,041

12% Interest, 30-Year Term, 20% Down

(2% of purchase price assumed for taxes and insurance; 33% of gross monthly income allowed for mortgage payment)

Monthly payment	Maximum mortgage Amount	P & I	Maximum price	Income to qualify Monthly	Annual
$495	$40,000	$411	$50,000	$1,484	$17,812
$515	$41,600	$428	$52,000	$1,544	$18,525
$534	$43,200	$444	$54,000	$1,603	$19,237
$554	$44,800	$461	$56,000	$1,662	$19,950
$574	$46,400	$477	$58,000	$1,722	$20,662
$594	$48,000	$494	$60,000	$1,781	$21,375
$614	$49,600	$510	$62,000	$1,841	$22,087
$633	$51,200	$527	$64,000	$1,900	$22,800
$653	$52,800	$543	$66,000	$1,959	$23,512
$673	$54,400	$560	$68,000	$2,019	$24,225
$693	$56,000	$576	$70,000	$2,078	$24,937
$712	$57,600	$592	$72,000	$2,137	$25,650
$732	$59,200	$609	$74,000	$2,197	$26,362
$752	$60,800	$625	$76,000	$2,256	$27,075
$772	$62,400	$642	$78,000	$2,316	$27,787
$792	$64,000	$658	$80,000	$2,375	$28,500
$811	$65,600	$675	$82,000	$2,434	$29,212
$831	$67,200	$691	$84,000	$2,494	$29,925
$851	$68,800	$708	$86,000	$2,553	$30,637
$871	$70,400	$724	$88,000	$2,612	$31,350
$891	$72,000	$741	$90,000	$2,672	$32,062
$910	$73,600	$757	$92,000	$2,731	$32,775
$930	$75,200	$774	$94,000	$2,791	$33,487
$950	$76,800	$790	$96,000	$2,850	$34,200
$970	$78,400	$806	$98,000	$2,909	$34,912
$990	$80,000	$823	$100,000	$2,969	$35,625
$1,009	$81,600	$839	$102,000	$3,028	$36,337
$1,029	$83,200	$856	$104,000	$3,087	$37,050
$1,049	$84,800	$872	$106,000	$3,147	$37,762
$1,069	$86,400	$889	$108,000	$3,206	$38,475
$1,089	$88,000	$905	$110,000	$3,266	$39,187
$1,108	$89,600	$922	$112,000	$3,325	$39,899
$1,128	$91,200	$938	$114,000	$3,384	$40,612
$1,148	$92,800	$955	$116,000	$3,444	$41,324
$1,168	$94,400	$971	$118,000	$3,503	$42,037
$1,187	$96,000	$987	$120,000	$3,562	$42,749
$1,207	$97,600	$1,004	$122,000	$3,622	$43,462
$1,227	$99,200	$1,020	$124,000	$3,681	$44,174
$1,247	$100,800	$1,037	$126,000	$3,741	$44,887
$1,267	$102,400	$1,053	$128,000	$3,800	$45,599
$1,286	$104,000	$1,070	$130,000	$3,859	$46,312
$1,306	$105,600	$1,086	$132,000	$3,919	$47,024
$1,326	$107,200	$1,103	$134,000	$3,978	$47,737

Monthly payment	Maximum mortgage		Maximum price	Income to qualify	
	Amount	P & I		Monthly	Annual
$1,346	$108,800	$1,119	$136,000	$4,037	$48,449
$1,366	$110,400	$1,136	$138,000	$4,097	$49,162
$1,385	$112,000	$1,152	$140,000	$4,156	$49,874
$1,405	$113,600	$1,169	$142,000	$4,216	$50,587
$1,425	$115,200	$1,185	$144,000	$4,275	$51,299
$1,445	$116,800	$1,201	$146,000	$4,334	$52,012
$1,465	$118,400	$1,218	$148,000	$4,394	$52,724
$1,484	$120,000	$1,234	$150,000	$4,453	$53,437
$1,504	$121,600	$1,251	$152,000	$4,512	$54,149
$1,524	$123,200	$1,267	$154,000	$4,572	$54,862
$1,544	$124,800	$1,284	$156,000	$4,631	$55,574
$1,564	$126,400	$1,300	$158,000	$4,691	$56,287
$1,583	$128,000	$1,317	$160,000	$4,750	$56,999
$1,603	$129,600	$1,333	$162,000	$4,809	$57,712
$1,623	$131,200	$1,350	$164,000	$4,869	$58,424
$1,643	$132,800	$1,366	$166,000	$4,928	$59,137
$1,662	$134,400	$1,382	$168,000	$4,987	$59,849
$1,682	$136,000	$1,399	$170,000	$5,047	$60,562
$1,702	$137,600	$1,415	$172,000	$5,106	$61,274
$1,722	$139,200	$1,432	$174,000	$5,166	$61,987
$1,742	$140,800	$1,448	$176,000	$5,225	$62,699
$1,761	$142,400	$1,465	$178,000	$5,284	$63,412
$1,781	$144,000	$1,481	$180,000	$5,344	$64,124
$1,801	$145,600	$1,498	$182,000	$5,403	$64,837
$1,821	$147,200	$1,514	$184,000	$5,462	$65,549
$1,841	$148,800	$1,531	$186,000	$5,522	$66,262
$1,860	$150,400	$1,547	$188,000	$5,581	$66,974
$1,880	$152,000	$1,564	$190,000	$5,641	$67,687
$1,900	$153,600	$1,580	$192,000	$5,700	$68,399
$1,920	$155,200	$1,596	$194,000	$5,759	$69,112
$1,940	$156,800	$1,613	$196,000	$5,819	$69,824
$1,959	$158,400	$1,629	$198,000	$5,878	$70,537
$1,979	$160,000	$1,646	$200,000	$5,937	$71,249

12½% Interest, 30-Year Term, 20% Down

(2% of purchase price assumed for taxes and insurance; 33% of gross monthly income allowed for mortgage payment)

Monthly payment	Maximum mortgage Amount	Maximum mortgage P & I	Maximum price	Income to qualify Monthly	Income to qualify Annual
$510	$40,000	$427	$50,000	$1,531	$18,369
$531	$41,600	$444	$52,000	$1,592	$19,103
$551	$43,200	$461	$54,000	$1,653	$19,838
$571	$44,800	$478	$56,000	$1,714	$20,573
$592	$46,400	$495	$58,000	$1,776	$21,308
$612	$48,000	$512	$60,000	$1,837	$22,042
$633	$49,600	$529	$62,000	$1,898	$22,777
$653	$51,200	$546	$64,000	$1,959	$23,512
$674	$52,800	$564	$66,000	$2,021	$24,247
$694	$54,400	$581	$68,000	$2,082	$24,981
$714	$56,000	$598	$70,000	$2,143	$25,716
$735	$57,600	$615	$72,000	$2,204	$26,451
$755	$59,200	$632	$74,000	$2,265	$27,186
$776	$60,800	$649	$76,000	$2,327	$27,920
$796	$62,400	$666	$78,000	$2,388	$28,655
$816	$64,000	$683	$80,000	$2,449	$29,390
$837	$65,600	$700	$82,000	$2,510	$30,125
$857	$67,200	$717	$84,000	$2,572	$30,859
$878	$68,800	$734	$86,000	$2,633	$31,594
$898	$70,400	$751	$88,000	$2,694	$32,329
$918	$72,000	$768	$90,000	$2,755	$33,064
$939	$73,600	$786	$92,000	$2,817	$33,798
$959	$75,200	$803	$94,000	$2,878	$34,533
$980	$76,800	$820	$96,000	$2,939	$35,268
$1,000	$78,400	$837	$98,000	$3,000	$36,003
$1,020	$80,000	$854	$100,000	$3,061	$36,737
$1,041	$81,600	$871	$102,000	$3,123	$37,472
$1,061	$83,200	$888	$104,000	$3,184	$38,207
$1,082	$84,800	$905	$106,000	$3,245	$38,942
$1,102	$86,400	$922	$108,000	$3,306	$39,676
$1,123	$88,000	$939	$110,000	$3,368	$40,411
$1,143	$89,600	$956	$112,000	$3,429	$41,146
$1,163	$91,200	$973	$114,000	$3,490	$41,881
$1,184	$92,800	$990	$116,000	$3,551	$42,615
$1,204	$94,400	$1,008	$118,000	$3,613	$43,350
$1,225	$96,000	$1,025	$120,000	$3,674	$44,085
$1,245	$97,600	$1,042	$122,000	$3,735	$44,820
$1,265	$99,200	$1,059	$124,000	$3,796	$45,554
$1,286	$100,800	$1,076	$126,000	$3,857	$46,289
$1,306	$102,400	$1,093	$128,000	$3,919	$47,024
$1,327	$104,000	$1,110	$130,000	$3,980	$47,759
$1,347	$105,600	$1,127	$132,000	$4,041	$48,493
$1,367	$107,200	$1,144	$134,000	$4,102	$49,228

Monthly payment	Maximum mortgage		Maximum price	Income to qualify	
	Amount	P & I		Monthly	Annual
$1,388	$108,800	$1,161	$136,000	$4,164	$49,963
$1,408	$110,400	$1,178	$138,000	$4,225	$50,698
$1,429	$112,000	$1,195	$140,000	$4,286	$51,432
$1,449	$113,600	$1,212	$142,000	$4,347	$52,167
$1,469	$115,200	$1,229	$144,000	$4,408	$52,902
$1,490	$116,800	$1,247	$146,000	$4,470	$53,637
$1,510	$118,400	$1,264	$148,000	$4,531	$54,371
$1,531	$120,000	$1,281	$150,000	$4,592	$55,106
$1,551	$121,600	$1,298	$152,000	$4,653	$55,841
$1,572	$123,200	$1,315	$154,000	$4,715	$56,576
$1,592	$124,800	$1,332	$156,000	$4,776	$57,310
$1,612	$126,400	$1,349	$158,000	$4,837	$58,045
$1,633	$128,000	$1,366	$160,000	$4,898	$58,780
$1,653	$129,600	$1,383	$162,000	$4,960	$59,515
$1,674	$131,200	$1,400	$164,000	$5,021	$60,249
$1,694	$132,800	$1,417	$166,000	$5,082	$60,984
$1,714	$134,400	$1,434	$168,000	$5,143	$61,719
$1,735	$136,000	$1,451	$170,000	$5,204	$62,454
$1,755	$137,600	$1,469	$172,000	$5,266	$63,188
$1,776	$139,200	$1,486	$174,000	$5,327	$63,923
$1,796	$140,800	$1,503	$176,000	$5,388	$64,658
$1,816	$142,400	$1,520	$178,000	$5,449	$65,393
$1,837	$144,000	$1,537	$180,000	$5,511	$66,127
$1,857	$145,600	$1,554	$182,000	$5,572	$66,862
$1,878	$147,200	$1,571	$184,000	$5,633	$67,597
$1,898	$148,800	$1,588	$186,000	$5,694	$68,332
$1,919	$150,400	$1,605	$188,000	$5,756	$69,066
$1,939	$152,000	$1,622	$190,000	$5,817	$69,801
$1,959	$153,600	$1,639	$192,000	$5,878	$70,536
$1,980	$155,200	$1,656	$194,000	$5,939	$71,271
$2,000	$156,800	$1,673	$196,000	$6,000	$72,005
$2,021	$158,400	$1,691	$198,000	$6,062	$72,740
$2,041	$160,000	$1,708	$200,000	$6,123	$73,475

13% Interest, 30-Year Term, 20% Down

(2% of purchase price assumed for taxes and insurance; 33% of gross monthly income allowed for mortgage payment)

Monthly payment	Maximum mortgage		Maximum price	Income to qualify	
	Amount	P & I		Monthly	Annual
$526	$40,000	$442	$50,000	$1,577	$18,929
$547	$41,600	$460	$52,000	$1,641	$19,687
$568	$43,200	$478	$54,000	$1,704	$20,444
$589	$44,800	$496	$56,000	$1,767	$21,201
$610	$46,400	$513	$58,000	$1,830	$21,958
$631	$48,000	$531	$60,000	$1,893	$22,715
$652	$49,600	$549	$62,000	$1,956	$23,472
$673	$51,200	$566	$64,000	$2,019	$24,230
$694	$52,800	$584	$66,000	$2,082	$24,987
$715	$54,400	$602	$68,000	$2,145	$25,744
$736	$56,000	$619	$70,000	$2,208	$26,501
$757	$57,600	$637	$72,000	$2,272	$27,258
$778	$59,200	$655	$74,000	$2,335	$28,016
$799	$60,800	$673	$76,000	$2,398	$28,773
$820	$62,400	$690	$78,000	$2,461	$29,530
$841	$64,000	$708	$80,000	$2,524	$30,287
$862	$65,600	$726	$82,000	$2,587	$31,044
$883	$67,200	$743	$84,000	$2,650	$31,801
$904	$68,800	$761	$86,000	$2,713	$32,559
$925	$70,400	$779	$88,000	$2,776	$33,316
$946	$72,000	$796	$90,000	$2,839	$34,073
$968	$73,600	$814	$92,000	$2,903	$34,830
$989	$75,200	$832	$94,000	$2,966	$35,587
$1,010	$76,800	$850	$96,000	$3,029	$36,344
$1,031	$78,400	$867	$98,000	$3,092	$37,102
$1,052	$80,000	$885	$100,000	$3,155	$37,859
$1,073	$81,600	$903	$102,000	$3,218	$38,616
$1,094	$83,200	$920	$104,000	$3,281	$39,373
$1,115	$84,800	$938	$106,000	$3,344	$40,130
$1,136	$86,400	$956	$108,000	$3,407	$40,888
$1,157	$88,000	$973	$110,000	$3,470	$41,645
$1,178	$89,600	$991	$112,000	$3,533	$42,402
$1,199	$91,200	$1,009	$114,000	$3,597	$43,159
$1,220	$92,800	$1,027	$116,000	$3,660	$43,916
$1,241	$94,400	$1,044	$118,000	$3,723	$44,673
$1,262	$96,000	$1,062	$120,000	$3,786	$45,431
$1,283	$97,600	$1,080	$122,000	$3,849	$46,188
$1,304	$99,200	$1,097	$124,000	$3,912	$46,945
$1,325	$100,800	$1,115	$126,000	$3,975	$47,702
$1,346	$102,400	$1,133	$128,000	$4,038	$48,459
$1,367	$104,000	$1,150	$130,000	$4,101	$49,217
$1,388	$105,600	$1,168	$132,000	$4,164	$49,974
$1,409	$107,200	$1,186	$134,000	$4,228	$50,731

Monthly payment	Maximum mortgage		Maximum price	Income to qualify	
	Amount	P & I		Monthly	Annual
$1,430	$108,800	$1,204	$136,000	$4,291	$51,488
$1,451	$110,400	$1,221	$138,000	$4,354	$52,245
$1,472	$112,000	$1,239	$140,000	$4,417	$53,002
$1,493	$113,600	$1,257	$142,000	$4,480	$53,760
$1,514	$115,200	$1,274	$144,000	$4,543	$54,517
$1,535	$116,800	$1,292	$146,000	$4,606	$55,274
$1,556	$118,400	$1,310	$148,000	$4,669	$56,031
$1,577	$120,000	$1,327	$150,000	$4,732	$56,788
$1,598	$121,600	$1,345	$152,000	$4,795	$57,545
$1,620	$123,200	$1,363	$154,000	$4,859	$58,303
$1,641	$124,800	$1,381	$156,000	$4,922	$59,060
$1,662	$126,400	$1,398	$158,000	$4,985	$59,817
$1,683	$128,000	$1,416	$160,000	$5,048	$60,574
$1,704	$129,600	$1,434	$162,000	$5,111	$61,331
$1,725	$131,200	$1,451	$164,000	$5,174	$62,089
$1,746	$132,800	$1,469	$166,000	$5,237	$62,846
$1,767	$134,400	$1,487	$168,000	$5,300	$63,603
$1,788	$136,000	$1,504	$170,000	$5,363	$64,360
$1,809	$137,600	$1,522	$172,000	$5,426	$65,117
$1,830	$139,200	$1,540	$174,000	$5,490	$65,874
$1,851	$140,800	$1,558	$176,000	$5,553	$66,632
$1,872	$142,400	$1,575	$178,000	$5,616	$67,389
$1,893	$144,000	$1,593	$180,000	$5,679	$68,146
$1,914	$145,600	$1,611	$182,000	$5,742	$68,903
$1,935	$147,200	$1,628	$184,000	$5,805	$69,660
$1,956	$148,800	$1,646	$186,000	$5,868	$70,417
$1,977	$150,400	$1,664	$188,000	$5,931	$71,175
$1,998	$152,000	$1,681	$190,000	$5,994	$71,932
$2,019	$153,600	$1,699	$192,000	$6,057	$72,689
$2,040	$155,200	$1,717	$194,000	$6,121	$73,446
$2,061	$156,800	$1,735	$196,000	$6,184	$74,203
$2,082	$158,400	$1,752	$198,000	$6,247	$74,961
$2,103	$160,000	$1,770	$200,000	$6,310	$75,718

13½% Interest, 30-Year Term, 20% Down

(2% of purchase price assumed for taxes and insurance; 33% of gross monthly income allowed for mortgage payment)

Monthly payment	Maximum mortgage		Maximum price	Income to qualify	
	Amount	P & I		Monthly	Annual
$542	$40,000	$458	$50,000	$1,625	$19,494
$563	$41,600	$476	$52,000	$1,689	$20,274
$585	$43,200	$495	$54,000	$1,754	$21,054
$606	$44,800	$513	$56,000	$1,819	$21,833
$628	$46,400	$531	$58,000	$1,884	$22,613
$650	$48,000	$550	$60,000	$1,949	$23,393
$671	$49,600	$568	$62,000	$2,014	$24,173
$693	$51,200	$586	$64,000	$2,079	$24,952
$715	$52,800	$605	$66,000	$2,144	$25,732
$736	$54,400	$623	$68,000	$2,209	$26,512
$758	$56,000	$641	$70,000	$2,274	$27,292
$780	$57,600	$660	$72,000	$2,339	$28,071
$801	$59,200	$678	$74,000	$2,404	$28,851
$823	$60,800	$696	$76,000	$2,469	$29,631
$845	$62,400	$715	$78,000	$2,534	$30,411
$866	$64,000	$733	$80,000	$2,599	$31,190
$888	$65,600	$751	$82,000	$2,664	$31,970
$910	$67,200	$770	$84,000	$2,729	$32,750
$931	$68,800	$788	$86,000	$2,794	$33,530
$953	$70,400	$806	$88,000	$2,859	$34,310
$975	$72,000	$825	$90,000	$2,924	$35,089
$996	$73,600	$843	$92,000	$2,989	$35,869
$1,018	$75,200	$861	$94,000	$3,054	$36,649
$1,040	$76,800	$880	$96,000	$3,119	$37,429
$1,061	$78,400	$898	$98,000	$3,184	$38,208
$1,083	$80,000	$916	$100,000	$3,249	$38,988
$1,105	$81,600	$935	$102,000	$3,314	$39,768
$1,126	$83,200	$953	$104,000	$3,379	$40,548
$1,148	$84,800	$971	$106,000	$3,444	$41,327
$1,170	$86,400	$990	$108,000	$3,509	$42,107
$1,191	$88,000	$1,008	$110,000	$3,574	$42,887
$1,213	$89,600	$1,026	$112,000	$3,639	$43,667
$1,235	$91,200	$1,045	$114,000	$3,704	$44,446
$1,256	$92,800	$1,063	$116,000	$3,769	$45,226
$1,278	$94,400	$1,081	$118,000	$3,834	$46,006
$1,300	$96,000	$1,100	$120,000	$3,899	$46,786
$1,321	$97,600	$1,118	$122,000	$3,964	$47,565
$1,343	$99,200	$1,136	$124,000	$4,029	$48,345
$1,365	$100,800	$1,155	$126,000	$4,094	$49,125
$1,386	$102,400	$1,173	$128,000	$4,159	$49,905
$1,408	$104,000	$1,191	$130,000	$4,224	$50,685
$1,430	$105,600	$1,210	$132,000	$4,289	$51,464
$1,451	$107,200	$1,228	$134,000	$4,354	$52,244

Monthly payment	Maximum mortgage		Maximum price	Income to qualify	
	Amount	P & I		Monthly	Annual
$1,473	$108,800	$1,246	$136,000	$4,419	$53,024
$1,495	$110,400	$1,265	$138,000	$4,484	$53,804
$1,516	$112,000	$1,283	$140,000	$4,549	$54,583
$1,538	$113,600	$1,301	$142,000	$4,614	$55,363
$1,560	$115,200	$1,320	$144,000	$4,679	$56,143
$1,581	$116,800	$1,338	$146,000	$4,744	$56,923
$1,603	$118,400	$1,356	$148,000	$4,809	$57,702
$1,625	$120,000	$1,375	$150,000	$4,874	$58,482
$1,646	$121,600	$1,393	$152,000	$4,938	$59,262
$1,668	$123,200	$1,411	$154,000	$5,003	$60,042
$1,689	$124,800	$1,429	$156,000	$5,068	$60,821
$1,711	$126,400	$1,448	$158,000	$5,133	$61,601
$1,733	$128,000	$1,466	$160,000	$5,198	$62,381
$1,754	$129,600	$1,484	$162,000	$5,263	$63,161
$1,776	$131,200	$1,503	$164,000	$5,328	$63,940
$1,798	$132,800	$1,521	$166,000	$5,393	$64,720
$1,819	$134,400	$1,539	$168,000	$5,458	$65,500
$1,841	$136,000	$1,558	$170,000	$5,523	$66,280
$1,863	$137,600	$1,576	$172,000	$5,588	$67,060
$1,884	$139,200	$1,594	$174,000	$5,653	$67,839
$1,906	$140,800	$1,613	$176,000	$5,718	$68,619
$1,928	$142,400	$1,631	$178,000	$5,783	$69,399
$1,949	$144,000	$1,649	$180,000	$5,848	$70,179
$1,971	$145,600	$1,668	$182,000	$5,913	$70,958
$1,993	$147,200	$1,686	$184,000	$5,978	$71,738
$2,014	$148,800	$1,704	$186,000	$6,043	$72,518
$2,036	$150,400	$1,723	$188,000	$6,108	$73,298
$2,058	$152,000	$1,741	$190,000	$6,173	$74,077
$2,079	$153,600	$1,759	$192,000	$6,238	$74,857
$2,101	$155,200	$1,778	$194,000	$6,303	$75,637
$2,123	$156,800	$1,796	$196,000	$6,368	$76,417
$2,144	$158,400	$1,814	$198,000	$6,433	$77,196
$2,166	$160,000	$1,833	$200,000	$6,498	$77,976

14% Interest, 30-Year Term, 20% Down

(2% of purchase price assumed for taxes and insurance; 33% of gross monthly income allowed for mortgage payment)

Monthly payment	Maximum mortgage		Maximum price	Income to qualify	
	Amount	P & I		Monthly	Annual
$557	$40,000	$474	$50,000	$1,672	$20,062
$580	$41,600	$493	$52,000	$1,739	$20,865
$602	$43,200	$512	$54,000	$1,806	$21,667
$624	$44,800	$531	$56,000	$1,872	$22,470
$646	$46,400	$550	$58,000	$1,939	$23,272
$669	$48,000	$569	$60,000	$2,006	$24,075
$691	$49,600	$588	$62,000	$2,073	$24,877
$713	$51,200	$607	$64,000	$2,140	$25,680
$736	$52,800	$626	$66,000	$2,207	$26,482
$758	$54,400	$645	$68,000	$2,274	$27,285
$780	$56,000	$664	$70,000	$2,341	$28,087
$802	$57,600	$682	$72,000	$2,407	$28,890
$825	$59,200	$701	$74,000	$2,474	$29,692
$847	$60,800	$720	$76,000	$2,541	$30,495
$869	$62,400	$739	$78,000	$2,608	$31,297
$892	$64,000	$758	$80,000	$2,675	$32,100
$914	$65,600	$777	$82,000	$2,742	$32,902
$936	$67,200	$796	$84,000	$2,809	$33,705
$959	$68,800	$815	$86,000	$2,876	$34,507
$981	$70,400	$834	$88,000	$2,942	$35,310
$1,003	$72,000	$853	$90,000	$3,009	$36,112
$1,025	$73,600	$872	$92,000	$3,076	$36,915
$1,048	$75,200	$891	$94,000	$3,143	$37,717
$1,070	$76,800	$910	$96,000	$3,210	$38,520
$1,092	$78,400	$929	$98,000	$3,277	$39,322
$1,115	$80,000	$948	$100,000	$3,344	$40,125
$1,137	$81,600	$967	$102,000	$3,411	$40,927
$1,159	$83,200	$986	$104,000	$3,477	$41,730
$1,181	$84,800	$1,005	$106,000	$3,544	$42,532
$1,204	$86,400	$1,024	$108,000	$3,611	$43,335
$1,226	$88,000	$1,043	$110,000	$3,678	$44,137
$1,248	$89,600	$1,062	$112,000	$3,745	$44,939
$1,271	$91,200	$1,081	$114,000	$3,812	$45,742
$1,293	$92,800	$1,100	$116,000	$3,879	$46,544
$1,315	$94,400	$1,119	$118,000	$3,946	$47,347
$1,337	$96,000	$1,137	$120,000	$4,012	$48,149
$1,360	$97,600	$1,156	$122,000	$4,079	$48,952
$1,382	$99,200	$1,175	$124,000	$4,146	$49,754
$1,404	$100,800	$1,194	$126,000	$4,213	$50,557
$1,427	$102,400	$1,213	$128,000	$4,280	$51,359
$1,449	$104,000	$1,232	$130,000	$4,347	$52,162
$1,471	$105,600	$1,251	$132,000	$4,414	$52,964
$1,494	$107,200	$1,270	$134,000	$4,481	$53,767

Monthly payment	Maximum mortgage		Maximum price	Income to qualify	
	Amount	P & I		Monthly	Annual
$1,516	$108,800	$1,289	$136,000	$4,547	$54,569
$1,538	$110,400	$1,308	$138,000	$4,614	$55,372
$1,560	$112,000	$1,327	$140,000	$4,681	$56,174
$1,583	$113,600	$1,346	$142,000	$4,748	$56,977
$1,605	$115,200	$1,365	$144,000	$4,815	$57,779
$1,627	$116,800	$1,384	$146,000	$4,882	$58,582
$1,650	$118,400	$1,403	$148,000	$4,949	$59,384
$1,672	$120,000	$1,422	$150,000	$5,016	$60,187
$1,694	$121,600	$1,441	$152,000	$5,082	$60,989
$1,716	$123,200	$1,460	$154,000	$5,149	$61,792
$1,739	$124,800	$1,479	$156,000	$5,216	$62,594
$1,761	$126,400	$1,498	$158,000	$5,283	$63,397
$1,783	$128,000	$1,517	$160,000	$5,350	$64,199
$1,806	$129,600	$1,536	$162,000	$5,417	$65,002
$1,828	$131,200	$1,555	$164,000	$5,484	$65,804
$1,850	$132,800	$1,574	$166,000	$5,551	$66,607
$1,872	$134,400	$1,592	$168,000	$5,617	$67,409
$1,895	$136,000	$1,611	$170,000	$5,684	$68,212
$1,917	$137,600	$1,630	$172,000	$5,751	$69,014
$1,939	$139,200	$1,649	$174,000	$5,818	$69,817
$1,962	$140,800	$1,668	$176,000	$5,885	$70,619
$1,984	$142,400	$1,687	$178,000	$5,952	$71,422
$2,006	$144,000	$1,706	$180,000	$6,019	$72,224
$2,029	$145,600	$1,725	$182,000	$6,086	$73,027
$2,051	$147,200	$1,744	$184,000	$6,152	$73,829
$2,073	$148,800	$1,763	$186,000	$6,219	$74,632
$2,095	$150,400	$1,782	$188,000	$6,286	$75,434
$2,118	$152,000	$1,801	$190,000	$6,353	$76,237
$2,140	$153,600	$1,820	$192,000	$6,420	$77,039
$2,162	$155,200	$1,839	$194,000	$6,487	$77,842
$2,185	$156,800	$1,858	$196,000	$6,554	$78,644
$2,207	$158,400	$1,877	$198,000	$6,621	$79,447
$2,229	$160,000	$1,896	$200,000	$6,687	$80,249

14½% Interest, 30-Year Term, 20% Down

(2% of purchase price assumed for taxes and insurance; 33% of gross monthly income allowed for mortgage payment)

Monthly payment	Maximum mortgage		Maximum price	Income to qualify	
	Amount	P & I		Monthly	Annual
$573	$40,000	$490	$50,000	$1,719	$20,634
$596	$41,600	$509	$52,000	$1,788	$21,459
$619	$43,200	$529	$54,000	$1,857	$22,284
$642	$44,800	$549	$56,000	$1,926	$23,110
$665	$46,400	$568	$58,000	$1,995	$23,935
$688	$48,000	$588	$60,000	$2,063	$24,760
$711	$49,600	$607	$62,000	$2,132	$25,586
$734	$51,200	$627	$64,000	$2,201	$26,411
$757	$52,800	$647	$66,000	$2,270	$27,236
$779	$54,400	$666	$68,000	$2,338	$28,062
$802	$56,000	$686	$70,000	$2,407	$28,887
$825	$57,600	$705	$72,000	$2,476	$29,712
$848	$59,200	$725	$74,000	$2,545	$30,538
$871	$60,800	$745	$76,000	$2,614	$31,363
$894	$62,400	$764	$78,000	$2,682	$32,189
$917	$64,000	$784	$80,000	$2,751	$33,014
$940	$65,600	$803	$82,000	$2,820	$33,839
$963	$67,200	$823	$84,000	$2,889	$34,665
$986	$68,800	$842	$86,000	$2,957	$35,490
$1,009	$70,400	$862	$88,000	$3,026	$36,315
$1,032	$72,000	$882	$90,000	$3,095	$37,141
$1,055	$73,600	$901	$92,000	$3,164	$37,966
$1,078	$75,200	$921	$94,000	$3,233	$38,791
$1,100	$76,800	$940	$96,000	$3,301	$39,617
$1,123	$78,400	$960	$98,000	$3,370	$40,442
$1,146	$80,000	$980	$100,000	$3,439	$41,267
$1,169	$81,600	$999	$102,000	$3,508	$42,093
$1,192	$83,200	$1,019	$104,000	$3,577	$42,918
$1,215	$84,800	$1,038	$106,000	$3,645	$43,743
$1,238	$86,400	$1,058	$108,000	$3,714	$44,569
$1,261	$88,000	$1,078	$110,000	$3,783	$45,394
$1,284	$89,600	$1,097	$112,000	$3,852	$46,219
$1,307	$91,200	$1,117	$114,000	$3,920	$47,045
$1,330	$92,800	$1,136	$116,000	$3,989	$47,870
$1,353	$94,400	$1,156	$118,000	$4,058	$48,695
$1,376	$96,000	$1,176	$120,000	$4,127	$49,521
$1,399	$97,600	$1,195	$122,000	$4,196	$50,346
$1,421	$99,200	$1,215	$124,000	$4,264	$51,171
$1,444	$100,800	$1,234	$126,000	$4,333	$51,997
$1,467	$102,400	$1,254	$128,000	$4,402	$52,822
$1,490	$104,000	$1,274	$130,000	$4,471	$53,648
$1,513	$105,600	$1,293	$132,000	$4,539	$54,473
$1,536	$107,200	$1,313	$134,000	$4,608	$55,298

Monthly payment	Maximum mortgage		Maximum price	Income to qualify	
	Amount	P & I		Monthly	Annual
$1,559	$108,800	$1,332	$136,000	$4,677	$56,124
$1,582	$110,400	$1,352	$138,000	$4,746	$56,949
$1,605	$112,000	$1,372	$140,000	$4,815	$57,774
$1,628	$113,600	$1,391	$142,000	$4,883	$58,600
$1,651	$115,200	$1,411	$144,000	$4,952	$59,425
$1,674	$116,800	$1,430	$146,000	$5,021	$60,250
$1,697	$118,400	$1,450	$148,000	$5,090	$61,076
$1,719	$120,000	$1,469	$150,000	$5,158	$61,901
$1,742	$121,600	$1,489	$152,000	$5,227	$62,726
$1,765	$123,200	$1,509	$154,000	$5,296	$63,552
$1,788	$124,800	$1,528	$156,000	$5,365	$64,377
$1,811	$126,400	$1,548	$158,000	$5,434	$65,202
$1,834	$128,000	$1,567	$160,000	$5,502	$66,028
$1,857	$129,600	$1,587	$162,000	$5,571	$66,853
$1,880	$131,200	$1,607	$164,000	$5,640	$67,678
$1,903	$132,800	$1,626	$166,000	$5,709	$68,504
$1,926	$134,400	$1,646	$168,000	$5,777	$69,329
$1,949	$136,000	$1,665	$170,000	$5,846	$70,154
$1,972	$137,600	$1,685	$172,000	$5,915	$70,980
$1,995	$139,200	$1,705	$174,000	$5,984	$71,805
$2,018	$140,800	$1,724	$176,000	$6,053	$72,630
$2,040	$142,400	$1,744	$178,000	$6,121	$73,456
$2,063	$144,000	$1,763	$180,000	$6,190	$74,281
$2,086	$145,600	$1,783	$182,000	$6,259	$75,107
$2,109	$147,200	$1,803	$184,000	$6,328	$75,932
$2,132	$148,800	$1,822	$186,000	$6,396	$76,757
$2,155	$150,400	$1,842	$188,000	$6,465	$77,583
$2,178	$152,000	$1,861	$190,000	$6,534	$78,408
$2,201	$153,600	$1,881	$192,000	$6,603	$79,233
$2,224	$155,200	$1,901	$194,000	$6,672	$80,059
$2,247	$156,800	$1,920	$196,000	$6,740	$80,884
$2,270	$158,400	$1,940	$198,000	$6,809	$81,709
$2,293	$160,000	$1,959	$200,000	$6,878	$82,535

264

〉

15% Interest, 30-Year Term, 20% Down

(2% of purchase price assumed for taxes and insurance; 33% of gross monthly
income allowed for mortgage payment)

Monthly payment	Maximum mortgage		Maximum price	Income to qualify	
	Amount	P & I		Monthly	Annual
$589	$40,000	$506	$50,000	$1,767	$21,208
$613	$41,600	$526	$52,000	$1,838	$22,056
$636	$43,200	$546	$54,000	$1,909	$22,905
$660	$44,800	$566	$56,000	$1,979	$23,753
$683	$46,400	$587	$58,000	$2,050	$24,601
$707	$48,000	$607	$60,000	$2,121	$25,450
$731	$49,600	$627	$62,000	$2,192	$26,298
$754	$51,200	$647	$64,000	$2,262	$27,146
$778	$52,800	$668	$66,000	$2,333	$27,995
$801	$54,400	$688	$68,000	$2,404	$28,843
$825	$56,000	$708	$70,000	$2,474	$29,691
$848	$57,600	$728	$72,000	$2,545	$30,540
$872	$59,200	$749	$74,000	$2,616	$31,388
$895	$60,800	$769	$76,000	$2,686	$32,236
$919	$62,400	$789	$78,000	$2,757	$33,085
$943	$64,000	$809	$80,000	$2,828	$33,933
$966	$65,600	$829	$82,000	$2,898	$34,781
$990	$67,200	$850	$84,000	$2,969	$35,630
$1,013	$68,800	$870	$86,000	$3,040	$36,478
$1,037	$70,400	$890	$88,000	$3,111	$37,326
$1,060	$72,000	$910	$90,000	$3,181	$38,175
$1,084	$73,600	$931	$92,000	$3,252	$39,023
$1,108	$75,200	$951	$94,000	$3,323	$39,871
$1,131	$76,800	$971	$96,000	$3,393	$40,720
$1,155	$78,400	$991	$98,000	$3,464	$41,568
$1,178	$80,000	$1,012	$100,000	$3,535	$42,416
$1,202	$81,600	$1,032	$102,000	$3,605	$43,264
$1,225	$83,200	$1,052	$104,000	$3,676	$44,113
$1,249	$84,800	$1,072	$106,000	$3,747	$44,961
$1,272	$86,400	$1,092	$108,000	$3,817	$45,809
$1,296	$88,000	$1,113	$110,000	$3,888	$46,658
$1,320	$89,600	$1,133	$112,000	$3,959	$47,506
$1,343	$91,200	$1,153	$114,000	$4,030	$48,354
$1,367	$92,800	$1,173	$116,000	$4,100	$49,203
$1,390	$94,400	$1,194	$118,000	$4,171	$50,051
$1,414	$96,000	$1,214	$120,000	$4,242	$50,899
$1,437	$97,600	$1,234	$122,000	$4,312	$51,748
$1,461	$99,200	$1,254	$124,000	$4,383	$52,596
$1,485	$100,800	$1,275	$126,000	$4,454	$53,444
$1,508	$102,400	$1,295	$128,000	$4,524	$54,293
$1,532	$104,000	$1,315	$130,000	$4,595	$55,141
$1,555	$105,600	$1,335	$132,000	$4,666	$55,989
$1,579	$107,200	$1,355	$134,000	$4,736	$56,838

Monthly payment	Maximum mortgage		Maximum price	Income to qualify	
	Amount	P & I		Monthly	Annual
$1,602	$108,800	$1,376	$136,000	$4,807	$57,686
$1,626	$110,400	$1,396	$138,000	$4,878	$58,534
$1,650	$112,000	$1,416	$140,000	$4,949	$59,383
$1,673	$113,600	$1,436	$142,000	$5,019	$60,231
$1,697	$115,200	$1,457	$144,000	$5,090	$61,079
$1,720	$116,800	$1,477	$146,000	$5,161	$61,928
$1,744	$118,400	$1,497	$148,000	$5,231	$62,776
$1,767	$120,000	$1,517	$150,000	$5,302	$63,624
$1,791	$121,600	$1,538	$152,000	$5,373	$64,473
$1,814	$123,200	$1,558	$154,000	$5,443	$65,321
$1,838	$124,800	$1,578	$156,000	$5,514	$66,169
$1,862	$126,400	$1,598	$158,000	$5,585	$67,018
$1,885	$128,000	$1,618	$160,000	$5,655	$67,866
$1,909	$129,600	$1,639	$162,000	$5,726	$68,714
$1,932	$131,200	$1,659	$164,000	$5,797	$69,563
$1,956	$132,800	$1,679	$166,000	$5,868	$70,411
$1,979	$134,400	$1,699	$168,000	$5,938	$71,259
$2,003	$136,000	$1,720	$170,000	$6,009	$72,107
$2,027	$137,600	$1,740	$172,000	$6,080	$72,956
$2,050	$139,200	$1,760	$174,000	$6,150	$73,804
$2,074	$140,800	$1,780	$176,000	$6,221	$74,652
$2,097	$142,400	$1,801	$178,000	$6,292	$75,501
$2,121	$144,000	$1,821	$180,000	$6,362	$76,349
$2,144	$145,600	$1,841	$182,000	$6,433	$77,197
$2,168	$147,200	$1,861	$184,000	$6,504	$78,046
$2,192	$148,800	$1,882	$186,000	$6,575	$78,894
$2,215	$150,400	$1,902	$188,000	$6,645	$79,742
$2,239	$152,000	$1,922	$190,000	$6,716	$80,591
$2,262	$153,600	$1,942	$192,000	$6,787	$81,439
$2,286	$155,200	$1,962	$194,000	$6,857	$82,287
$2,309	$156,800	$1,983	$196,000	$6,928	$83,136
$2,333	$158,400	$2,003	$198,000	$6,999	$83,984
$2,356	$160,000	$2,023	$200,000	$7,069	$84,832

Index

Abstract of title, 19
Acceleration clause, 19, 22
Adjustable convertible mortgage, 132–134
Adjustable-rate mortgage (ARM), 19, 36, 48–49, 62–89, 165
   adjustment date, 19, 78–79, 81–83, 89, 133
   advantages of, 65–66, 73
   assumption of, 21, 73
   buy-downs and, 145–146
   catch-up clause, 83
   convertible, 23, 128–130, 132–134
   graduated-payment mortgage and, 25, 175–176
   hybrid, 79
   index, 25, 74–78, 83, 118
   interest rate cap, 63, 64, 67, 79–81, 89
   interest rate steps, 81–83, 87, 89, 133
   margin, 26, 77–78, 118
   negative amortization, 26, 84–87, 89, 192, 213
   qualifying for, 68–70, 72
   teaser rate, 10, 48, 64–72, 146
   (*See also* Lines of credit)
Adjusting values, 53–54
Adjustment date, 19, 78–79, 81–83, 89, 133
AIM (all-inclusive mortgage), 111
Alienation clause, 19, 22
All-inclusive mortgage (AIM), 111
ALTA (American Land Title Association), 20, 30
American Institute of Real Estate Appraisers (MAI), 26
American Land Title Association (ALTA), 20, 30
American Society of Appraisers (ASA), 20
Amortization, 20, 79, 90–92
   schedules, 100, 229–230
Annual percentage rate (APR), 20, 67, 221

Appraisal, 5, 20, 22, 26, 33, 34, 51, 53–54
   fee, 223
   private mortgage insurance and, 201
   in refinancing, 155–156, 158, 159
   for VA loan, 22, 184
   (*See also specific appraisal organizations*)
Appreciation, negative amortization and, 87
APR (annual percentage rate), 20, 67, 221
ARM (*see* Adjustable-rate mortgage)
ASA (American Society of Appraisers), 20
Assignment of mortgage, 20–21
Assumption, 21, 27, 29, 72–73
   of adjustable-rate mortgage, 21, 73
   of fixed-rate mortgage, 21, 72–73
   foreclosure and, 21
   of government loans, 21, 27, 72, 112, 119, 178, 179, 202, 203
   in seller financing, 111–113, 119–122
Assumption fee, 223
Attorney, 116
Attorney's fees, 224
Automatic funding, 184–185
Automatic guarantee, 21
Automobile loans, 14
Average mortgage rate, 74–76

Back-end ratio, 35, 45–50
Balloon payment, 20, 21, 90, 124–127, 130
   late payment penalty, 116
   paying off, 127
   in seller financing, 127
Bank, 9, 11–12, 33, 140, 146, 153
Banking Act of 1933, 11
Bankruptcy, 56
Basis points, 27
Beneficiary, 18, 30
Biweekly mortgage, 21, 90, 95–101
   disadvantages of, 96–98
   establishment of, 97–99

Blanket mortgage, 21, 110
Borrower, 17, 18
Bridge loan, 5
Buy-down mortgage, 22, 143–146
  lender sources, 146
  qualifying for, 146
  requirements for, 145–146
  types of, 146

Call provision, 22, 79
Cap, 22, 26
Carries back paper, 103
Catch-up clause, 83
Certificate of Eligibility (CE), 184
Certificate of reasonable value (CRV), 22, 184
Chain of title, 22, 30
Clauses (*see specific clause*)
Closing, 5, 22, 222, 227–228
CLTV (combined loan-to-value) ratio, 34, 105, 141
Combined loan-to-value (CLTV) ratio, 34, 105, 141
Commercial loans, 11, 12, 36, 111
Commitment, 23
Construction loan, 12, 23
Consumer loan, 14
Consumer Price Index (CPI), 189
Conventional loan, 23
Convertible mortgage, 23, 128–131
  adjustable, 128–130, 132–134
  conversion window, 133–135
  fee, 135–136
  types of, 129–131
Cosigner, 23, 58
Cost-free lines of credit, 153
Cost-of-funds index, 74–76, 118
CPI (Consumer Price Index), 189
Creative financing, 102, 103
Credit card, 147, 148
Credit rating, 2, 3, 23, 50, 68
Credit report, 6, 8, 23–24, 34, 55–61, 137
  assessment of, 56
  bad credit, 57–61
  fee, 5, 158, 159, 224
  foreclosure and, 23, 56–59
  no credit rating, 56, 60–61
  personal letter of explanation, 57–60
Credit union, 9, 14, 15, 141, 146, 153

CRV (certificate of reasonable value), 22, 184

Debt to income ratio, 34
Deed, 29–30
Deed of trust, 17, 18
Deficiency judgment, 18, 27–28
Discount, 24
Discount points, 24, 224–225
Disintermediation, 31
Document preparation, 225
Down payment, 58, 61, 68, 107, 118, 151, 152
  for government loans, 181–182
Due-on-encumbrance clause, 24
Due-on-sale clause, 24, 72–73, 111–113

Encumbrances, 19
Entitlement, 183
Equity, 24, 52, 101
  reverse annuity mortgage, 194–197
  (*See also* Home-equity loan)
Equity of redemption, 17, 18
Equity return, 163, 215, 216
Escrow, 222, 226
Escrow company, 10, 24, 158, 159

Fannie Mae, 9
FDIC (Federal Deposit Insurance Corporation), 10, 11
Federal Home Loan Bank Board, 75, 86–88, 175
Federal Housing Administration (FHA), 34
Federal Housing Administration (FHA) loan, 21, 25, 178–182
  advantages of, 179–180
  assumption of, 21, 27, 72, 112, 119, 178, 179, 202, 203
  disadvantages of, 180
  down payment, 181–183
  FHA-HUD GPM plan, 171–174
  foreclosure, 202–203
  Home Equity Conversion Mortgage, 194–196
  impound account, 185
  lender sources, 11, 12
  maximum loan amount, 180

Federal Housing Administration (FHA) loan (*Cont.*):
  mortgage insurance premium, 180, 181, 198, 202–204, 2226
  origination fee, 26
  owner-occupancy requirement, 180, 185
  points, 224
  prepayment penalties, 180
  programs, 179
  qualifying for, 35, 180–181
  second mortgage and, 181
Federal Reserve Board, 75
Federal Savings and Loan Insurance Corporation (FSLIC), 10
FHA (Federal Housing Administration), 34
FHA-HUD GPM plan, 171–174
FHA loan (*see* Federal Housing Administration loan)
15-year mortgage, 92–95, 99–101
Finance companies, 153
Fire insurance, 225
Firm commitment, 23
Fixed-rate mortgage, 2, 10, 23, 25, 27, 36, 165
  adjustable-rate mortgage and, 62, 65–67, 72, 73, 78
  assumption of, 21, 72–73
  convertible mortgage and, 128–130, 132–135
Float, 99
Foreclosure, 24, 28, 29, 33, 47, 52, 69, 105–106
  assumption and, 21
  court action for, 17, 18
  credit reports and, 23, 56–59
  on Federal Housing Administration loans, 202–203
  refinancing and, 169
Fraud, 106, 138
Freddie Mac, 9, 35, 50
Front-end ratio, 35–45, 49
FSLIC (Federal Savings and Loan Insurance Company), 10

Ginnie Mae, 9, 35, 48, 50
GMI (*see* Gross monthly income)
Good faith estimate, 221–223

Government mortgages, 9, 12, 23, 35, 48, 50, 178–185
  assumption of, 21, 27, 76, 112, 119, 178, 179, 202, 203
  insurance, 180, 181, 198, 202–204, 226
  (*See also* Federal Housing Administration loan; Veteran's Administration loan)
Graduated-payment mortgage (GPM), 25, 170
  adjustable-rate mortgage and, 175–176
  advantages of, 177
  FHA-HUD plan, 171–174
  negative amortization, 175, 176
  recasting, 176
  schedule chart, 171
Great Depression, 33, 34, 203
Gross monthly income (GMI), 34, 37–39, 45, 48, 49
  sources of, 37–38
Gross monthly payment, 41–44, 47
Growing-equity mortgage, 25
Guaranteed mortgages, 12, 23, 35

Hard-money second, 103, 107
Home Equity Conversion Mortgage (HECM), 194–196
  annuity version, 196
  line of credit, 196
  qualifying, 196
  tenure option, 196
Home equity loan, 148–154, 160, 166, 169
  lender sources, 153–154
  tax considerations, 212
Hybrid adjustable-rate mortgage, 79
Hypothecation, 31

Impound accounts, 52, 185, 225–226
Imputed interest, 213
Income property loans, 11, 12, 36
Income (*see* Gross monthly income)
Index, 25, 74–78, 83
  stability of, 74, 76, 77
  types of, 74–76, 118
Individual Retirement Account loan (*see* IRA loans)
Insurance companies, 9

Interest:
    imputed, 213
    on mortgage payment, 91–93, 96, 97,
        99, 100, 226
    personal, 212
    on swing loans, 108
    tax considerations, 205, 208–209, 212,
        214, 218
Interest-only mortgage, 126, 130
Interest rate:
    fluctuation of, 6, 62–63, 66
    lock-ins, 5–7
    refinancing reduction, 162, 165, 166
    seller financing and, 106–110, 113–116
    (See also Teaser rate)
Interest rate caps, 63, 64, 67, 79–81
    advantages of, 80–81
    mortgage payment caps and, 88–89
Interest rate steps, 81–83, 87, 89, 133

Jumbos, 11, 50–51, 131, 132

Late mortgage payments, 212–213
Late payment penalty, 116
Lender, 2, 5, 8, 17
    (See also Mortgage sources; specific type of
        lender)
Letter of credit, 5, 147
Libor (London Interbranch) rate, 74, 76
Liens, 19, 25, 30
    mechanic's, 25, 166
    tax, 25
Life insurance, 201–202
Lines of credit, 52–53, 107, 147–148
    clauses, 150
    credit card, 147, 148
    home equity, 148–154, 160, 166, 169
    Home Equity Conversion Mortgage,
        194–196
Loan application, 5–6, 8
Loan fees, 5, 24
Loan-to-value (LTV) ratio, 25–27, 34,
    38–41, 47, 53, 54, 141, 155
Lock-ins, 5–7
Lo-doc (low-documentation) mortgage,
    2, 6, 137, 140–142
    advantages of, 140–141
    documentation for, 142
    lender sources, 141

Long-term-debt ratio, 35, 45–50
    maximum total, 45
Low-documentation mortgage (see Lo-doc
    mortgage)
LTV (loan-to-value) ratio, 25–27, 34,
    38–41, 47, 53, 54, 141, 155

MAI (American Institute of Real Estate
    Appraisers), 26
Margin, 26, 77–78, 118
Maximum monthly mortgage payment,
    39–41, 43
Maximum mortgage amount, 41, 44, 48,
    50, 131
Mechanic's lien, 25, 166
MIP (mortgage insurance premium),
    180, 181, 226
Mortgage, 17
    maximum amount, 41, 44, 48, 50, 131
    options, 2
    time constraints, 3
    (See also specific type of mortgage)
Mortgage banker, 9, 12–15, 139, 141, 146,
    154
Mortgage broker, 2, 7, 9, 12–15, 35–36,
    48, 139
Mortgage companies, 13
    (See also Mortgage; Wraparound
        financing)
Mortgage insurance, 198–204
    government, 180, 181, 198, 202–204, 226
    life insurance, 201–202
    private, 27, 103–104, 178, 198–201
Mortgage insurance premium (MIP),
    180, 181, 226
Mortgage loan officer, 15
Mortgage obtaining steps, 4–15
    closing, 5, 22, 222, 227–228
    loan application, 5–6, 8
    lock-ins, 5–7
    decide on mortgage type, 5
    (See also Appraisal; Credit report;
        Mortgage sources; Qualifying)
Mortgage papers, 5
Mortgage paybacks, 33, 56, 90–92
    maximum monthly payment, 39–41, 43
    monthly payments, 93–95
    refinancing savings, 161–162
    seller financing and, 106–110
    (See also specific mortgage types)

Mortgage payment caps, 83–89
    cap rate comparison chart, 88
    interest rate cap and, 88–89
Mortgage-payment-to-income ratio, 38–39
Mortgage prepayment, 214–219
    cash reserve, 218–219
    equity return, 215, 216
    prepayment penalty, 27, 98–100, 157,
        180
    tax considerations, 217–218
    (*See also* Refinancing)
Mortgage sources, 5, 8–15
    for buy-downs, 146
    for government loans, 11, 12
    for home equity loan, 153–154
    for lo-docs, 141
    referral sheet, 10, 15
    retail lender, 9, 10, 12, 14, 35
    secondary lender, 9, 11–13, 24, 35, 48,
        49, 146
    (*See also* Seller financing; *specific type of
        lender*)
Mortgage yield index, 118
Mortgagee, 17, 18
Mortgagese (*see specific term*)
Mortgagor, 17

Negative amortization, 26, 84–87, 89, 192
    appreciation and, 87
    ARM-GPM, 175, 176
    causes of, 85
    tax considerations, 213
Negotiating, 7
    in refinancing, 158–159
    in seller financing, 113, 122–123, 145
No-doc (no-documentation) mortgage, 5,
    137, 139–141
No-interest, no-payment second, 108–110
No payments swing loan, 108
No-qualifying, 51–52
Nonconforming loan, 139, 169

Once-in-a-lifetime $125,000 exclusion, 211
1/1/1/1 buy-down, 146
$125,000 exclusion, 211
Option reduction mortgage, 192–193
Origination fee, 26, 226–227
Owner-occupancy requirement, 138, 180,
    185

Payment-to-income ratio, 35–45, 49
Personal interest, 212
Personal property, 26–28
Piggybacks, 51, 131–132
PITI (principal, interest, taxes, and
    insurance), 27, 41–44, 47
PLAM (price-level-adjusted mortgage), 2,
    189–192
PMI (*see* Private mortgage insurance)
Points, 26, 27, 66, 144, 145
    basis, 27
    buy-down mortgage, 144, 145
    discount, 24, 224–225
    margin, 26, 77–78, 118
    refinancing and, 159, 160, 165
    tax considerations, 205–207
Portfolio lender, 11, 35, 36, 49, 50,
    198–199
Portfolio loans, 11
Prepayment (*see* Mortgage prepayment)
Prepayment penalty, 27, 98–100, 157, 180
Prequalification, 5, 7–8
Price-level-adjusted mortgage (PLAM), 2,
    189–192
Prime rate index, 74, 75
Principal, 91, 93, 96, 98–101, 192
Principal, interest, taxes, and insurance
    (PITI), 27, 41–44, 47
Private mortgage insurance (PMI), 27,
    103–104, 178, 198–201
    appraisal and, 201
    disadvantages of, 200–201
    payment length, 199–201
Property, occupation of, 106, 138, 180,
    185
Property appraisal (*see* Appraisal)
Property qualifying, 11, 195
Purchase money mortgage, 27–28,
    245–247

Qualifying, 5–8, 32–54
    for adjustable-rate mortgage, 68–70, 72
    adjustable values, 53–54
    for buy-down mortgage, 146
    documents for, 137–138, 142
    for government loans, 35, 180–181,
        183–184
    gross monthly income, 34, 37–39, 45,
        48, 49
    gross monthly payment, 41–44, 47

Qualifying (*Cont.*):
  history of, 33–35
  for Home Equity Conversion Mortgage,
    196
  for jumbos, 50–51
  lines of credit, 52–53
  maximum mortgage amount, 41, 44,
    48, 50, 131
  no-qualifying, 51–52
  prequalification, 5, 7–8
Qualifying ratios, 35–50
  back-end, 35, 45–50
  flexibility of, 35, 48–50
  front-end, 35–45, 49
  loan-to-value, 25–27, 34, 38–41, 47, 53,
    54, 141, 155
  long-term-debt, 35, 45–50
  mortgage-payment-to-income, 38–39
  underwriting standards, 35–36, 48, 53

RAM (*see* Reverse annuity mortgage)
Real estate, 28
Real estate agent, 8, 10, 13
Real Estate Settlement Procedures Act
    (RESPA), 28, 220–221, 228
Real property, 28, 29
Recasting, 176
Red-lining, 188–189
Refinance clause, 117–118
Refinancing, 25, 27, 29, 155–169
  age of existing mortgage, 162–165
  appraisal, 155–156, 158, 159
  costs of, 156–160
  data needed for, 166–168
  decision-making factors, 156, 161,
    166–168
  financing the costs, 158
  foreclosure and, 169
  interest rate reduction, 162, 165, 166
  negotiating, 158–159
  reasons for, 155, 163, 165–166, 168–169
  rental property, 160, 161
  savings calculations, 161–163
  tax considerations, 209–211
  time factors, 163–165
  (*See also* Mortgage prepayment; Second
    mortgage)
Rental property:
  income from, 37–38
  refinancing, 160, 161
  tax considerations, 207, 209, 212

Repos, 182
RESPA (Real Estate Settlement
    Procedures Act), 28, 220–221, 228
Retail lender, 9, 10, 12, 14, 35
Reverse annuity mortgage (RAM),
    194–197
  history of, 197
  Home Equity Conversion Mortgage,
    194–196
Rip-off financing, 103
Roosevelt, Franklin D., 34

Sale of property, taxes on, 205, 209–211
SAM (shared appreciation mortgage),
    186–187
  disadvantages of, 188–189
  red-lining, 188–189
Savings and loan association (S&L), 9–12,
    33–36, 49, 62–63, 66, 140, 141, 146,
    153
Savings banks, 9–11, 14, 35, 49, 153
Sears, Roebuck and Company, 40
Second mortgage, 11, 21, 24, 28, 29, 30,
    51, 148, 154
  government loans and, 181
  seller financing and, 103–106, 108–111,
    113–118, 120–122
  time frame, 105–106
Secondary lender, 9, 11–13, 24, 35–36, 48,
    49, 146
Self-employed, 138–140
Seller financing, 102–123
  balloon payment in, 127
  for buy-down, 146
  conditions, 116–118
  for first mortgage, 118–119
  imputed interest in, 213
  interest rate in, 106–110, 113–116
  late payment penalty, 116
  mortgage assumption, 111–113,
    119–122
  negotiating, 113, 122–123, 145
  reasons for, 106–110
  refinance clause, 117–118
  for second mortgage, 103–106,
    108–111, 103–118, 120–122
  subordination clause, 116–117
  term, 114–116
  time frame, 103, 105–106
  wraparound mortgage, 110–114, 120
Servicing, of loans, 12

Settlement costs, 220–228
  appraisal fee, 223
  assumption fee, 223
  attorney's fees, 224
  complaints about, 227–228
  credit report fee, 5, 158, 159, 224
  discount points, 24, 224–225
  document preparation, 225
  fire insurance, 225
  good faith estimate, 221–223
  impound accounts, 52, 185, 225–226
  mortgage insurance premium, 180,
    181, 226
  origination fee, 26, 226–227
  Real Estate Settlement Procedures Act,
    28, 220–221, 228
  settlement statement, 222–223
  title insurance, 10, 20, 30, 158, 159,
    220–221, 226
  (*See also* Interest)
Shared appreciation mortgage (*see* SAM)
Shearson Lehman Mortgage Company,
  192
Short-term debt, 48
Short-term loan:
  swing loan, 107–109, 151–152
  (*See also* Lines of credit)
Silent second, 105, 106
Society of Real Estate Appraisers (SREA),
  28
Soft-money second, 103
SREA (Society of Real Estate Appraisers),
  28
Stake holder, 18
Standard factual, 55
Subject to, 29
Subordination clause, 29, 116–117
Superpiggy mortgage, 131, 132
Swing loan, 107–109, 151–152

Tax considerations, 152, 205–213
  home equity loan, 212
  imputed interest, 213
  interest, 205, 208–209, 212, 214, 218
  late mortgage payments, 212–213
  mortgage prepayment, 217–218
  negative amortization, 213
  once-in-a-lifetime $125,000 exclusion,
    211
  points, 205–207
  refinancing, 209–211

Tax considerations (*Cont.*):
  for rental property, 207, 209, 212
  sale of property, 205, 209–211
Tax lien, 25
Teaser rate, 10, 48–49, 64–72, 146
  advantages of, 71–72
  disadvantages of, 68–71
  effect of, 67–68
  qualifying and, 68–70
Termite report, 158, 159
30 due in 5 mortgage, 131, 132
30 due in 7 mortgage, 129–132
30 due in 10 mortgage, 126, 131, 132
30-year mortgage, 91, 93–95, 99–101
3/2/1 buy-down, 143, 146
Title, 19, 22, 25, 29–30, 103
Title insurance, 10, 20, 30, 158, 159,
  220–221, 226
Title insurance company, 18, 19
Treasury securities index, 74–77, 118
Trick second, 105, 106
Trust deed, 17, 18
Trust fund account, 185
Trustee, 18
Trustor, 18
2/3/1 buy-down, 146

Underwriting standards, 35–36, 48, 53
Usury laws, 114

VA loan (*see* Veteran's Administration
  loan)
Variable-rate loan, 10
Veteran's Administration (VA) loan, 11,
  30, 35, 182–185
  appraisal, 22, 184
  assumption of, 21, 27, 72, 112, 119
  automatics, 184–185
  down payment, 182–183
  eligibility requirements, 184
  entitlement, 183
  impound account, 185
  lender sources, 12
  maximum loan amount, 182
  origination fee, 26
  owner-occupancy requirement, 185
  qualifying, 183–184

Wraparound financing, 30–31
  in seller financing, 110–114, 120

About the Author

Robert Irwin has been a successful real estate broker for over 25 years and has steered countless buyers and sellers through every kind of real estate transaction imaginable. He has been a consultant to lenders, investors, and other brokers and is one of the most knowledgeable and prolific writers in the field. His books include *Tips and Traps When Buying a Home; Tips and Traps When Selling a Home; Buy, Rent, & Hold: How to Make Money in a Cold Real Estate Market; How to Find Hidden Real Estate Bargains;* and *The McGraw-Hill Real Estate Handbook.*